Explain Rabbi Elmer ~~~~
outlook on Zion and Diaspora.

Bersers overall stance on Zion vs. Diaspora

— Compare and contrast him
w/ figures discussed in class (including
Phillip Roth)

RABBI OUTCAST

Related Titles from Potomac Books

Does Israel Have a Future? The Case for a Post-Zionist State,
by Constance Hilliard

*Transforming America's Israel Lobby: The Limits of Its Power
and the Potential for Change,* by Dan Fleshler

RABBI
OUTCAST

Elmer Berger and American Jewish Anti-Zionism

Jack Ross

Potomac Books
Washington, D.C.

Library of Congress Cataloging-in-Publication Data

Ross, Jack.
Rabbi outcast : Elmer Berger and American Jewish anti-Zionism / Jack Ross.
    p. cm.
Includes bibliographical references and index.
ISBN 978-1-59797-697-8 (hardcover)
1. Berger, Elmer, 1908-1996. 2. Berger, Elmer, 1908-1996—Views on
Zionism. 3. Zionism—United States—History—20th century 4. Rabbis—
United States—Biography. 5. Jews—United States—Biographhty. I. Title.
DS149.5.U6R67 2011
320.54095694092—dc22

                    2011007571

ISBN 978-1-59797-697-8

(alk. paper)

Printed in the United States of America on acid-free paper that meets the
American National Standards Institute Z39-48 Standard.

Potomac Books, Inc.
22841 Quicksilver Drive
Dulles, Virginia 20166

First Edition

10 9 8 7 6 5 4 3 2 1

Dedicated to the memory of Tony Judt, most learned scourge of the neoconservatives, of Jewish nationalism, and their enabling in the name of liberalism, who by simple use of his pen brought liberal Jewish anti-Zionism back to life

CONTENTS

PROLOGUE

In January 2008 Ehud Olmert, then prime minister of Israel, addressed the annual Herzliya conference, where he declared the following:

> Once we were afraid of the possibility that the reality in Israel would force a binational state upon us. In 1948, the obstinate policy of the Arabs, our strength, and the leadership of David Ben-Gurion saved us from such a state. For 60 years, we fought with unparalleled courage in order to avoid living in a reality of binationalism, and in order to ensure that Israel exists as a Jewish and a democratic state with a solid Jewish majority. We must act to this end and understand that such a reality is being created, and in a very short while it will be beyond our control.[1]

This was a virtually unnoticed, but nonetheless shocking, admission, reverberating to the very foundations of Zionism itself. Olmert declared, in other words, that three generations of propaganda about the Arab desire to "push the Jews into the sea" was nothing but a lie, and that a century of some of history's bloodiest and most protracted ethnoreligious warfare had been an effort not to stave off such a genocidal threat but to avoid "binationalism," meaning nothing more than to exist as normal citizens of the place where they had chosen to live, rather than in an idealized state, real or imagined, of the Zionist ideology.

But it was nothing new for a representative of Zionism to take such deep personal offense to the mere suggestion that Israel should be at peace with both the internal and external Arab populations on anything other than its own terms. As far back as 1954, a firestorm erupted when Assistant Secretary of State for Near Eastern Affairs Henry Byroade gave a speech saying that Israel must reconcile itself to becoming "a Middle Eastern state, and not a worldwide grouping of people of a particular faith who have special rights within and obligations to the Israeli state." Though Byroade was only artic-ulating official U.S. policy at that time, as articulated by Secretary of State John Foster Dulles, that Israel should become "a part of the Near East com-munity and cease to look upon itself as an alien to this community," the speech ultimately cost Byroade his job.[2]

The man who very possibly ghostwrote that speech, in his brief period of favor with the State Department, was Elmer Berger, an ordained Reform rabbi who for nearly sixty years until his death in 1996 was at the forefront of Jewish opposition to Zionism, and for much of that time was its most well-known and widely despised Jewish antagonist. After a decade of ministering to two congre-gations in Michigan—first in Pontiac, then in Flint—Berger became executive director in 1942 of a new organization, the American Council for Judaism (ACJ). The ACJ was formed to combat the Reform movement's embrace of Zionism as well as the movement's drift away from its origins and toward a kind of ortho-doxy that would only reach its climax in the years after his death, including and perhaps especially on the issue of Zionism.

What prompted Elmer Berger to his lifelong active opposition to Zionism from virtually the outset of his career was his early confrontation with the very historic duplicity illustrated by the above quotation from Ehud Olmert. Berger had observed Zionist recruitment and fund-raising efforts in the Michigan communities he served, which stressed support for cultural devel-opment and humanitarian aid to the Jewish communities of Palestine and obfuscated the reality—the raising up of militias, often engaged in terror-ism, acting with the goal of an exclusively Jewish state. When the Zionist goal of nothing short of complete sovereignty over the British Mandate of Palestine became unambiguous with the Biltmore Program of 1942, many of these "cultural Zionists" became fierce advocates of binationalism, among them Martin Buber and Albert Einstein, and were led by the first president of the Hebrew University of Jerusalem, Judah Magnes. One of the great losses of this period was the failure to forge an effective alliance of these bination-alists with the Reform rabbis of the ACJ.

There were many twists and turns in the long remainder of Berger's life after 1948. Ironically, it appeared for a time that the ACJ might prosper in the years to come as it looked inward and recommitted itself to the religious preservation of Classical Reform Judaism, a question of priorities that had dogged the Council from the very beginning. Added to this were the opportunities afforded it while its views still coincided, at least officially, with U.S. policy in the Middle East under Dwight Eisenhower and John F. Kennedy, and rank-and-file movement Zionism was still a force to be reckoned with in American life. But by the 1960s, Israel became an unambiguous Cold War ally of the United States, and organized rank-and-file Zionism declined sharply, giving way to the elite-led Israel lobby of late infamy; this all collapsed in the face of a triumphant, nationalistic Jewish religion and its increasingly powerful self-appointed political leadership.

After the Six Day War of 1967, a long simmering clash finally occurred between Berger, the last of the original rabbis of the ACJ still active, and a lay leadership with markedly different priorities. This ultimately led to Berger's resignation in 1968 from the ACJ, an organization with which he had long been virtually synonymous. For the remainder of his life, under the banner of American Jewish Alternatives to Zionism, Elmer Berger planted the seeds of serious Jewish opposition to the Zionist domination of American Jewish life at a time when the reckoning would come with all that Zionism had wrought—for America, for the world, and for the Jews. Rabbi Berger would not live to see this reckoning, which came amid the crisis that began on September 11, 2001.

Little about Elmer Berger and his colleagues who formed the ACJ can be understood without understanding the political climate to which they were responding. To do so one must grasp and then deconstruct the stereotypes that surrounded the Council and their frequent contradictions with reality. As the Zionist movement in the United States relied so heavily on first- and second-generation immigrant Jews who came predominantly from the Russian Empire, it was able to arouse hatred of the Jewish opposition to Zionism along lines of ethnic resentment against the more established and Americanized Jewish communities, which went back three and four generations, largely from Germany. The politics of the era, including but not limited to the impact of the Holocaust, added to this picture the insinuation that the ACJ was cold and indifferent to anti-Semitism. There was also an added dimension based in the politics of the New Deal era, which bred an ostensible class conflict among American Jews.

Although some of these charges may have been fairly leveled against certain laymen of the Council or the rabbis who founded and led the organization, for the most part they could not have been further from the truth. The leading rabbis of the ACJ included Samuel Goldenson of New York, a Polish immigrant who was a strong voice of Progressive-era social reform in the communities he served before gaining the pulpit of New York's prestigious Temple Emanu-El. Even more remarkable were Irving Reichert of San Francisco, an outspoken supporter of California's radical labor movement of the 1930s and later an equally outspoken opponent of Japanese internment, and Abraham Cronbach of Cincinnati, a well-known pacifist leader and widely admired professor at Hebrew Union College. The rabbis all had a deep commitment to social justice, much of it influenced by the contemporary trends of liberal Protestantism, which remained relatively conservative and antiwar in the New Deal era.

Indeed, the vast majority of German American Jews, by virtue of that origin, were if anything even more roused to action by the rise of Nazi Germany, and those who were opposed to Zionism were certainly not an exception. As the leading historian of the ACJ, Thomas Kolsky, has compellingly argued: "Both the ACJ and the American Zionists were wrong on the issue of rescue. Once they had learned about the Holocaust, they should have made peace and diverted all their resources to saving Jews. Thus, from a Jewish standpoint, the wartime behavior of neither the Zionists nor the anti-Zionists was defensible."[3] This is true enough, but it ignores the successful Zionist efforts to sabotage efforts to relocate Jews anywhere besides Palestine.

The campaign by the American Zionists, and particularly by the Zionists in the Reform rabbinate, to disaffect, isolate, and effectively purge their opponents had a uniquely frightening quality in its seamless combination of both religious and modern ideological fervor. The ad hominem attacks on anti-Zionists varied from describing them as "quislings" and "internal enemies of the Jewish people" to vintage religious admonitions that the leaders of the ACJ "will be marked down in history to the undying shame of their descendants."[4] The Zionists would even frequently call into question the mental health of their opponents, with titular leader of the Reform Zionists Stephen Wise declaring that opposition to Zionism was "a Jewish sickness, a condition created by centuries of Jewish homelessness."[5]

This perfectly reflects how Wise, probably more than anyone else, was responsible for displacing the original doctrine of Reform Judaism with a secular ideology, largely inspired by the militant progressive John Dewey, in religious garb. And it was in keeping with the spirit of the age. Wise and his allies such as Abba Hillel Silver were, in many ways, merely echoing the ascendant "smearbund," as it was labeled by the journalist John Flynn, who was just one of many liberal and progressive stalwarts who were savagely and without mercy cast into the wilderness by the end of the 1930s as the new "far right" and perhaps even a Nazi fifth column for their dissent from the culmination of the New Deal and the drive to enter the Second World War. This brown scare, as some scholars have come to call it, would make the McCarthyism of a later era pale in comparison and would even foreshadow it.

To a remarkable degree, the hate campaign against the ACJ was part and parcel of the brown scare. In addition to the outspoken opposition of Rabbis Reichert and Cronbach to the U.S. entry into the Second World War, the president of the ACJ in its most active years, Lessing Rosenwald, had served on the board of the America First Committee, the largest antiwar organization in U.S. history. One of the most remarkable philanthropists in U.S. history, Rosenwald would also be a voice in the wilderness during and after the war for a generous U.S. policy toward all European refugees, not exclusively the Jews, and against the cynical Zionist manipulation and prolonging of the refugee crisis.[6] It would be a stretch to say that the ACJ was an extension of what had been the core of Jewish opposition to intervention, as it also included rabbis who were active on the interventionist side of the debate. But certainly the upheaval that was taking place in the Reform movement reflected the larger struggle that was taking place between classical liberalism, at least as it was understood by its partisans, and the progressivism of the New Deal era, which some older liberals would go so far as to name "totalitarian liberalism."

A most curious manifestation of this entire problem, which also happens to touch heavily on the controversies in Judaism of this era, presented itself in the past decade; a bizarre novel of counterfactual history by Philip Roth, *The Plot Against America*.[7] The novel begins with the absurd premise of Charles Lindbergh being elected president of the United States in 1940 and keeping America out of war as though, in the Orwellian formulation, war is peace and freedom is slavery. On top of libeling some of the greatest progressive politicians in U.S. history, Roth threads into the narrative a horrifically unironic spasm of parochial Jewish fear and loathing of their fellow Americans, revolving largely around what can only be interpreted as his caricature of an ACJ rabbi, the fictional Lionel Bengelsdorf. Anyone with a cursory knowledge of the period covered by Roth can recognize its malicious absurdities, but there has been so great a blackout of the history of the ACJ, and the larger history of Reform Judaism of which it is a part, that reviewers of *The Plot Against America* seemed to have had no clue what Roth's ranting about the assimilated German Jews and their rabbi was all about.[8]

The classical doctrine of Reform Judaism, which prevailed for the first century of its existence until about the 1930s, based its opposition to Zionism on two premises: first, that Judaism was a religion only and not the basis of an ethnic or national identity; and second, the renunciation of any messianic expectation, be it the coming of a personal messiah, the restoration of a Jewish state, or of the ancient sacrificial religion and priesthood. For over one-and-a-half millennia, the messianic idea in Judaism had consisted of some variation and combination of those two things. The Reform movement began early in the nineteenth century in Germany, where it renounced rabbinical law, or halacha, and the messianic idea in favor of the principles of the German Enlightenment. The movement would succeed as spectacularly in America as it would fail in Germany. History has largely placed the tragedy of the movement in Germany on the rise of Adolf Hitler, but the fact is that the German Enlightenment, and German Reform Judaism with it, were defeated and discredited arguably as early as Otto Von Bismarck and German unification. By the time the tragedy of the German Jews began with the First World War, Reform was, at best, a living fossil from another age. Most non-Orthodox Jews by then, and until the rise of Hitler, were secular liberals or socialists, if they had not, as many had, committed outright apostasy.

Both Reform and Zionism can only be understood in the context of the larger history of the Jews in modernity, which began in the seventeenth century with the climax of 1,500 years of messianic expectation: the spectacular rise and fall in little over a year of Shabtai Tzvi, who by 1666 had anywhere from half to nearly all of the world's Jews believing he was the messiah before converting to Islam when Mehmed IV gave him the choice between conversion or death.[9] In addition to anticipating the rise of Zionism with the most brazen, albeit fanciful, propaganda toward reconquering Palestine since Bar Kochba, the advent of Shabtai Tzvi also served as midwife to the birth of Christian Zionism. Coming as it did in the wake of the devastation of Puritanism by the overthrow of Oliver Cromwell and the Stuart Restoration, there was a great messianic expectation among the Puritans that many saw fulfilled by this Oriental Jewish messiah, with some going so far as to believe he was the Second Coming of Christ himself. It is indeed a grave and embarrassing omission on the part of such propagandists as Michael Oren and Martin Peretz, who write of the great and historic kinship of Anglo-American pietism and Zionism, that their narrative ultimately relies on the most notorious false messiah in the history of the Jews.[10]

Once the dust had settled by the eighteenth century from this apparently once-and-for-all discrediting of the messianic idea in Judaism, two paths lay open. One was the path of renunciation, Enlightenment, and Reform, begun already at roughly the same time as the messianic upheaval with the heresy of Baruch Spinoza. Following him at the dawn of the German Enlightenment was Moses Mendelssohn, who upon being given the chance to study at the great academies of Berlin and Prussia became an advocate for dialogue between Judaism and modern philosophy and for the Enlightenment itself among the Jews, which he called *haskalah* in Hebrew. Although *haskalah* at first advocated only assimilation into German society as an end in itself, Reform soon followed. The original Reform Temples, which sprouted up spontaneously across the German states in the early decades of the nineteenth century, promoted a doctrine that at times more closely resembled Freemasonry, most famously the Hamburg Temple founded in 1819, as well as the first American temple, in Charleston, South Carolina, in 1824. These would be short lived, but by midcentury many of its surviving advocates would bring to America a more developed and recognizably Jewish faith, where it would prosper.[11]

The second, more ominous path, was that of retreat into religious fervor defined by mysticism, enthusiasm, and utopian expectation, not at all unlike the contemporaneous Great Awakening in Protestantism. This was led by the founder of Hasidic Judaism, the enigmatic Baal Shem Tov, whose movement at its best, like many of the more anarchist-minded sects of the Great Awakening, encouraged a populist revolt against Orthodoxy and a healthy communitarianism. Although the vast majority of his followers would retreat after his death into an even more ossified kind of Orthodoxy, he also faced a formidable competitor in Jacob Frank, who revived the doctrines of Shabtai Tzvi into the basis of a utopian sect easily the equal of the most debased pre-Lutheran and Catholic heretical sects. These sects would be cited by many scholars as the ominous precursors to Marxism-Leninism, perhaps most notably by onetime ACJ member Murray Rothbard in his epic two-volume *An Austrian Perspective on the History of Economic Thought*.[12]

Out of the ferment in which, at the dawn of the nineteenth century, the followers of Jacob Frank and the French Revolutionary terror—by no means

mutually exclusively, as the historian Gershom Scholem would later document—would wreak havoc on Orthodox Jewish communities across the
German realm would emerge a man of extraordinary consequence to the rise
of Zionism and of totalitarianism generally: Moses Hess. Rebelling against
his Orthodox upbringing, he joined a vanguard that by the 1840s was promoting a sort of Jewish counterenlightenment, not by means of religious orthodoxy, but by applying to Judaism the authoritarian philosophy of Wilhelm
Friedrich Hegel, which portended the rise of nationalism. Hess was in an especially forerunning role because he cast his lot with the so-called Young
Hegelians, a band of young German radicals whose other principals were Karl
Marx, Friedrich Engels, and Heinrich Heine. By the time Marx and Engels took
up residence in London, Hess had broken with them over their emerging "scientific socialism" in favor of staying true to the romanticism of Hegel.

Although Hess had always exhibited, to one degree or another, a
parochial interest in "the Jewish question," he made his debut as an unabashed champion of the new nationalism that had swept Europe upon
Hegel's inspiration, with his 1862 pamphlet "Rome and Jerusalem." The
pamphlet served to propagandize on behalf of the Roman Republic, which
was seeking to forcibly unify Italy against the resistance of the Vatican and
some other principalities, and which Hess saw as the greatest fulfillment of
the revolutionary upheaval that swept across Europe in 1848. In sharp contrast to Marx, who had denounced the consequences of 1848 with one of
his most famous pamphlets, attacking the rise of Napoleon III in France,
Hess praised the self-appointed monarch for his imperial ambitions that led
him to occupy Italy, ostensibly in support of the Republic while frequently
being forced by expediency to switch support to the Vatican and back again.

The echo of George W. Bush and his misadventure in Iraq hardly stops
here, for Hess expressed the hope that like his namesake, Napoleon III would
march all the way into the Levant where he would establish a Jewish socialist commonwealth in Palestine and, of course, secure the national liberation
of the Arabs in Egypt and Syria as well. As Hess would declare: "With the liberation of the Eternal City on the Tiber begins the liberation of the eternal
city on Mount Moriah, with the resurrection of Italy begins the resurrection
of Judea. The orphaned children of Jerusalem will too be permitted into the
great renaissance of the nations."[13]

Not only are all the evils that history most commonly assigns to Marx more
properly laid at the feet of Hess, the vastness of his legacy has hardly ever
been addressed. With eerie foresight Moses Hess anticipated and celebrated

the whole horrible drama of the twentieth century. His central role in the genesis of Marxism was complemented by his anticipation of fascism with his panegyrics to the Roman Republic. With respect to Zionism specifically, his abiding faith in socialism made him not only a forefather of Labor Zionism, but the nexus he proposed with "Rome and Jerusalem" was stunningly borne out by the role of Italian fascism in the origins of the Israeli Right. Finally, whereas Hegel was but a repentant ex-radical of the Enlightenment whose "right turn" led him to be a mere court propagandist for the Prussian Crown, Hess went so far as to qualitatively preserve his abiding ideology by putting it to the service of an ambitious ruling class, making him, very plausibly, the first neoconservative.[14]

Small wonder, then, that the pivotal defeat for the bourgeois enlightenment embraced by the great majority of the German Jews was brought on by the event most directly affected by the rise of the Roman Republic—the unification of Germany. Though it had been inevitable ever since the failure of the 1848 revolutions, it was rather appropriately ushered in when Napoleon III engaged in a degree of recklessness such that Moses Hess had urged upon him and went to war against Bismarck, who deposed him in a matter of days in 1871. Thus did the era of *haskalah* and the German Enlightenment of which it was a part come to a close, but Reform Judaism would join many other exiled products of the great upheavals that led to German unification in a new land of opportunity—in America.

When the first permanent Reform congregation in America was established in Charleston, South Carolina, in 1841, it was boldly declared in the dedication that "this house of worship is our Temple, this free city our Jerusalem, this happy country our Palestine." This unabashed optimism and virtually messianic faith in the promise of America would define Reform Judaism for nearly a century to come. Within just two decades of the Charleston dedication, some version of the Reform doctrine was the dominant mode of Jewish practice in America, propelled by massive immigration from Germany in which the Jews were often barely distinguished from their fellow immigrants. In 1846 a recent arrival from Bohemia, Isaac Mayer Wise, joined the fledgling Temple Emanu-El in New York, where he was urged by Rabbi Max Lilienthal to join him in that calling. In 1850 Wise would begin his career as the father of American Reform Judaism, ministering to a largely Orthodox community in Albany, New York.

Wise's time in Albany was not a happy one, as his championing of Reform deeply divided his congregation and more than once led to open brawling.

But by 1854 he had moved on to the greener pastures of Cincinnati, then the third largest city in America, where he would put down roots that would be most fruitful. There he would find a more favorable congregation to which he could minister and begin his national leadership with the publication of a newspaper, *The Israelite*. In 1857 he wrote the first liturgy for the Reform movement in America, which led the movement away from its origins in German Freemasonry and toward a rough approximation and revision of traditional liturgy. With an initial ambition to totally unify American Jews under his movement, Wise founded the Union of American Hebrew Congregations in 1873 and finally a seminary, Hebrew Union College, which graduated its first class in 1883.[15]

From relatively early in his career Wise made his prophetic spirit felt. Although consistently opposed to slavery (indeed, his mentor Max Lilienthal was a noted abolitionist), Wise cast his lot with the antiwar Northerners known as the Copperheads, declaring on the eve of the Civil War that "force will not hold together this Union, it was cemented by liberty and can stand only by the affections of the people."[16] In 1863 Wise was briefly a Democratic candidate for the state senate, when that party in Ohio was led by the Copperhead firebrand Clement Vallandigham. This, along with Wise's later unsparing damnation of Zionism, would mark a record of prophetic dissent unmatched even by the most steadfast rabbis of the ACJ, who as a general rule yielded to none in the religious nationalism of postbellum America. For herein lay a paradox that would confront the Classical Reform movement and would become especially salient to and ultimately within the ACJ: the conflict between devotion to America and the need for prophetic dissent therein.

The definitive statement of Reform Jewish belief was finally issued in 1885, reflecting the classical liberalism borne witness by Isaac Mayer Wise and instilled in his now legion disciples. This was the Pittsburgh Platform, so named because it was issued from the leading Reform temple in that city, Rodef Shalom, and drafted by two of Wise's closest students, Rabbis Kauffman Kohler and Emil Hirsch.[17] The platform read in part:

> We maintain that Judaism preserved and defended, midst continual struggles and trials and under enforced isolation, this God-idea as the central religious truth for the human race. . . . We hold that all such Mosaic laws as regulate diet, priestly purity, and dress originated in ages and under influences of ideas altogether foreign to our present mental and spiritual state. They fail to impress the modern Jew with a spirit of holiness. . . . In full accordance with the spirit of Mosaic legislation,

which strives to regulate the relation between rich and poor, we deem it our duty to participate in the great task of modern times, to solve, on the basis of justice and righteousness, the problems presented by the contrasts and evils of the present organization of society.[18]

Most relevant to the issue of Zionism, and to its ultimate consequences, was this passage:

> We consider ourselves no longer a nation, but a religious community, and, therefore, expect neither a return to Palestine, nor a sacrificial worship under the sons of Aaron, nor the restoration of any laws concerning the Jewish state. We recognize in Judaism a progressive religion, ever striving to be in accord with the postulates of reason. We are convinced of the utmost necessity of preserving the historical identity with our great past. Christianity and Islam, being daughter religions of Judaism, we appreciate their providential mission to aid in the spreading of monotheistic and moral truth.[19]

These words would form the basis of the argument against Zionism by the Classical Reform movement as well as the counterargument against it, asserting that the denial of a Jewish national identity was fundamentally ahistorical.

Without question the idea that the Jews constituted a religious community alone was novel in the history of the Jews, but the idea of a mere religious community, as put forward by the advent of Protestantism and by the American ideal of religious liberty, is itself a very new and novel one in human history, not more than a few centuries old. Newer and more novel still, around for barely two centuries if that, is the modern idea of nationalism. The point with respect to Judaism is that, since the time of Shabtai Tzvi, the Orthodox rabbinic faith that had prevailed for well over a thousand years, with a few notable dissenters along the way, was no longer tenable by the dawn of modernity. By the eighteenth century, the two paths appeared to be *haskalah*, the path of enlightenment, and Hasidism, the path of piety. Both of these, in their own way, put forward the idea of a mere religious community. Only by the dawn of the twentieth century, as nationalism was already beginning to show signs of decline and fall, did it become anything remotely approaching a viable option for the Jews. For at the dawn of the twentieth century, just as secular Zionism was taking off, the conservative backlash to the apparent triumph of Reform would give religious expression to the nationalist idea of Judaism developed by Moses Hess.

The undoing of Isaac Mayer Wise's dream of American Jewish unity under his banner of Reform came at the commencement of the first class of rabbis ordained by the new Hebrew Union College in 1883, when shellfish was served at the commencement banquet. Prompted by this, and by the release two years later of the Pittsburgh Platform, two leaders of long-standing orthodox dissent from the triumph of Reform in America founded the Jewish Theological Seminary (JTS) in New York. Sabato Morais and Pereira Mendes were typical of the orthodox dissenters who emerged in virtually every established Jewish community, based mostly in the older, Sephardic communities that dated back to the colonial period. JTS would align itself with Zionism effectively from the very beginning, with Mendes attending the second and third Zionist Congresses and considered by Theodor Herzl himself to be his key American recruit.[20]

Part of the reason that the history of Reform Jewish anti-Zionism has become so obscure has been the prominence and notoriety, in recent years, of Orthodox opposition to Zionism. Although this was the dominant position in Europe until the Holocaust, the Orthodox community in America would be mostly Zionist from the start. In the beginning, the Orthodox were unified under the leadership of JTS, with the first schism only occurring in 1902 when JTS brought in as its president, Solomon Schechter, a Cambridge lecturer on medieval Jewish thought and ardent Zionist. Drawing inspiration from Maimonides, Schechter asserted a middle path between Orthodoxy and Reform, asserting that halacha was valid but subject to constant revision and amendment. These first dissenters from JTS would affiliate with the international movement Agudath Israel, whose almost schizophrenic relationship with Zionism would become a matter of scorn from Zionists and anti-Zionists alike. Schechter would then lead JTS in founding the Conservative movement, premised explicitly on the idea of Judaism as a national religion and always devoted to Zionism. The Orthodox Union that prevails today would only break from the conservatives in the 1950s over the issue of whether driving is allowed on the sabbath.[21]

So by the close of the nineteenth century, when Theodor Herzl fatefully published *Der Judenstaat*, the die was cast for the vital legitimacy that the Zionist project would ultimately receive from religious American Jews, but at the time this was anything but obvious. The story has been told that when the Zionist agent Joseph Klausner asked an American rabbi if there were any Zionists in America, the rabbi replied, "Yes, there are two. A mad man named Stephen Wise and a mad wench named Henrietta Szold."[22] Typical of liberal

and elite Jewish opinion in both Europe and America of Herzl and his movement were the words of one German publisher: "If Herzl needs to be taken
to a lunatic asylum, I shall happily put my carriage at his disposal."[23] But the
most bold and forthright denunciation would come from the great Isaac
Mayer Wise, just a few short years before his death in 1900:

> That new Messianic movement over the ocean does not concern us at
> all. But the same expatriated, persecuted, and outrageously wronged
> people came in large number also to us, still imbued with their home
> ideals and beliefs, and compromised in the eyes of the public the
> whole of American Judaism as the fantastic dupes of a thoughtless
> utopia, a momentary inebriation of morbid minds, a prostitution of
> Israel's holy cause to a madman's dance of unsound politicians.[24]

But there would soon emerge a man who would, almost singlehandedly,
give currency to the idea that the proposition of Judaism as a "national religion" implied in full that the essence of Judaism was indeed the modern
concept of nationalism, and would seek, with astonishing if little-appreciated
success, to totally fashion the Jewish religion into the dystopian image foreseen for it by Moses Hess. Mordecai Kaplan, who joined the faculty of JTS immediately upon his ordination there in 1909, would in 1912 be among the
founders of a quasisect of Orthodoxy called Young Israel, modeled explicitly
on contemporary protofascist movements of the various European nationalisms. Young Israel would seek to proselytize Orthodoxy of a particularly
Zionist flavor among American Jews. Though they can only be given so much
of the credit, the nationalist idea became, for the vast majority of those who
dissented from Reform, the ultimate and abiding touchstone of their Jewish
identity, perhaps for little more reason than that they knew it was an idea especially outrageous to Reform.

Kaplan, however, would soon grow distant from Young Israel, increasingly drifting away from rabbinic Orthodoxy and into the orbit of John
Dewey, the reigning philosopher of the Progressive era, which was coming to
prevail in America, rapidly displacing the zeitgeist of relative liberalism in
the America so loved by Isaac Mayer Wise. Representing the ultimate fulfillment of Hegelian Romantic nationalism as it was anticipated by Hess, Dewey
heralded the rise of an abstraction called democracy, which would lead to the
ultimate glory of the state through the perfected, egalitarian new man, by
what he called "education," meaning little more than the rigid indoctrination
of the masses in the glories of the new age. Convinced that "Jewish civilization"

required nothing less than a revolution to attain the Deweyan ideal, Kaplan began to advocate radical changes in Judaism. These included a previously unheard of degree of gender egalitarianism, with Kaplan giving his daughters the first bat mitzvah ceremonies (the Reform, still by this time, gave only the confirmation ceremony to both sexes at fifteen, two years later than the traditional thirteen). But in an ultimate act of hubris, Kaplan brought God himself into question, promoting a "naturalist" conception of God advocated by Dewey. Kaplan would be formally excommunicated by Young Israel in 1945.

The key turning point in the rise of Zionism would come with the great cataclysm that shattered the liberal optimism that had inspired the Reform movement, and it would mark the beginning of the horrible epoch generally known as the twentieth century and would be welcomed with delight by John Dewey and all his cothinkers: the First World War. Although Zionism had been adrift since the death of Herzl in 1904, and with him his fantastic appearances before the rulers of all the empires of Europe, the Great War gave the Zionists the crucial chance to win the favor of a great power. To some, the obvious choice was Germany, where in the most hopeful affair of Herzl's lifetime, the kaiser considered securing a protectorate in Palestine from his increasingly supplicant Ottoman ally. The ultimate stumbling block was the so-called *kaiserjuden*, Germany's Jewish power elite, such as they were, who remained loyal to the Reform tradition.

The prize that tempted the kaiser for the first three years of the war was the prospect that if he were to come out in favor of Zionism, it would win for Germany a valuable fifth column in the Jews of the Russian Empire. However, the likely consequence of this would have been that the czar would then beat Hitler to the punch; in other words, the Russians would have then done to the Jews as the Ottomans, earlier in the war, had done in their genocide of the Armenians to stave off the potential that they could have been just such a fifth column for Russia. Moreover, the leaders of German Jewry knew all this perfectly well, and their actions were surely motivated in great measure by that knowledge. Nonetheless, the tragedy of the Jews of Germany was sealed by their devotion in the Great War, which only allowed them to be the subject of the "stabbed in the back" myth that would make way for the rise of Hitler.

One man was shrewd enough to sense this, the new leader of the Zionists whose ruthlessness and abiding belligerence would set the tone for the leadership of Zionism for generations to come: Chaim Weizmann. A Lithuanian who had settled in England where he achieved success as an innovator in the production of chemical weapons, he redirected Zionist lobbying efforts to the British, who in 1917 issued the momentous—but, in actual fact, quite ambiguous—Balfour Declaration, by which the Zionist project would forever after be tied to the policies and legacy of the British Empire. Thus did the Zionist project definitively demonstrate itself to be the very thing that the Prophets, so venerated by the Classical Reform doctrine, took their stand directly against: the instrument of a rapacious empire, though it would be as the ancient kingdoms of the Pharisees in service to the empires of antiquity.

The issuance of the Balfour Declaration came within a month of U.S. entry into the war, two events that together would cast an ominous shadow. Considering that a durable stalemate had taken hold until the United States entered the war, and that on top of all the horrors set in motion by Versailles, the saving of the British Empire by America's entry into the war allowed them to concoct so fantastic a new scheme as to endorse Zionism, it would not be an exaggeration to say that America's entry into the First World War was the ultimate root cause of all the tragedy and horror of the twentieth century. However, as armed Wilsonianism ushered in not only these terrors but an American domestic situation that was as close as ever to martial law, Reform Judaism (with the prophetic voice of Isaac Mayer Wise long in passing) was shamefully quiescent. Of Jewish members of congress at that time, only one, the Socialist Meyer London of New York's Lower East Side, would vote against entry, while on the other extreme was Julius Kahn of San Francisco, who would be one of Wilson's closest Republican allies during the war, and after the war would go so far as to try to ram through peacetime conscription against a majority of Democrats.

Kahn, however, would arguably represent the high point of American Jewish opposition to Zionism when he personally lobbied Woodrow Wilson to oppose the Zionist project at Versailles, ultimately leading to the King-Crane Commission, which concluded that any effort to establish a Jewish state in Palestine was neither viable nor desirable. When he died in 1924, he was succeeded in his seat in congress by his wife, Florence, who would go on to be a supporter of both the America First Committee and then the ACJ. Julius Kahn's success on the issue is all the more remarkable in that it successfully intervened against one of Wilson's most trusted advisers, Louis Brandeis, who had baldly declared that one must be a Zionist in order to be a good American. Though couched in language suggesting that this meant nothing more than that one must belong to any and numerous fraternal societies to be a good American, in the political climate of the First World War this had ominous implications, especially since Zionism was now official British policy at a time when any anti-British speech was subject to suppression and prosecution.

On the one hand, Reform stayed true to its convictions, passing a resolution against the Balfour Declaration and denouncing the new American Jewish Congress, with Rabbi David Philipson testifying against pro-Zionist congressional resolutions in 1922.[25] On the other hand, it began to crack under the pressure of what the First World War's new realities implied. Many pressures had contributed, beyond the mood of the moment, to their unflinching support of Wilson's war policies. Not only did loyalty to America have such a central role in Classical Reform doctrine, but the urge asserted itself to prove loyalty doubly so by standing with America against the old Fatherland. Ethnic and class resentments also played a role, since for many German Jews there was the fear of being associated with the alleged anarchism and "bolshevism" of the Yiddish-speaking immigrants.

Finally, Zionism would enter the mix as the influence of Brandeis conspired with events to convert many of America's Jewish power elite of that era to Zionism, notable among them the jurist Felix Frankfurter and the banker Jacob Schiff. This would prove ironic as the ethnic and class resentments of first- and second-generation immigrants against these very Jews would provide much grist for their attachment to Zionism, and this resentment would find itself erroneously directed toward the ACJ. This was a problem foreseen by Isaac Mayer Wise in his firsthand experience with the failures of Reform in Germany and with his political radicalism: the fundamental problem of the Enlightenment itself, which lay at the heart of the upheavals that were beginning to take place in U.S. politics and society and would be reflected in the upheavals of the Reform movement.

The most fundamental mistake of the founders of the Reform movement was that while they rejected the belief in a personal messiah and in the return to Zion, they did not forthrightly reject the proposition that there could ever be a "new Zion," which was exactly how they regarded Germany. This declaration of Germany as the new Zion, at the most fevered peak of the German Enlightenment while the idea of a single unit called Germany was still but an abstraction, should be especially telling, as it was of a piece with the romanticism that would marry the theories of Hegel in forging nationalism itself. The mistake would be repeated in America—in perhaps not so explicit and ominous a way, but such that would be deeply felt, even, fatefully, in the precincts of the ACJ itself.

Thus was there evident a plausible and legitimate basis in philosophy for Reform to accept and even embrace Zionism. If any country of the modern world could be a new Zion, why couldn't it be in Palestine? If the new Zion was being heralded by the advance of democracy by the bayonet, as Wilson decreed should be the new order of things, why shouldn't there be a great colonial endeavor to extend this to Palestine? For just as the republicanism of the enlightenment led naturally to armed progressivism, the republican assumptions of Classical Reform would only logically lead to the proposition that there must be a similar new dispensation in Judaism. This, of course, was provided by Mordecai Kaplan, whose ideology of reconstructionism would make its presence felt even in the Reform movement. Nevertheless, the exorcism of the anti-Zionists from the Reform movement would undeniably be among the most vicious and merciless purges of heretics in the history of American religion, perhaps rivaled only by the suppression of Mormon polygamy.

The man who all but singlehandedly converted Reform Judaism from the optimistic faith of the German Enlightenment to a kind of watered-down Kaplanism was Stephen Wise, whose family immigrated from Budapest when his father was called to serve as rabbi for a fledgling but growing Conservative congregation in New York, Rodef Shalom. The son would begin his own rabbinical career in Portland, Oregon, in 1900, where he would immerse himself in Zionist activities, openly derisive of his ministering duties, declaring that Zionism gave meaning to his life as it fulfilled all his wildest romantic hopes. When his Zionism kept him from claiming the pulpit of New York's prestigious Temple Emanu-El in 1905, Wise would establish his own rival Free Synagogue.[26] During this time he would further immerse himself in Progressive-era activism, contributing to what would eventually become a seamless fusion of his politics and religion. In the abuse he hurled toward the anti-Zionists, Wise would uniquely possess at once the religious fervor of the inquisitor and the ideological fervor of the commissar.

Continuing with his novel yet shrewd strategy of advancing Zionism in the Reform movement through an adaptation of what in the context of labor radicalism was called "dual unionism," in 1922 Stephen Wise founded in New York the Jewish Institute for Religion, a rival seminary to Hebrew Union College. The Institute, like Wise himself, would be deeply influenced by the Reconstructionist ideology of Mordecai Kaplan, which in Wise's hands would perfectly suit his unholy marriage of the new religion of Jewish nationalism with the fulfillment of the armed progressive epoch in New Deal liberalism.

The same year as he founded the Jewish Institute for Religion, Wise would singlehandedly reconvene the abortive American Jewish Congress, an effort during the First World War to have a governing representative body of all American Jews by the power elite fair-weather friends of Zionism recruited by Brandeis who in the struggle of the coming years would incredibly be most commonly identified as the "non-Zionists." By the 1930s Wise could exploit the rise of Hitler to take it to the next level and convene a World Jewish Congress.

Thus, even before the rise of Hitler, the die was already cast—the "progressive" nationalist zeitgeist of the twentieth century was well in the saddle and was slowly but surely having its way with Reform Judaism, whose classical doctrine was an authentic faith inspired by the principles of liberal enlightenment as possibly no other could claim to be. The prophetic path of standing against the tide would be a lonely one, as it always is, but it would be met by men worthy of the task. They included Morris Lazaron, a disillusioned Zionist whose witness would be the equal of other disillusioned ideologists of that era. They included Irving Reichert, who would be second to none in standing for the prophetic faith in the face of the century's darkest hours. And they included Elmer Berger, who would be forever shaped by the old faith's last days of glory at Hebrew Union College.

1

AN EARNEST DISCIPLE

In 1867 eighteen-year-old David Turk arrived at the port of Galveston to serve as an agent for the rapidly growing mercantile operation in central Texas known as J. Loewenstein and Walter. The sixth of nine children and the first to be born after the family arrived in New York from the Prussian city of Posen, this young man set out west to fulfill the American dream by the most parochial means of the Old World—to seek the benevolent employment of filial relations. In this case, it would be from the brothers Joseph and Benjamin Loewenstein, who arrived in Texas from Posen around the same time and by 1873 had a successful operation based in the small town of Rockdale, Texas (fifty miles northeast of Austin), selling dry goods, clothing, boots, shoes, and groceries.[1]

Turk's employment ultimately led him to Marion, Texas, just outside San Antonio, where in March 1882 he married Esther Lowenstein, who with her older sister Adelaide had come to Texas from Philadelphia to find husbands in the community in which their relatives had become so prosperous.[2] The couple's first child, Selma, was born in 1883, about which time the young family moved to Texarkana, where David sought to make it with a store of his own. They were beset by tragedy when Esther died while giving birth to their second child, Sidney, in 1887. At that time, David married Adelaide in keeping with the Orthodox Jewish practice known as Levirate marriage.[3] Within several years, the family left Texas behind and settled in Cleveland, where David was able to reestablish his business and had three more children with Adelaide.

Selma Turk likely came of age in Cleveland with a pathos of downward mobility, the daughter of a more hopeful frontier community that was part of the tremendous success story of German American Jews in the nineteenth century, now living in an industrial Midwestern city that was one of the leading destinations beyond New York for the huddled masses of Jewish immigrants just coming over from the Russian Empire. And in this she would seem to have found a kindred spirit in the man she would marry, Samuel Berger. Born in 1885 in Hungary, he was the second of four children and was brought with his family to America as a small child. His father, Leon, immediately established himself in Cleveland as a grocer. Though the father would retain at least a degree of traditional Jewish practice, the son would go to considerable lengths to fully Americanize himself. In addition to having a career as a railroader, a very uncommon profession for a Jewish immigrant, Samuel would eventually change his middle name from the Yiddish "Sendor" to "Saunders" and would claim to have been born in Austria rather than Hungary.[4]

Samuel Berger and Selma Turk were married in Cleveland on March 24, 1907, and their first son, Elmer, was born May 27, 1908. He would be followed by another son, Melvin, less than two years later, and a daughter, Adelaide, in 1919. The family lived comfortably, with Samuel enjoying lifelong employment with the Pennsylvania Railroad, first as a locomotive fireman, then as an engineer, and ultimately as a junior executive.[5] It is not clear exactly what motivated the family to affiliate as Reform Jews, as both Samuel and Selma largely bore the markings of a more traditional, if lapsed, background. Both Elmer and Melvin attended the Sunday school of Cleveland's Euclid Avenue Temple and were confirmed there, though, as Elmer recalled generations later, "without the hoopla that you sometimes get with the Bar Mitzvahs nowadays."[6]

The family would always attend High Holiday services at the temple and would observe Passover at the home of their grandfather, Leon. It was, in Berger's own words, "a Reform Jewish home, we just accepted it as a normal part of who we were and otherwise never let it impinge on our daily lives."[7] Growing up, Elmer's passion was athletics, the origins of which provide an interesting window into his early Jewish identity, such as it was. After being diagnosed with anemia, he received a doctor's recommendation to enlist in regular athletics. Though Cleveland did at that time have a Young Men's Hebrew Association (YMHA), a branch of the Cleveland Young Men's Christian Association (YMCA) was closer to Berger's home, and he was thus enrolled there. When Elmer came to qualify to be a junior leader at the YMCA, his coach, whom he recalled to have been an Armenian, asked him if he had any problems associating with non-Jews before agreeing to appoint him.[8]

But as Elmer Berger came of age, and even well before, such an assimilationist attitude was increasingly an anomaly in the Jewish world of Cleveland. If in most of the cities east of the Mississippi the older, more Americanized Jewish communities managed to hold their own with the rising tide of the new Jewish immigrants, and if in the Southern and Western states the German influence remained dominant, Cleveland was exceptional in having its Jewish community so totally overwhelmed by Ellis Island. In the period of Eastern European immigration to America, the Jewish population of Cleveland increased by over an astounding twenty times, from 3,500 in 1880 to 85,000 in 1925. Perhaps most tellingly, by the first decade of the twentieth century, the garment industry of Cleveland was considered the equal of New York's.

The booming Jewish immigrant community in Cleveland would also become home to a rabbi of extraordinary charisma who would become the principal leader of American Zionism in the period of the founding of the State of Israel, Abba Hillel Silver. Born Abraham Silver in Lithuania, he was heir to a local rabbinic dynasty and the son of a committed Zionist. On the Lower East Side of New York, he would emerge as the wunderkind of the struggling Zionist movement in America before being ordained by Hebrew Union College in 1915. Silver was installed just two years later at Cleveland's oldest Reform congregation, Tifereth Israel, which under Silver's charismatic leadership would become simply known as The Temple. Ironically, the Euclid Avenue Temple, also called Anshe Chesed, was formed by a more moderate split from Tifereth Israel.

Silver's predecessor, Moses Gries, had been one of several more radical contemporaries of Isaac Mayer Wise, who would abolish all use of Hebrew, including in Torah readings, and hold sabbath services on Sunday. Though as a committed Zionist Silver immediately restored Hebrew in all capacities, Sunday services were still held at The Temple as late as the 1970s.[9] Indeed, in contrast to his bitter rival for the Zionist leadership, the confirmed ideologue Stephen Wise, Silver was a man of many contradictions: a product of the Lower East Side and stalwart Zionist who nonetheless sought to join the Classical Reform elite, and outspoken as anyone in the rabbinate toward social justice yet a committed Republican who was likely responsible for securing the Zionist loyalties of "Mr. Republican," Robert Taft.

It is likely, therefore, that it is because neither of Berger's parents were of a Reform background that the family belonged to the more moderate Euclid Avenue Temple, which was nonetheless very deeply committed to Classical Reform practices and whose rabbi would emerge as a leading voice against the opponents of Classical Reform, including but not limited to the Zionists. Louis Wolsey, the son of Russian immigrants in Michigan, would study directly under Isaac Mayer Wise and be a member of the last class that Wise would live to see ordained in 1899. As ambitious as he was committed to his ideals, and a fair rival in the charisma department to Abba Hillel Silver, Wolsey became the rabbi of Euclid Avenue Temple in 1907 after starting out in Little Rock, Arkansas. Long before he would issue the call that ultimately led to the founding of the American Council for Judaism, Wolsey entered the fray as an anti-Zionist immediately as the issue first reared its head on the American scene at the close of the First World War, engaging in a frenzied correspondence with like-minded rabbis against the pro-Zionist congressional resolutions of 1922.[10]

As a top student at his technical high school in Cleveland, the adolescent Elmer Berger was pulled between two poles: the rabbinate and chemistry. Though encouraged toward chemistry by his teachers, he held Rabbi Wolsey in high regard and continued to have an interest in the temple after he was confirmed. In his words, competing with his interests in science was an interest in "having some impact on social problems."[11] He came down decisively in favor of becoming a rabbi a year before finishing high school, when Wolsey asked him to give the sermon at a children's High Holiday service. Berger recalled finding Wolsey to be somewhat discouraging toward his ambitions, eager for him to pursue the rabbinate but unsure of whether he could handle the rigors and multifaceted portfolio of being a congregational rabbi. But after meeting with both Elmer and his father, Wolsey gave his blessing for his erstwhile disciple to be admitted in 1925 to Hebrew Union College through its undergraduate track program at the neighboring University of Cincinnati.[12]

Though Berger was extremely vague in his reminiscences about what appealed to him in the rabbinical calling toward social justice, there are significant clues. As a railroad engineer, his father was likely involved in the Conference for Progressive Political Action, largely sponsored by the Brotherhood of Locomotive Engineers, which gathered in Cleveland in 1924 to nominate for president the legendary "Fighting Bob" LaFollette. But Berger was no doubt greatly influenced by Louis Wolsey's defense from his pulpit of a colleague who would ultimately prove to be a more enduring influence on Berger and his thought. Abraham Cronbach, an Indianapolis native ordained by Hebrew Union College in 1906, ministered to congregations in South Bend, Indiana, and Akron, Ohio, before becoming radicalized as a prison and hospital chaplain, and he would become an outspoken and radical pacifist in reaction to the First World War.

In January 1924 Cronbach wrote and distributed a "Pledge for Jewish Pacifists" in hopes that he could organize a solid bloc of Reform rabbis that could prevent a repeat of the movement's acquiescence to the war fever of the First World War.[13] The pledge became a subject of much abuse, and within six months he was rebuked by the board of the Hebrew Union College—where he was now a professor and would remain until his death—for causing "a public relations problem too serious to be overlooked in the name of academic freedom."[14] But Louis Wolsey, who did not often become politically engaged (though he gave the invocation at the 1940 Republican Convention), eloquently spoke in Cronbach's defense from his pulpit:

> Some may ridicule such a thoroughgoing pacifism, and others may taunt it with the hackneyed criticism of being visionary and impractical, while professional soldiers and war makers might call it the counsel of cowardice. It would not be the first time in history that some world redemptive idea was sneered at. That has been the usual fate of every revolutionary thought that has gradually incarnated itself into an accepted institution of life.[15]

At the same time, however, the challenges to Classical Reform Judaism were making themselves very well known, especially in Cleveland and at the Euclid Avenue Temple itself. The same year that Wolsey's earnest disciple left Cleveland for Hebrew Union College, Wolsey himself left for a more prestigious pulpit at Philadelphia's Rodef Shalom, where he would establish himself as a zealous partisan of Classical Reform. Wolsey's successor at Anshe Chesed was Barnett Brickner, a staunch supporter of Stephen Wise who would become a key Zionist leader in his own right. As the new rabbi, Brickner would be notable for reintroducing a number of traditional practices that had been eschewed by Classical Reform, among these the bar mitzvah ceremony, the observance of Simchat Torah, and the use of the shofar during the High Holidays, which had been replaced by a trumpet.[16]

Much of this no doubt seems extremely odd to the modern Jewish reader. How bizarre, in retrospect, that such rites and practices to which Jews today

would never give a second thought should have become so closely identi-
fied with Orthodoxy in the minds of the early Reform Jews and moreover
would eventually become so closely associated with what it was that many
Reform Jews felt they were defending against the encroachment of Zionism.
One may even wonder the extent to which "Zionism" was for many of these
Jews and their rabbis simply a catch-all term for all that they found undesir-
able in the changes that the recent immigrants had brought about in
American Jewish life.

That many, but certainly not all, Zionists in the Reform movement were
pushing for a significant return to traditional ritual reveals two things: first, that
they were able to seize on it as a wedge issue by which to win over newer immigrants coming into Reform, who may not have been necessarily predisposed
to Zionism. But by the same token, as would become clear in the most active
years of the American Council for Judaism, those who identified with it did so
primarily for religious and not political reasons. In other words, far from being
"self-hating Jews" of the Zionist imagination, most of the resistance to the
Zionist encroachment of the Reform movement came from those who were
deeply committed to their own understanding of Judaism and their Jewish
identity. Furthermore, if somewhat ironically given his later reputation and priorities, Elmer Berger was clearly set on a path toward the rabbinate by his earnest
commitment to an idea of Judaism that was clearly beginning to be challenged
at the time of the initial commitment. There may be a good deal to criticize
in this understanding of Judaism, but it must be understood on its own terms
in order to have an honest understanding of the anti-Zionism it engendered.

The idea central to Classical Reform theology, upheld as such by both its
proponents and its detractors, is the centrality of the biblical prophets. That
is, that the essence of Judaism is not in the "national narrative" that ostensibly constitutes the Old Testament but rather in the example of those,
namely the prophets, who spoke out against the kings and priests who cor-
rupted the nation and the people. It has been said by many that there is no
greater polemic against arbitrary power in all of human literature than the
warning of the Prophet Samuel against the Israelites' desire for a king. Also
widely celebrated has been the message of the minor prophets with respect
to the just treatment of the poor and the corrupting power of wealth. Binding
all of this together were the backward-looking rebukes of Isaiah and
Jeremiah, with their emphasis on the all-corrupting nature of war.

Implicit in all of this is the overarching premise that the downfall of biblical Israel was its eagerness to define itself as a temporal kingdom—in other

words, a state, with all its trappings of power. Though many Zionists would invoke the Prophets, interpreting them as yearning for a national restoration, this would bear many of the marks of the standard Christian understanding of the Prophets, anticipating the Son of David. Indeed, grounding this Classical Reform invocation of the Prophets was their rejection of a personal messiah and its replacement with the Prophets' message of social justice. When seen in this light, therefore, it is difficult to argue that the prophetic call for social justice was not meant, in its own context, as a rebuke of yearning for either temporal or messianic redemption.

The genesis of rabbinic Judaism provides a great degree of validity to the relevance of these ideas to the challenges that confronted Judaism at the beginning of the modern era. Founded as the state religion of the Hasmonean Kingdom, which existed for just less than a century from the triumph of the Maccabean revolt to the beginnings of Roman rule in Palestine, the establishment of the kingdom itself had been a betrayal of the majority of its leaders (including those celebrated at Hanukkah) who wished to restore the system of the Judges, a prophetic aim if ever there was one. Many of these dissenters would eventually become the sect known as the Essenes.[17] In the beginnings of the modern Jewish era, the Hasidim sought to return to the ideal set by the Essenes.[18] But the founders of Reform sought to reach even farther back to first principles, back to the Prophets themselves in their forewarning of what would become of a restored Jewish state. Indeed, insofar as rabbinic Judaism can be said to have always implicitly sought the restoration of the state it was created to serve, anti-Zionism was absolutely a matter of first principle for Reform.

The logic of this narrative for Reform Judaism closely mirrored that of Protestantism, which is not surprising given Reform's origins in the German Enlightenment. The founders of Reform, in short, sought to return to the ideal represented by the pre-Hasmonean Judaism of the Prophets, just as the Protestants sought to restore an idealized early church of the Roman era. Reform Judaism, however, was far more fundamentally rationalist than historical Protestantism, whose more extreme and enthusiastic sects closely resembled the Hasidim that Classical Reformists despised. The difference, which may or may not be fundamental to the difference between Judaism and Christianity, lay in the desire, in the phrase of the twentieth-century German Jewish philosopher Eric Voegelin, to "immanentize the eschaton."

Taken from the terminology of Gnosticism, Voegelin used this phrase to describe the process sought out by secular ideology, attaching a religious "end of days" significance and fervor to political action and events. It is true that many of the founders of Reform in Germany attached such significance to their doctrines in the larger context of German Romanticism, but this was a mistake that the movement's leaders in America tried, though ultimately failed, to correct. But it would be precisely the purpose of Zionism to immanentize the eschaton, and its genius would be in seizing upon both religious and secular messianic yearning as though they were one and the same, and thus make them so. Any alternative faith in simple human progress, such as that of Elmer Berger in prophetic Judaism, could never have stood a chance.

For his first four years in Cincinnati, Berger would take university courses in the morning and Hebrew Union College courses in the afternoon, graduating Phi Beta Kappa from the University of Cincinnati in 1929. At that time, Hebrew Union College was a markedly different place than one might recognize it today, home to a dormitory lifestyle for young men of a long lost place and time. Berger would recall his years at the college as a particularly happy time in his life. In addition to finding it a positive academic environment, it would be marked by memories of camaraderie, late night bull sessions with piano and card playing, and even a popular amateur basketball club. A handful of the students who were given private lessons in modern Hebrew by request were regularly mocked by the others as "heebs."[19]

Still, Berger came to the college as an outsider. He was already at a disadvantage, entering the rabbinate from a relatively marginal Jewish background, to the point of even requiring some tutoring in basic Hebrew before arriving in Cincinnati.[20] Only a minority of students in those years were of a Reform background. A large number were of Orthodox background, often the sons of rabbis or other Orthodox functionaries such as *mohels* or kosher butchers for whom the Reform rabbinate was practically the only path to upward social mobility in the New World. Partly for this reason, Berger was perceived by many of his peers and professors as pompous, interested primarily in his studies and having no interest in teaching or other extracurricular Jewish activities during his years at the college.[21]

Nevertheless, the Classical Reform outlook continued to flourish in these years at Hebrew Union College, and if anything this likely only served to reinforce that which made Berger a man apart, instilling in him the aspiration for prophetic greatness. In contrast to the norm in Jewish history, the Classical Reform concept of a rabbi was not primarily as a scholar but as a preacher, that is, one in the mold of the biblical prophets who holds forth in matters of great social and moral import. Thus rabbinic training in this era placed great emphasis on oratory and homiletics. Complementing this was a related emphasis on biblical studies and on the Prophets especially.

It is not surprising then that the professor who would have the most formative influence on Elmer Berger was Moses Buttenweiser. Born in Germany and educated there in biblical scholarship at the state academies, he was hired by Hebrew Union College in 1897 and would write four major scholarly works in both German and English. Even in his last years, Berger would recall: "I can still see Buttenweiser walking up the hill on Clifton Avenue just like it were yesterday, in his white beard looking just like one of the Prophets. While other professors could be dry as dust and give lectures from 3×5 cards they held up to their nose, he could read from the original sources like poetry. He made the Prophets live."[22] Buttenweiser died in 1939, but his son Herman, a New Englander, would be a loyal member of the American Council for Judaism.

Also making a great impact on Hebrew Union College in this period was the return to Cincinnati of a group of professors who had just received their German doctorates. Among them was Jacob Rader Marcus, who was rare among those at the college of Orthodox background for having come to Reform out of personal conviction as an adolescent. Completely enamored of the original movement's remnants in Weimar Germany, he would with great tragedy publish in 1932 an optimistic tome titled *The Rise and Destiny of the German Jew*. No doubt greatly haunted by his error, he became deeply committed to the flourishing of the field of American Jewish history, recognizing that it would undoubtedly be the essential Jewish civilization of the modern era. In addition to producing a wealth of scholarship on the subject (it was often joked that Marcus was personally acquainted with each of the 3,000 Jews who lived in the thirteen colonies in 1776), Marcus would found the American Jewish Archives in 1947 at Hebrew Union College and would be a revered professor there until his death in 1995.

But joining Marcus was the ostensible successor to Moses Buttenweiser in biblical scholarship, an accomplished archaeologist who would be Elmer Berger's dissertation adviser and eventually go on to become president of Hebrew Union College, Nelson Glueck. The son of Orthodox immigrants in Cincinnati, after being ordained by Hebrew Union College, he spent most of the 1920s in Palestine as a protégé of William Foxwell Albright, the product of a Methodist missionary family widely regarded as the father of biblical archaeology. Though Glueck was aware that he was unwittingly assisting the Zionist movement by providing ostensible "scientific" evidence to back Jewish

claims to Palestine, he remained for the most part a non-Zionist and cultivated excellent relations with both the British and the Arabs throughout the
era of the Mandate and would also become close to Judah Magnes.

When Glueck became Elmer Berger's adviser at Hebrew Union College,
critical study of biblical texts was still a new and largely unexplored field.
Even Isaac Mayer Wise had stubbornly maintained the divine origin of the
Torah, but higher criticism would be embraced by his successors, Gotthard
Deutsch and Kauffman Kohler. Nelson Glueck, it would not be an exaggeration to say, was the first to bring a Jewish perspective to biblical archaeology and thus to put the Hebrew Union College on the cutting edge of an
academic approach to Jewish biblical exegesis. To Berger and his fellow students, who would sit enrapt at Glueck's telling of his various expeditions,
perhaps most notable among them the tracing of the route of the Exodus
through the Sinai and Transjordan, this opened up exciting possibilities for
the future of Judaism, perhaps as the ultimate fulfillment of the promise of
Reform itself.[23]

At least, this is how Berger likely saw it. Whereas others might have taken
the promise held forth by biblical archaeology as an academic license to embrace the Zionist narrative of Jewish history and its implicit critique of the
Jewish religion, it also held forth a contrary possibility of giving the ultimate
empirical validation to the Classical Reform narrative of Jewish history. This
narrative, which would be most directly expressed and argued by Berger in
his 1951 book *A Partisan History of Judaism*, would hold that the bulk of historical events chronicled by the Old Testament reflected little more than a
long saga of tribal warfare through the Iron and Bronze Ages, which may not
even have been subject to as much fundamental continuity as widely believed, and that fundamentally the Jewish religion is not the tribal religion
of this history but the faith of the prophets who proclaimed the possibility
of a more just and righteous way of life.

It would seem, then, that long before he approached the barricades to
battle Zionism with such remarkable fortitude, Elmer Berger's original aspiration was to use the new "science" of higher biblical criticism through archaeology and linguistics, the latter of which would be the area of his thesis
research, to establish the prophetic narrative of Jewish history once and for
all as the most empirically valid. It was just such a calling to prophetic greatness that had set him on the path to the rabbinate, whether in its first initial
and vague form from Louis Wolsey or in his later rabbinic training from such
stalwarts of the Classical Reform faith as Moses Buttenweiser, Abraham

Cronbach, and Jacob Marcus. But his path would ultimately lead elsewhere. In perhaps the most consequential decision of his life, Berger rejected an offer by Nelson Glueck to accompany him on a new expedition just after his ordination, which would surely have led his life to have been very different, though still very possibly arriving at the same convictions. But Berger felt he had "had enough schooling for a while."[24]

Berger's rabbinical thesis, "An examination of the meanings of *selichah*, *hemlah*, *rotzon*, and *hen* in The Bible," would be completed in 1932, no doubt modeled on Glueck's own German doctoral dissertation, on the meanings of the word *chesed*.[25] At first glance, such a vague thesis on linguistics and theological ethics would not be rich in foreshadowing of Berger's ultimate claim to fame, but it proves otherwise. The terms examined in the dissertation deal primarily with the compassion, mercy, and forgiveness of God; and thus with respect to their appearances in scripture, there is great emphasis on the episodes dealing with the downfall of the biblical kings and the Prophets who stood against them.

Particular emphasis was paid to the episodes surrounding the Prophets Jeremiah, Isaiah, and Elijah, all rich in allegories against Zionism. Several years hence, Berger would allude to the latter of the three in describing his initial negative reaction to organized Zionism as "a new form of Baal worship."[26] Also significant about the dissertation was its constant allusion to the standard religious understanding of repentance and its consequent mercy and forgiveness, which was very much grounded in the God-centered understanding of Classical Reform Judaism, that is, emphasizing man's humility before the infinite. Not only does this reveal the fundamentally religious basis for Berger's anti-Zionism, but it is also an expression of the God-centered outlook that motivated the majority of rabbis in the American Council for Judaism with whom Berger would ultimately fail to identify.

At the very peak of the Great Depression, Berger was extremely fortunate to find a pulpit placement immediately upon his ordination. In Pontiac, Michigan, there had been since the mid-1910s a small community with both Reform and Orthodox-leaning elements that decided for the first time to hire a rabbi. Having owned a building since 1925 and simply calling themselves the Jewish Community Center, in 1932 they elected Elmer Berger to become their first rabbi and formally became a congregation, taking the name Temple Beth Jacob. The following year, Berger would return to Cleveland to be married. His bride, who would prove to be the first of three, was Seville Schwartz, whose brother Gilbert was Elmer's classmate at Hebrew Union College. She received her law degree from Case Western Reserve University in 1930. At that point, Elmer Berger could have gone on to live a quiet if personally rewarding life as a simple congregational rabbi in Michigan. But he was clearly destined for other things.

2

THE LINES ARE DRAWN

The Jewish community of Pontiac that Elmer Berger found himself ostensibly leading was deeply divided between its Reform and Conservative factions. Much of it was strange to him, in his words, "besides a little bit from my paternal grandfather really all I knew about Orthodox Judaism was what we had learned about it academically at the College."[1] Though he recalled not having anything against Orthodox ritual, it was nonetheless foreign to him, and so ultimately he declared that while he could accommodate those who would want a traditional service for a private function such as a wedding or a funeral, he had to lead regular temple services in the fashion with which he was familiar, though as a concession to the traditionalist camp he did cover his head in these services. By Berger's own account, this arrangement was accepted with little conflict, and by 1934 Beth Jacob had voted to affiliate Reform. Still, there was apparently enough dissension with the decision that it played a role in influencing Berger to eventually make the move to Flint.[2]

By Berger's own recollection, the issue of Zionism was never a significant one in his years in Pontiac, and indeed, the Zionist Organization of America did not have a district organization in Pontiac until 1938.[3] This gave Berger a rare opportunity for experimentation in developing a perspective on Reform Jewish practice generally. The occasion Berger would most fondly recall occurred at a Sukkot celebration at Beth Jacob. Throughout his career, Berger would often make the point that Judaism, being in all its particulars the product of an agricultural society, had never come to terms with the

31

overwhelming movement of Jews away from agriculture in modernity, and nowhere more conspicuously than in the United States. Thus, for the holiday most conspicuously representing this dilemma, the members of Berger's congregation, who were employed overwhelmingly by the auto industry, decided to decorate their sukkah with auto parts, to more genuinely represent the fruits of their labor.[4]

In 1935, the year that Nazi Germany passed the Nuremberg Laws that began the long march toward the Final Solution, the Zionists began their major assault on the official anti-Zionism of the Reform movement. Led by Abba Hillel Silver and joined by Barnett Brickner, James Heller, and Felix Levy, they originally introduced a resolution stating that the Central Conference of American Rabbis (CCAR) "at present harbors no opposition to Zionism," which would be defeated. They did, however, score a major victory by getting the CCAR to agree to a resolution that stated that they "took no official stand on the subject of Zionism." In addition, they were able to elect Felix Levy as president of the CCAR for a two-year term, though even he had to concede that his election was a reflection of the CCAR's magnanimity.[5]

Levy's term at the head of the CCAR gave the Zionists the critical opportunity to replace the old Pittsburgh Platform, which had defined Reform Judaism for half a century. The document that was adopted by just a single vote in 1937 was called "The Columbus Platform: The Guiding Principles of Reform Judaism." In somewhat muted language as to be acceptable to non-Zionists, the platform declared: "In the rehabilitation of Palestine, the land hallowed by memories and hopes, we behold the promise of new life for many of our brethren. We affirm the obligation of all Jewry to aid in its upbuilding as a Jewish homeland by endeavoring not only a haven of refuge for the oppressed but also a center of Jewish cultural and spiritual life."[6]

Although a number of Zionist and other critics of the Pittsburgh Platform have charged that it ascribed messianic significance to Jewish emancipation, a far more serious charge to this effect can be leveled against the Columbus Platform. However ambiguously the platform stated its hopes for Palestine, the relevant clause concluded by stating flatly that "this is our messianic goal."

Though he remained outside the CCAR, the public face of this new religion of Jewish nationalism continued to be Stephen Wise, who by the 1930s was an increasingly prominent self-appointed spokesman for American Jews in both politics and the media. But with his growing prominence in American life, Wise also attracted a growing amount of scrutiny and outright opposition from those rabbis who were adamantly opposed to his vision for the future of American Judaism. Prominent among these of course was Louis Wolsey, who had his first significant clash with Wise in 1935. This came after the publication of Mahatma Gandhi's famous comments on the plight of the Jews of Europe, in which he prophesied that Jewish nationalism was going to corrupt the people who were historically "the untouchables of Europe," possibly to a degree beyond conceiving.

No doubt moved by the same pacifist sympathies that had rallied him to the defense of Abraham Cronbach ten years earlier, Wolsey passionately wrote to Gandhi declaring: "The Jewish people are greatly divided between those who believe in utilizing the doctrine of replying to force with force and those who are impressed with your contribution to the problem of human relationships, whom I should like to call Jewish Gandhists who believe in answering the Hitler persecutions with non-resistance and non-violence." Wise furiously responded with his own open letter to Gandhi with great presumption and condescension: "Never, as far as we know, have you urged that non-resistance means passive submission to the will of a persecutor. I have often thought of appealing to your support of that non-cooperation of Nazi Germany which takes the form of an economic and moral boycott. You have spoken as if you understood the injustice of a Jew alluding to the boycott as if it were violent because it is resistant."[7]

Wolsey would respond more than competently, comparing the desired goals of the boycott to the starvation blockade the Allies imposed on postwar Germany to force it to sign the Versailles Treaty, going on to deliver one of the most damning indictments of the Zionist "left" of all time: "I might say in passing that Gandhi ought to be grateful to you for enlightening him as to the meaning of Satyagraha. The important thing is that I have not misrepresented Judaism, and particularly your Judaism. You cannot in sanity be a non-resistant and a fighter all at the same time. You cannot pillory Jews who disagree with you and call yourself irenic and tolerant. You cannot eat your cake and have it too."[8]

The first direct challenge to the claims of Stephen Wise on the destiny of American, and indeed world Jewry would not be made until 1938, two years after the founding of the World Jewish Congress. That challenge would be issued by Samuel Goldenson, the senior rabbi of the prestigious Temple Emanu-El of New York. Born in Kalvaria, Poland, in 1878 and arriving in America at the age of twelve, he would be ordained by Hebrew Union College in 1904 and begin with pulpit positions in Lexington, Kentucky, and Albany, New York, distinguishing himself in the latter city by running as the mayoral candidate of the Progressive or Bull Moose Party in 1914.

The quintessential Classical Reform rabbi, Goldenson was a prolific sermonizer, very often dwelling on themes of Americanism. Contrary to Zionist and modern liberal sensibilities, this hardly made him a reactionary. In 1918 Goldenson was awarded the prestigious pulpit of Rodef Shalom in Pittsburgh, the very seat from which the Pittsburgh Platform had been issued. Here he became nationally known for his outspokenness in matters of social justice, most notably in 1928 when he spoke from his pulpit in support of the coal miners' strike that was sweeping western Pennsylvania that year. He arrived at Temple Emanu-El in 1934.

Goldenson fired what may well have been the first shot in the battle for the survival of Classical Reform Judaism with a sermon he gave on May 28, 1938, titled "Can we achieve Jewish Unity by a referendum?," responding to the attempt just that month by Stephen Wise and his new World Jewish Congress to do exactly that. Goldenson thundered:

> How strange it is that in the present circumstances when civilization
> is so threatened and troubled by totalitarian states, that the Jewish
> people should now be asked by certain of their leaders to establish an
> agency which, in its "single and all-inclusive" character, appears very
> much like a totalitarian organization. Indeed, these very leaders in
> their call to the Jewish people already use the language of supreme authority, for they speak of having "decreed" the referendum. And all
> this is done in the name of unity and democracy![9]

With a keen and prophetic foresight, Goldenson foresaw what the consequences of such designs, which would lay the foundation of the modern Israel lobby, would be for American Jewish life. On the political implications of organizing such a Congress, he continued:

> In effect, such an organization is an indirect acceptance of the racial
> philosophy of the Hitler regime. It seems to give notice to the rest of
> the world that in the promotion of our interests and in the defense of
> our rights, we as American citizens cannot be effective enough
> through availing ourselves of the agencies of our government, but that
> we must have our own national organizations so that our leaders may
> speak for us as a single unit. This endeavor separates us at one stroke
> from the rest of the population on the sole ground that we are Jews.[10]

And on the dire ultimate consequences of such a reconstruction of Jewish identity, Goldenson was no less forthright:

As long as the Jew feels he has a heritage worth cherishing, a heritage informed with the spirit of his lawgivers, prophets, psalmists, and sages, and that through this heritage he can realize the best in himself and make significant contributions to the moral and spiritual life of mankind, he can feel personally justified to carry on and can claim the right to remain a Jew in any society. The moment he gives up these convictions, he abandons his special reason for existence and his warrant to survive as a member of a separate group. Thereafter, every claim that he makes in behalf of Jewish life and Jewish identity becomes less and less intelligible to others and loses force in their minds.[11]

Naturally, this provoked the outrage and full furor of Stephen Wise and his confederates. Wise himself waxed especially demagogic, belittling Goldenson for condemning racialism, "the thing most dreaded by the Jewish members of Temple Emanu-El, or the Jewish members of St. Thomas Church. This is but another expression of Jewish self-contempt and self-belittlement, too common among the earlier groups of Jewish immigrants of whom Dr. Goldenson chooses to be a representative."[12] On the very same page of the very same periodical, Louis Lipsky of the Zionist Organization of America accused Goldenson of "raising fears and dangers that are unworthy of courageous men."[13] These attacks were accompanied by a press release from the three leading Conservative rabbis of New York, who unironically invoked the totalitarian argument that a Jew was obligated to join the American Jewish Congress in order to be a good American.

On the other end of the continent, the equally prestigious Temple Emanu-El of San Francisco had already heard the gauntlet thrown down against Zionism two years earlier. Home to an especially prosperous community of German Jews who established themselves from the earliest years of the Gold Rush, rising with the city and the country to the point where they would become known as the "San Francisco aristocracy," San Francisco would achieve special notoriety in the Zionist imagination as the most stubborn stronghold of resistance to their aims from the kind of Jews they most loved to hate. But if the pioneer families of Emanu-El, some of whom would be too assimilated even to identify with the American Council for Judaism, were uncomfortably close to the stereotype of reactionary and prosperous German Jews, the rabbi who would lead them in these tumultuous and consequential years could not have been farther from it.

Irving Reichert, the son of a Lower East Side rabbi born in 1895, grew up in extremely modest means before attending Hebrew Union College and was a politically precocious young man who wrote his dissertation on the Dreyfus Affair before being ordained in 1921. While he spent the next decade ministering to struggling immigrant communities in his native New York, first in the Jamaica section of Queens and then in the Tremont section of the Bronx, his brother Victor would also be ordained by Hebrew Union College and eventually become the successor to the Cincinnati pulpit of David Philipson. A member of the first class ordained by Isaac Mayer Wise in 1883, Philipson led the Reform movement's charge against Zionism in the early Mandate period and would in his last years be a stalwart of the American Council for Judaism.

Reichert arrived in San Francisco in 1930, where he did not let the potential pressures from his wealthy congregation prevent him from becoming an outspoken advocate of the radical labor movement of Depression-era California, made famous by the novels of John Steinbeck. At least once taking the side of California farm workers against some of his own congregants who employed them, he was also active in the defenses of Tom Mooney and the Scottsboro Boys in the era that a general strike nearly paralyzed San Francisco in 1934.[14] Probably best remembered was Reichert's close collaboration with Lincoln Steffens in protesting Governor Jim Rolph's openly voiced support of antilabor vigilantes. To Steffens he would write: "I am convinced that you have failed most lamentably as a revolutionary because you have a sense of humor, which is the most damning indictment I can lay at your door."[15]

No milquetoast liberal of the type that epitomized the Reform rabbinate of the postwar era, Irving Reichert was also a vocal opponent of American entry into the Second World War and after Pearl Harbor was a leader of the Committee for Fair Play, which protested Japanese internment. As Fred Rosenbaum would put it in his history of Temple Emanu-El, "He cited the blistering indictment by the Prophet Amos of ancient Israel, but the shepherd of Tekoa merely set the stage for Reichert's own critique of his own inequitable society."[16] It is not surprising then that in matters of religion he zealously adhered to Classical Reform, to the point of admitting privately that he could just as easily be a Unitarian. This made Emanu-El an auspicious place for Reichert, who, though succeeding two severe critics of Classical Reform in its pulpit, was thence preceded by Jacob Voorsanger, who had been second only to Isaac Mayer Wise in denouncing Zionism during the time of Herzl.[17]

Though he voted for the CCAR neutrality resolution in 1935 in the spirit of compromise, Reichert made his first significant declaration of his anti-Zionism in a January 1936 sermon. This was prompted by a recent article in the *Atlantic Monthly* crowing over the apparent victory for Zionism within the Reform movement the preceding year. The author of the article was Ludwig Lewisohn, a native of Berlin whose family converted to Methodism on arriving in America, but who himself returned to Judaism and became a fervent Zionist ideologue after his ancestry barred him from becoming an English literature professor. This ultimately apt victory lap on behalf of Zionism forced Reichert to come forward on an issue that, despite his convictions, he preferred to avoid at this stage. Reichert was so bold as to even challenge the essential Zionist premise of Judaism's attachment to historic Palestine:

> If my reading of Jewish history is correct, Israel took upon itself the yoke of the Law not in Palestine, but in the wilderness at Mount Sinai, and by far the greater part of its deathless and distinguished contribution to world culture was produced not in Palestine but in Babylon and the lands of the Dispersion. Jewish states may rise and fall, as they have risen and fallen in the past, but the people of Israel will continue to minister at the altar of the Most High God in all the lands in which they dwell.[18]

Not hesitating either to call out the totalitarian nature of Zionism, as Goldenson would two years later, Reichert continued:

> There is too dangerous a parallel between the insistence of some Zionist spokesmen upon nationality and race and blood, and similar pronouncements by Fascist leaders in European dictatorships. Some types of propaganda may prove too tragically successful for our comfort. If we succeed in teaching America that Zionism is the only instrument of our political salvation, we may live to regret it. Last summer, an American rabbi declared before the World Zionist Congress "We are not asking the world, we are telling it. We are not inviting decisions by the nations, we are apprising the nations of our decisions." No swashbuckling, saber-rattling German Nazi or Japanese jingo ever used more provocative language than that.[19]

For the American rabbi probably most active up to that point in anti-Nazi activities—going on three separate fact-finding missions to Germany between 1933 and 1937 and second to none in providing for German refugees in his congregation—these were fighting words that earned him the confidence of Louis Wolsey as he began to plan for the inevitable.[20]

Thus it was as combative anti-Zionist voices began to be heard in the Reform rabbinate that Elmer Berger accepted the pulpit of Temple Beth El in Flint, Michigan, in 1936. A younger congregation, but with a more solidly Reform culture than Beth Jacob (they would not formally affiliate Reform until after Berger left Flint during the Second World War), the congregation was founded in 1927, largely at the instigation of Harry Winegarden. Winegarden lived the classic Horatio Alger story of a Russian immigrant who rose from peddling fruit in the streets of Detroit to become a large retailer of furniture and appliances with his Winegarden's Store, which dominated downtown Flint until the early 1960s, eventually growing to be the largest property owner. He was able to apply his business acumen to the rapid growth of the new congregation, attracting several Jewish businessmen of Flint, including Charles Fisher of auto body fame.

The fledgling congregation was therefore able to afford its own building by 1935 and the following year was able to hire Berger as its first rabbi.[21] It was an awkward time for the young rabbi to be making the transition from a lower middle-class community in Pontiac—many of whom, to Berger's dismay, were even attracted to the economic message of the controversial "radio priest" Charles Coughlin in neighboring Royal Oak[22]—to a congregation comprised largely of the captains of industry in Flint. Within his first year in Flint, the city was rocked by the much-storied sit-down strike that marked the arrival of the United Auto Workers and their recognition by General Motors. Fisher Body had been a major target of the strike, and nearly all male members of the congregation were small manufacturers who supplied General Motors.

As his future career would make abundantly clear, Elmer Berger was not one who was shy about expressing his honest opinions, but he did not distinguish himself one way or the other during this upheaval as perhaps the most important Jewish leader in Flint. No doubt there had to have been pressure to bear from the bulk of his congregants, but it would certainly not behoove him to appeal to their baser instincts and give an antilabor sermon from his pulpit, as on other occasions he would express his admiration for the Jewish labor movement.[23] In fairness also, for all its explosiveness, the strike was relatively short, lasting only seven weeks. But most of all, Berger was never terribly interested in politics, and this would hardly be mutually exclusive from his anti-Zionism, even in his later years as its original religious motivation grew dimmer. Perhaps it was an early indicator of the irrepressible optimism of his faith, that even at a moment of merciless pitched battle between capital and labor, he held to older ideals of social justice and noblesse oblige.

It was not long after that exciting first chapter of his rabbinate in Flint that the issue of Zionism finally asserted itself into Berger's ministry. Though his family background and training at Hebrew Union College clearly grounded him in the basic assumptions behind Reform anti-Zionism, his friendship and shared interests with Nelson Glueck suggest that under the right circumstances he could have been open to binationalism. This, moreover, would seem to confirm Berger's own claim to have not been passionate either way on the issue until it began to interfere in the life of his congregation in Flint. It was what may have otherwise been a benign incident in the everyday life of a house of worship that set off the spark that led Elmer Berger to his ultimate notoriety.

The sisterhood of Beth El had adopted the perfectly quintessential function of buying floral arrangements for Friday services each week and then after the services donating the flowers to a local hospital. As it happened, one Friday evening Berger arrived at the temple expecting to see the floral arrangements fully in place, only to find the sanctuary barren. When he asked the member of the sisterhood responsible for flowers that week what had happened, with complete nonchalance she informed him that she had unilaterally decided to give the money instead to the United Palestine Appeal. Berger did not react angrily, but he did resolve to take a closer look at the Appeal to get a better idea of what exactly it was doing in the community.[24]

What he discovered alarmed him. Specifically, he found that the literature of the United Palestine Appeal deliberately misrepresented itself as a movement that aided refugees from the Nazis by settling them in Palestine, while it was an open secret that the money was going to the militias of the Jewish Agency or *Yishuv*. Berger particularly detested the theatrics used in the literature and in public campaigns, which involved the hosting of "secret" fundraisers in order to add a cloak-and-dagger drama to the efforts, as though the tragedy of European Jewry was being sold to American Jews as some kind of adventure of which they could be a part.[25] In addition, at the peak of the terrible Jewish-Arab rioting that wracked Palestine in the late 1930s, the Appeal literature was pushing a pure fiction that "responsible Jews and responsible Arabs will unite in an independent state to fight alongside the Allies."[26] Although it was easy enough to refute this just by reading the newspapers, as Berger quickly found, there was simply no source of information from the Arabs in America at that time.

And so by the eve of the Second World War, Elmer Berger became unalterably convinced that this subordination of all charitable and civic functions

of the Jewish community to the service of an armed Jewish nationalist movement amounted to exactly the sort of malevolent folly that had been the constant target of righteous hatred by his venerated Prophets. Though Berger
was not secretive of his views, it would not be until 1942, after some years
had passed, that this issue would become the cause for serious dissension in
the Jewish communities of and around Flint. Berger even in this period
hosted a Zionist speaker at Beth El, Melbourne Harris, assistant rabbi in
Cleveland to Abba Hillel Silver.[27] However, this did not stop Berger's committed Zionist successor in Pontiac, Eric Friedland, from denouncing Berger
from his pulpit as early as 1939, and it was between the two men that the
drama in Flint would ultimately climax.[28]

It could not have been immediately obvious what the ultimate significance would be of the disillusionment with Zionism of this young and obscure rabbi, but in another such case around the same time, it was. Morris
Lazaron, the nationally famous rabbi of Baltimore Hebrew Congregation
who had testified in favor of the 1922 congressional resolutions, was finding his way into the anti-Zionist camp. Born in 1888 in Savannah, Georgia,
he was descended on his mother's side from one of the original Sephardic
families to have settled in the Georgia colony at its founding in 1733, and on
his father's side from a leading rabbi of the Prussian city of Konigsberg. He
spent but a year after being ordained in 1914 in Wheeling, West Virginia, before earning his prestigious Baltimore pulpit and was succeeded in Wheeling
by none other than Abba Hillel Silver, who in a yet greater irony would marry
the sister of Lazaron's wife.

Lazaron rapidly distinguished himself in Baltimore as a leading Jewish
military chaplain during the First World War and thereafter as a founder of the
Military Chaplains Association. Also an early pioneer of interfaith dialogue,
which would be for him a deep lifelong commitment, Lazaron was a founder
of the National Conference of Christians and Jews. Like many in the privileged class of American Jews during and after the First World War, Lazaron's
initial interest in Zionism was likely inspired by Louis Brandeis and his specifically philanthropic interests in Palestine. Like his friend and fellow Hebrew
Union College alumni Judah Magnes, he was also a fundamental believer in
the prophetic tradition of universalism, if also cognizant of Classical Reform's
failings. Philip Roth's fictional Lionel Bengelsdorf, a Southerner who traveled
in elite social circles, appears to have been loosely based on Lazaron.

At most a nominally active but largely lapsed member of the Zionist
Organization of America (ZOA), Lazaron experienced a disillusionment that

appears to have begun with the disaffection of Brandeis from the Zionist movement. Brandeis's belief that the political goals of Zionism were fully met by the establishment of the British Mandate ultimately forced him and his lieutenants out of the movement by the American allies of Chaim Weizmann, notably Louis Lipsky, by the 1930s.[29] (This would not, however, prevent Zionists from the invocation of Brandeis, even to this very day.) Hardly alone in considering the Brandeis position perfectly compatible with the faith of Isaac Mayer Wise and the Pittsburgh Platform, while still a member of the ZOA, Lazaron joined the growing chorus of opposition to Stephen Wise and denounced the World Jewish Congress from his pulpit in 1937.

This won Lazaron the plaudits of his friend and fellow leading citizen of Baltimore H. L. Mencken. Over the years Mencken would consider Lazaron a man of the cloth in whom he could confide his ravings about whatever two-bit evangelist had him agitated that week. When they discovered in each other kindred spirits on Zionism and nationalism generally, Mencken would write to his friend with the bluntness that would make him one of America's most beloved men of letters:

> I needn't tell you that I agree completely with the doctrine set forth in your speech. It seems to me that the brethren of the Jewish Congress are most imprudent, to put it very mildly. I am especially uneasy about the frequent rantings of Stephen S. Wise. Whether intentionally or not, he is constantly propagating the notion that Jews are a separate people, with interests quite distinct from those of the countries in which they live. This is the sort of thing that gives anti-Semitic demagogues their chance.[30]

Lazaron decisively crossed the Rubicon with the publication of a book the following year titled *Common Ground: A Plea for Intelligent Americanism*, which set out his views on Jewish issues and larger world affairs, Lazaron having closely consulted Mencken on the manuscript.[31] The book immediately won him the praises of his new allies such as Samuel Goldenson, David Philipson, and Jacob Marcus. A delighted Mencken informed Lazaron: "I have just sent a copy of your book to an anti-Semite in New York who bombards me with literature. He seems to be a perfectly honest man and is certainly not violent, but nevertheless his credulity is apparently endless."[32] Also in 1937 Lazaron began to sound the alarm to the officially "non-Zionist" American Jewish Committee, catching the ear of its most anti-Zionist regular, Joseph Proskauer, who began to warn of a "serious disruption in non-Zionist ranks."[33]

It is imperative to note, in the case of Morris Lazaron, that he did not become an anti-Zionist because his views on the question of Palestine had changed, but precisely because they had not. He was consistently in favor of binationalism, and perhaps more important, the position of non-Zionism as it was understood by the American Jewish Committee. That is, the imperative of philanthropic and other support by the American Jewish community for the cultural and civic institutions of Jews in Palestine, most especially the Hebrew University founded by Judah Magnes, with the disavowal of any political aims relating thereto, either in Palestine or for themselves as American Jews. It also bears emphasis, again, that this "non-Zionism" was indeed the unwavering position of Louis Brandeis.

In keeping with the spirit of this position, Lazaron's major statement came in 1940, when war had already begun to rage in Europe, in a pamphlet titled "Homeland or State: The Real Issue." Lazaron directly challenged the Zionists over their fundamental dishonesty and their complementary position of attack on any who dared stand in their way:

> The political Zionist group charges all of us who do not accept their program with Jewish disloyalty and labels us antagonists of Palestine. Some go so far as to read us out of Jewish life. It would be unfortunate if we permit these charges to go by default. American Jews who are not secularists or political nationalists will not let themselves be jockeyed into this position. They will not permit themselves to become involved in political maneuverings under the guise of philanthropy or friendship for Palestine.[34]

The pamphlet thus struck an optimistic tone: "This is the time to set the Jewish problem in the matrix of the world situation, to see it as a part of the world picture. The spiritual and ethical life of humanity is involved, the future of mankind."[35] But Lazaron would receive a note of prophetic foreboding from his dear friend H. L. Mencken in praising him for the pamphlet:

> Unhappily, I have some doubt that you will be able to convince the majority of Jews that you are right. They have been so horribly misled by foolish leadership that they seem to be in an almost irrational state of mind. If I had the time and the energy I think I'd do a pamphlet on the origins of anti-Semitism. They have never been discussed with any real candor. Tactless leadership is certainly one of them.[36]

And it was surely an hour of foreboding. As a desperate measure to contain and even hopefully quell the violence that had been ongoing between the Jews and Arabs of Palestine since the beginning of the Arab revolt against the British in 1936, in May 1939 the British severely restricted Jewish immigration into the Mandate. This of course led to a disastrous impact on the prospects for the rescue of European Jewry once the Second World War commenced in September. In turn this led to an unparalleled opportunity for the Zionists. When the war broke out, the World Zionist Organization resolved to set up in the United States, the neutral country with the largest Jewish population, an "emergency council" that could take command of the Zionist movement were its leadership incapacitated either in Europe or Palestine by the circumstances of the war. This, the American Zionist Emergency Council, in the 1950s became known as the American Zionist Council for Public Affairs, and a decade later changed its name once more to American Israel Public Affairs Committee, the infamous AIPAC.

Immediately, the Emergency Council was able to effect the fundamental coup upon which all of the financial power of the modern Israel lobby—and more important the complete control of Jewish organizational life that eluded Stephen Wise and his World Jewish Congress—ultimately rests. Exploiting the crisis, the Zionists were able to strong-arm a merger of the United Palestine Appeal with the philanthropic arm of the American Jewish Committee, the Joint Distribution Committee, into the United Jewish Appeal. Indeed, the continued existence of the United Jewish Appeal after the founding of the State of Israel, and the means by which it only continued to expand its control of American Jewish organizational life for the political and military ends of that state, would be a principal cause for the continued activity of the American Council for Judaism in that same time. However, because the activities of the Zionists remained mostly under the radar until after America entered the war, for fear of arousing suspicion, serious objections from anti-Zionist members of the American Jewish Committee (AJC) were not raised until that time.[37]

Still, those members of the AJC who objected to what was happening (concentrated heavily in the New York German Jewish elite, which became known colloquially as "our crowd") generally let it be known. Foremost among them was Joseph Proskauer, the son of a successful cotton broker in Mobile, Alabama, who remained in New York after receiving his law degree from Columbia University. A leading aide to New York governor Al Smith and able defender of his later criticisms of the New Deal, he spent many years as a judge before founding the prestigious law firm of Proskauer and Rose and serving as a longtime leader of the AJC. He was fortunate enough to be joined in New York by two relatives of the great Isaac Mayer Wise—his youngest son Jonah Wise, the rabbi of New York's prestigious Central Synagogue, and Arthur Hays Sulzberger, the husband of his eldest grand-daughter and distinguished publisher of the *New York Times*.

All three men had been intimately involved in the efforts of the Joint Distribution Committee toward the rescue of the Jews of Europe, but they had a colleague in Philadelphia whose deep commitment to that cause was matched only by the depth of his outrage at the cynical and unscrupulous way in which that cause had been seized by the Zionists to whom he had always been opposed. Lessing Rosenwald was roused to action after he was stonewalled by Abba Hillel Silver upon first raising the issue in a private meeting, and then on his own initiative when consulting a team of accountants about his suspicions.[38] The tremendous success story of the German American Jews represented by "our crowd" was anchored in, for all practical purposes, the invention of the retail industry as we know it today. Virtually every major department store chain in U.S. history was founded by German Jews, and though the name Rosenwald was not attached to any store, it was the proverbial 800-pound gorilla of them all.

Julius Rosenwald was born in 1862 in Springfield, Illinois, where his immigrant parents ran a dry goods store. When he took over the family business, he was already expanding into a more broad mercantile operation when he bought the failed mail-order firm of Sears Roebuck and Company. Combining his new and highly successful Sears Catalog with a far-flung retail operation had made Rosenwald by 1900 one of the richest men in America. With this wealth, he would become one of the most accomplished philanthropists in U.S. history, not only with such conventional endowments as Chicago's Museum of Science and Industry and the University of Chicago Library, but also with the Rosenwald Fund, which built over a thousand rural schools for southern black children and may well have been all that kept them above abject serfdom in the darkest days of Jim Crow. Indeed, many black homes in that era would have his picture on the wall alongside those of Abraham Lincoln and Booker T. Washington.

Also a major patron of American Reform Judaism in its formative years, Rosenwald would be a founder of the Chicago Sinai Congregation, whose first rabbi was Emil Hirsch, coauthor of the Pittsburgh Platform and leader of the movement's radical wing. Rosenwald also spoke out against Zionism in the aftermath of the First World War and was the prime mover behind the settlement of Jewish refugees in America in the early years of the Joint Distribution

Committee. It was against this backdrop that Lessing Rosenwald, the second of five children born in 1891 in Chicago, came of age.[39] Beginning his career as a shipping clerk in the Philadelphia warehouse, he was soon running it and eventually worked his way up to succeed his father as the chairman of Sears Roebuck after his death in 1932. When Lessing first took charge of the company at the peak of the Great Depression, he went around the country offering an employee buyout but was met with an overwhelming response of confidence in the company and his leadership.

Lessing Rosenwald retired from Sears Roebuck in 1939 to devote his full energy to his own philanthropic activities, which in addition to his devotion to the Joint Distribution Committee included the prolific collection of art and rare books, which were ultimately all donated to the National Gallery of Art and the Library of Congress, respectively. After witnessing with horror the Zionist seizure of the Joint Distribution Committee, Rosenwald was further alarmed by the increasing politicization and consequent polarization of American Jewish identity. When he endorsed Wendell Willkie in the presidential election of 1940 and allowed his name and public statements to be distributed by the Independent No Third Term Committee, he was deeply disturbed by the campaign rhetoric that identified the Jewish vote with Franklin Roosevelt and the specter of anti-Semitism with Willkie.[40] Even when Rosenwald joined another Jewish Willkie supporter, Sidney Sternbach, in organizing a "Committee of 100,000" to protest the especially outrageous statements in this connection of FDR's running mate Henry Wallace and New York governor Herbert Lehman, he was still disturbed by that declaration's talk of a "Jewish vote."[41]

In that same political season, Rosenwald joined the national board of the America First Committee, founded that September on the Yale University campus to oppose the U.S. entry into the Second World War. The largest antiwar organization in U.S. history, peaking at 800,000 members, its national chairman was Rosenwald's successor at Sears Roebuck and dear friend Gen. Robert Wood. The Committee grew rapidly at the end of 1940 in the wake of FDR's reelection, with supporters from the better-established and left-wing Keep America Out of War Committee, whose leaders such as Norman Thomas and John Flynn embraced America First. Thomas in particular brought other notable Jewish supporters to America First, namely Sidney Hertzberg (father of the journalist Hendrik Hertzberg) and James Lipsig.[42]

These strides were largely thwarted, however, after a solicitation for membership was sent to Ira Hirschmann, an executive with Bloomingdale's who had previously supported the Keep America Out of War Committee. Hirschmann expressed his sympathy for the group and its objectives but stated he could not join because of the presence on the board of the notorious anti-Semite Henry Ford.[43] Recently added to the Committee in what was immediately recognized by all to have been a tragic blunder, Ford was hastily given the boot, but Rosenwald was so disheartened by the whole episode that he too resigned. Rosenwald emphasized, however, that he was "still in accord with the basic principles"[44] of America First and took on all comers in the pro-war onslaught of the following year, defending his friend General Wood's "courageous and impeccable character."[45]

The anti-Zionist rabbis would be split on the question of America's entry into the war, not withstanding that the original platform of the American Council for Judaism, written at the height of wartime, would be steeped in the rhetoric of Allied war aims. Samuel Goldenson had been active in anti-Nazi organizing since 1933 and was a founding member of America First's nemesis, the Committee to Aid and Defend the Allies, led by the journalist William Allen White. Lazaron, though likely conflicted for most of the period before Pearl Harbor, finally would denounce America First from his pulpit in October 1941. For the better part of that year, however, he kept up an extensive correspondence with his good friend, Undersecretary of State Sumner Welles, about the evolving picture of American Jewish politics and what it portended for wartime. Berger himself, according to his friend Justus Doenecke, was generally sympathetic to intervention and had no sympathy for America First but was unlikely to have ever discussed the world situation from his pulpit before Pearl Harbor, no doubt pulled in the other direction by the influence of his pacifist mentors Wolsey and Cronbach.[46]

Cronbach, for his part, was as firm in his pacifist convictions as ever, as early as July 1941 founding the Jewish Peace Fellowship, allied with the Fellowship of Reconciliation led by A. J. Muste, to advocate for Jewish conscientious objectors. But it would be Irving Reichert to make the boldest protest, bravely giving an antiwar Rosh Hashanah sermon at the peak of vitriol against America First in September 1941:

> What makes war possible? War seizes hold of some of the noblest elements in human personality—courage, loyalty, heroism, faith, willingness to die for a cause—and uses them for fearful ends. Despite the fact that modern man no longer prostrates himself before images of carved wood or hewn stone or molten metal, it is nevertheless a fact that most of the world's unhappiness today springs from the cardinal

sin of idolatry. Just see how we take the worthy elements of human life and lay them at the feet of false gods—nationalism, racism, selfish acquisitiveness—giving to these idols what belongs to God, to selfish groups what belongs to all mankind.[47]

Only some realized it, but when America finally entered the war, it was ultimately the end of the America with which Classical Reform Judaism had such an incredible love affair. Out of this war would come the American colossus that would sooner or later bestride the globe, and it would be as a part of that new world order that the Zionists would succeed in establishing their state. Consequently, American Jewish identity would never be the same, as the claims of Zionism thereupon would be increasingly treated by all concerned as a given. No matter to what degree the partisans of Classical Reform did or did not realize that the end of the old America would mean the end of the Jewish identity they cherished, they would not surrender it hastily.

3

STAKING EVERYTHING

Effectively, the Zionists declared victory in their struggle to secure the loyalty of Reform Judaism in 1941 when they elected James Heller as president of the Central Conference of American Rabbis (CCAR). The son of Max Heller, an early disciple of Isaac Mayer Wise who had himself flirted with Zionism from his pulpit in New Orleans, James would join the Zionist hardcore after other youthful political flirtations. Immediately upon his election, Heller proclaimed, as though by decree, that Reform Judaism was no longer anti-Zionist, and that the matter was closed as far as he was concerned.[1] It would not be long before he would have the opportunity to test the force of his declaration, as Zionist agitation began to take full force in the early months of America's participation in the Second World War.

It was around this time that the standoff over Zionism between Elmer Berger and his successor in Pontiac, Eric Friedland, finally came to the boiling point. Perhaps becoming just too insufferable in repeating the crowing of Heller and his associates upon their victory, Friedland had finally pushed the limits of what Berger's remaining friends in Pontiac could tolerate. Led by Norman Buckner, a founding member of Beth Jacob who was originally from the Upper Peninsula of Michigan, they appealed to their old friend in Flint to confront Friedland in a public debate. The debate was held on March 17, 1942, at the Flint Jewish Community Center. Though the only existing account comes from Berger himself, it relates that Berger was widely thought to have won the debate, "demolishing" Friedland. The president of Beth El said to Berger that he was "absolutely unmerciful," though Berger would recall many years later that "if indeed the outcome was all that one-sided, it was more a demonstration of the general lack of information about the entire problem than any particularly brilliant insights on my part."[2]

The text of Berger's speech in the debate was soon after published in the form of a pamphlet titled "Why I Am a Non-Zionist," a title that would take on a deeply ironic twist as the term "non-Zionism" increasingly came to designate for Berger a tragic, if not downright malevolent, fecklessness on the part of those who claimed it. In many ways merely an extended essay that would eventually be expanded into his book *The Jewish Dilemma*, the speech anchored Berger's analysis in forthright declarative statements of the forces that were afflicting American Jewish life:

> Jewish life is deeply and profoundly troubled. It is troubled not only by nearly ten years of brutal, unrelenting battering at the hands of the brutalitarians of the world, it is troubled by a deep-seated and profoundly stirring internecine warfare. Today, having accommodated itself somewhat to the universal confusion, the superficial unity which the first attacks against it produced is disappearing from the areas of Jewish life. That Jewish life and thought are today again showing signs of internal conflict testifies only to the profundity with which the opposing opinions in Jewish life have found root and soil in Jewish attitudes and Jewish living.[3]

No less forthrightly did Berger state the reasons for his views:

> I am a non-Zionist because I do not believe that any exclusively Jewish salvation program, in and of itself, can be permanently beneficial to Jewish life for the Jew is inseparably a part of civilization. I believe this is true in defense work, in philanthropy, and in the area of Zionism. Zionism offers neither a practical nor a spiritual solution to the Jewish problem and indeed, it can offer neither. For the "Jewish problem" is not really Jewish at all, though the Zionist is well on his way to making it so by seeking this thoroughgoing exclusiveness of Jewish life. The destiny of the Jew still lies with the destiny of the liberal world. Because fundamentally, Zionism has no faith with that world, I am a non-Zionist.[4]

The pamphlet would be widely distributed as the controversy over Zionism in those parts of the Jewish community that had been most resistant to it reached its climax and earned Berger the confidence of his allies. He rapidly became the public face of Jewish anti-Zionism. Among those who sent letters to Berger praising the pamphlet were Joseph Proskauer and Julian Morgenstern, president of Hebrew Union College.[5]

"Why I Am a Non-Zionist" was published and distributed with the financial backing of Myron "Mike" Winegarden, the son of Beth El's founding patron, who would join his cousin Jerome in funneling the family fortune into a prosperous law practice; both men would be long-standing members of the American Council for Judaism. The debate with Rabbi Friedland would, however, mark the beginning of the end for Elmer Berger in Flint. For all the success of the debate, Berger's increasingly outspoken views could not have been very popular in the Jewish community there, where, as in Pontiac, he had the support of a vocal minority, but still a minority. This was reflected in his increasing eagerness to find his way out of the "ghetto" of Flint, as he was wont to refer to it.[6] In this he found a kindred spirit who would prove as providential as scandalous. When his erstwhile patron Mike Winegarden shipped out that year, Berger began an affair with Winegarden's wife.[7] The former Ruth Rosenthal, the daughter of a wealthy furniture manufacturer in Evansville, Indiana, had graduated from the University of Michigan law school and was the first woman ever admitted to the bar in Genesee County, Michigan.

But while the Flint tempest brewed, events were unfolding rapidly on the national scene. The last week of February 1942 was the occasion of the first meeting of the CCAR since James Heller's elevation to its presidency. Heller and his Zionist allies decided to use this occasion to conduct a test of the extent of their control. It is telling, however, that even with their triumph coinciding almost perfectly with American entry into the war and the first reports of the Final Solution, the Zionists still felt a need to hedge their bets by manipulating protocol to the fullest extent possible. On the morning of Friday, February 27, the last day of the conference, when over half of the 236 rabbis attending had left, Heller led thirty-three Zionist rabbis in introducing the following resolution: "Be it resolved that the Central Conference of American Rabbis is in complete sympathy with the demand of the Jews of Palestine that they be given the opportunity to fight in defense of their homeland on the side of the democracies, under allied command to the end that the victory of democracy may be hastened everywhere."[8]

This demand for a "Jewish army" had been the central demand of the *Yishuv* since Britain's declaration of war against Germany. A symbolic Jewish unit had been formed in the period of British occupation of Ottoman Palestine toward the end of the First World War, which Zionist propaganda to this very day celebrates as "the first Jewish army in 2,000 years." Specifically, the Jewish Agency was now demanding that the British raise an army of "Palestinian and stateless Jews" with the status conferred to the Free French and Belgian forces. The Winston Churchill government had formally endorsed the plan in October 1940, but practical considerations militated against its actual implementation for the remainder of the war. This was contrary to the sympathies of many in British politics—Churchill had, after all, been the colonial secretary who drew the borders of the modern Middle East, including the formal establishment of the Mandate.

Not only was a resolution by the CCAR endorsing this scheme a direct violation of the 1935 neutrality resolution, which technically remained in effect, but in the circumstances of wartime, and the clear implication that such an army was intended toward the establishment of a state after the war, this amounted to a wholesale, if backdoor, endorsement of Zionism by the Reform movement. While the rabbis opposing the resolution spoke directly to these broader implications, which could even directly lead to a redefinition of "Jew" from a religious to a national identity by Reform, the supporting rabbis focused the debate on the specifics of what was called for in the resolution itself. The exception here would come from Philip Bernstein, a militant Zionist who would become the leading anti-anti-Zionist in the years to come, arguing frankly that "much of what Jews get at the peace table will depend on what Jews do as Jews during the war."[9]

After a failed attempt to table the resolution by Solomon Freehof, Samuel Goldenson's successor in Pittsburgh and generally a non-Zionist, the "Jewish army" resolution passed by a vote of 64 to 38.[10] But the anti-Zionist response would be immediate. At the suggestion of Lewis L. Strauss, a U.S. Navy captain and active member of the American Jewish Committee who was then serving as president of Temple Emanu-El, Samuel Goldenson wrote an open letter just days later, which would be signed by sixty-three rabbis and telegrammed to the British War Office, expressing Jewish dissent on the army question. Stephen Wise, naturally, went immediately to the ramparts to denounce the endorsers of the Goldenson telegram, while Morris Lazaron was consulting with Sumner Welles about the desirability of formally organizing Jewish anti-Zionist sentiment.[11] Lazaron also consulted with Nelson Glueck, serving with the Office of War Information, who at Lazaron's suggestion began to urge his British contacts to establish an army of "all loyal Palestinians."[12]

Almost naturally, the leadership of the "rebellion," as it was becoming known, fell to Louis Wolsey, who just months earlier had been struck by tragedy when his wife and son were found dead in his garage under bizarre circumstances, suggesting a suicide pact.[13] Wolsey was also growing increasingly close to a fellow rabbi in Philadelphia of equally strong anti-Zionist convictions, William Fineshriber, of Philadelphia's most elite Reform congregation, Keneseth Israel, whose members would come to include many prominent leaders of the American Council for Judaism. Born in 1878 in St. Louis and ordained in 1900, Fineshriber held pulpits in Davenport, Iowa, and Memphis, Tennessee, before arriving in Philadelphia. In Memphis he had distinguished himself as a leading opponent of the Ku Klux Klan and a vocal supporter of women's suffrage and the teaching of evolution.[14]

On April 15 an invitation was sent out with the signatures of Wolsey, Fineshriber, Goldenson, and Jonah Wise for a two-day conference in Atlantic City described as "a meeting of non-Zionist Reform Rabbis to discuss the problems that confront Judaism and Jews in the world emergency."[15] From the outset they could bank the support of such rabbis as Lazaron; Cronbach; Louis Binstock of Chicago; David Marx of Atlanta; David Lefkowitz of Dallas; Samuel Koch of Seattle; Julian Feibelman of New Orleans; Edward Calisch of Richmond, Virginia; Isaac Landman and Samuel J. Levinson of Brooklyn, New York; Solomon Foster of Newark, New Jersey; Milton Greenwald of Evansville, Indiana; Solomon Starrels of Albuquerque, New Mexico; and Henry Cohen of Galveston, Texas.

An exuberant David Philipson wrote from Cincinnati, "My heart is so full of happiness that it is difficult for me to express myself adequately. You and your colleagues who are calling this meeting are doing a deed of great loyalty to the high significance of our universalistic Judaism."[16] Wolsey wrote as excitedly to Philipson, "The Zionists have definitely overreached themselves and have completely Nazified their movement. Their hatred of freedom of opinion and expression, their totalitarianism in the name of a specious unity, their dictatorialness and cock-suredness, are a bubble that must be pricked. We have tried to appease them too long, but I think you know what President Roosevelt said about appeasing a certain animal."[17] Irving Reichert also wrote to Wolsey with great enthusiasm and expressed complete solidarity but felt duty-bound to stay in San Francisco while the fear of a direct attack by the Japanese remained palpable.[18]

None, however, were more excited than Wolsey's erstwhile disciple from his Cleveland days, Elmer Berger. Declaring to Wolsey that he was completely at Wolsey's service, he remained that spring excited about the progress of his work in Flint and noted that already at this early stage he had become a target of attack from beyond Michigan, with a representative of the United Jewish Appeal giving a speech there consisting of little more than an extended personal attack on Berger.[19] But also evident was Berger's anticipation for what the future held:

> It has always been in my mind that there was hope that this meeting might provide the beginnings of a lay-rabbinic organization of non-nationalistic Jews in America. Then, the sovereignty of the Conference would not even be involved. We might then lend our strength and support to such a movement with quite as much impunity as the Zionists in the Conference provide the leadership to American Zionism.[20]

Also anticipating things to come was Norman Buckner, Berger's loyal friend in Pontiac, who elatedly wrote: "You really have started something and before you get through, the Jews of this country are going to know that you are not only just another Rabbi. Of that I have been certain ever since you first came to Pontiac."[21]

The Zionists were divided over exactly how to respond to these developments. Abba Hillel Silver, whose star was rising with so much of Zionism's fortunes now invested in the United States, urged that the anti-Zionists simply be given the silent treatment. Stephen Wise, on the other hand, was never a believer in the silent treatment and, true to form, could not help but push for a fight with "Cardinal Wolsey and his Bishops." Belligerent as ever, Wise called for the "moral decapitation" of his adversaries.[22] But facing the most pressing dilemma was James Heller, who, for all his devotion to the cause, knew that it was incumbent upon him, as president of the CCAR, to maintain its unity as best he could. Not only would a formal split, which was impossible to rule out, be an indelible black mark on his reputation, but he also likely felt he had to exhibit some degree of statesmanship in the long-term interests of Zionism as well.

In the meantime, from May 9–11, 1942, the American Zionist Emergency Council convened a most momentous public conference at the Hotel Biltmore in New York. With representatives from seventeen countries and the attendance of Jewish Agency leaders Chaim Weizmann, David Ben-Gurion, and Nahum Goldman, the gathering was, for all practical purposes, an official Zionist congress, along exactly the lines by which the Emergency Council had been set up to function. It was at this conference where the

Zionists finally began to openly state their aims: free Jewish immigration
into Palestine and the establishment therein of a "Jewish commonwealth."
The question of how to deal with non-Zionists or anti-Zionists was now effectively moot. The duplicity by which the Zionists in the past two generations were able to secure the support of committed binationalists and
unassuming philanthropists was now totally locked away in storage. No
longer would there be any question of the goal of statehood.

The Zionists, however, would make a serious blunder in implementing
their first objective—securing the complete loyalty of American Jewry to the
Biltmore Program—largely by seeking a memorandum of understanding
with the American Jewish Committee (AJC), thereby giving a temporary
boon to the anti-Zionists. With the initial contacts beginning over a year before the Biltmore Conference, within a month of the conference the AJC
committee assigned to oversee the negotiations was ready to act. Led by AJC
President Maurice Wertheim and Executive Secretary Morris Waldman, the
committee of eleven met at Wertheim's home in Cos Cob, Connecticut, to
approve the following formula: that the AJC would endorse the complete
demands of the Biltmore Conference in exchange for a Zionist renunciation
of Jewish national identity outside of Palestine. Known as the "Cos Cob formula," the committee approved it by a vote of eight to three.[23]

Since there were three nay votes (Joseph Proskauer, Henry Ittleson, and
Morris Wolf, a prominent Philadelphia lawyer who would be active in the
American Council for Judaism), Wertheim and Waldman decided to wait
until they could persuade the dissenters toward consensus before bringing
the formula to a full vote of the executive committee of the AJC. This back-
fired, however, when Waldman shared the material in confidence with a
prominent member of the executive committee, James Rosenberg, who proceeded to write a forty-five-page brief attacking the proposal. Placing emphasis on the inherently undemocratic nature of any exclusively Jewish state
in Palestine, Rosenberg galvanized anti-Zionist sentiment in the AJC to the
point that the costs would have been too great to try to impose the Cos Cob
formula. Especially galvanized was Proskauer, who quite accurately predicted
that "if the American Jewish Committee doesn't make itself the mouthpiece
of this public position, some other organization will have to."[24]

On May 11, the day that the Biltmore Conference concluded, Heller met
with Rabbis Wolsey and Goldenson in Pittsburgh, through the mediation of
Solomon Freehof, who had attempted to cut the controversy off in February
and who would go on to be one of the leading scholars of the postwar

Reform rabbinate. Heller presented Wolsey and Goldenson with a generous offer—having the Jewish army resolution stricken from the record, reaffirming the 1935 neutrality resolution and enacting a bylaw to enforce it, and affirming the Reform movement's support for "non-Zionist" philanthropic activities in Palestine.[25] By a vote of seventeen to two (with Berger in the minority), the ad-hoc group planning the Atlantic City conference decided to accept Heller's offer provided that it be approved by a special session of the CCAR, to replace the Atlantic City meeting.[26] Days had barely passed, however, when Heller sent an incensed telegram insisting that he had never called for the army resolution to be stricken from the record.[27] After several days of sorting through the confusion, in which Wolsey was closely consulted by Norman Gerstenfeld, a young Austria native who held the pulpit of the prestigious Washington Hebrew Congregation in the nation's capital, it was finally agreed by May 20 that the meeting in Atlantic City would go on.[28]

The meeting was held on June 1. The first paper delivered was by David Philipson, the last living link to the heyday of Isaac Mayer Wise, on "The Message of Reform Judaism to American Israel and World Jewry."[29] This was followed by Morris Lazaron on "Jewish Postwar Problems," which struck a note squarely in the camp of binationalism:

> We agree that, if large scale emigration is necessary immediately after the war, Palestine would be able to receive considerable numbers. There the administrative machinery for receiving immigrants already exists, and for many Jews the spiritual attraction will undoubtedly play a large part in making settlement more successful than it would be in other countries. For such settlement to be possible, it is not necessary to urge the creation of a Jewish state. To found a state based on race or creed is fundamentally wrong and indeed is the antithesis of one of the principles for which this war is being fought. We cannot imagine any basis for a Jewish state which is not wholly inconsistent with the principles of the Atlantic Charter.[30]

The star attraction of the day though was Elmer Berger, who gave a talk detailing his activities in Flint to illustrate a model for a national organization with active lay participation, emphasizing that he was able to organize his group in a part of the country that could not have been considered its most promising terrain:

> When I had first come to Flint there had been several resignations from the congregation, with other excuses offered, but obviously because I

had refused to cooperate with the Zionists. Otherwise, there had been the constant pressure and the frequent sniping of the usual Zionist tactics, but no serious impairment of the congregation's life. Besides, our group promised a transfusion of increased interest and support. In short, we were no longer to be intimidated by the usual cries for unity and charges of secession from Jewish life.[31]

With a bold call to action, Berger concluded: "It is not enough that we fight this evil, poisonous growth, belonging to 19th century European philosophies, as individuals or even as a group of Rabbis. To refuse to join the issue because it may produce a quarrel is to duplicate the short-sighted diplomacies of liberals everywhere in the world who constantly appeased because they hated war."[32]

The next day, the conference approved a statement of principles, which read in part:

> We believe that the present tragic experiences of mankind abundantly demonstrate that no single people or group can hope to live in free-dom and security when their neighbors are in the grip of evil forces either as perpetrators or sufferers. To this general rule the problems of our Jewish people constitute no exception. . . . We declare our unwa-vering faith in the humane and righteous principles that underlie the democratic way of life, principles first envisaged by the Prophets of Israel and embodied in our American Bill of Rights. . . . We cannot but believe that Jewish nationalism tends to confuse our fellow men about our place and function in society and also diverts our attention from our historic role to live as a religious community wherever we may dwell.[33]

With thirty-six rabbis attending the Atlantic City conference, the state-ment of principles was ultimately endorsed by a grand total of 104. The con-ference also established a Committee on Lay-Rabbinical Cooperation, whose first order of business was to publish a pamphlet with the statement of prin-ciples and Berger's address, which became known as the Flint Plan.

Following the meeting, as the consensus grew among the rabbis that what was necessary was a lay-led organization that would directly challenge the Zionist agenda, several rabbis who professed to be involved merely out of in-terest in the defense of Classical Reform Judaism dropped out of the anti-Zionist ranks, including a few who had been involved in Wolsey's consultations from the very beginning. The Zionist reaction to the Atlantic

City statement was swift as usual; James Heller and Philip Bernstein gathered the signatures of an astonishing 757 rabbis from all three branches of Judaism for an open letter asserting that "anti-Zionism, not Zionism, is the departure from the Jewish religion." In a sign of things to come, the student body of Hebrew Union College endorsed this statement by a vote of forty-two to nine. By autumn, lay groups were organized in Chicago, Philadelphia, San Francisco, and Dallas. The first pledges of major financial backing were made by Aaron Strauss, a nephew and heir of Levi Strauss of blue-jeans fame who was a prominent member of Lazaron's congregation in Baltimore. By November, everything was set for the formation of a national organization.[34]

Throughout autumn, Berger had been seeking to enlist as a chaplain. He had written to Barnett Brickner in Cleveland, who was in charge of administering naval chaplaincies, receiving only a form letter saying that the navy posts were all filled and to apply for an army chaplaincy. A similar response was thus forthcoming from Philip Bernstein, a member of the first class to be graduated by the Jewish Institute of Religion founded by Stephen Wise and who would clash with Berger many times in the future.[35] Bernstein's professions of pacifism throughout the 1930s apparently did not disqualify the militant Zionist from a leading position to enforce Zionist control of the chaplaincy through the Jewish Welfare Board led by Heller and Brickner.[36] Most of all, Berger was extremely eager to move on from Flint, and likely from the congregational rabbinate altogether. So naturally he was overjoyed when Wolsey informed him that he was being offered the position of executive director of a new national anti-Zionist organization. The words he wrote Wolsey in accepting the offer were as forthright an embrace of his destiny as any man would ever utter: "I am willing to stake everything I have on the fight with the Zionists, I cannot have peace as long as Reform Rabbis are predominantly Zionists rather than religious men."[37]

The American Council for Judaism was incorporated on December 7, 1942, in a meeting at the Hotel New Yorker. In addition to appointing Berger, the decision was made to hire a public relations adviser, Sidney Wallach, who had previously worked for the American Jewish Committee. Hopes were high early on when within weeks Joseph Proskauer was elected the new president of the AJC. Proskauer immediately declared upon accepting the presidency that he favored an allied trusteeship to govern Palestine after the war, and that Palestine alone could not provide the answer to postwar Jewish rehabilitation. This led the Council to believe it might be able to operate under the direct sponsorship of the AJC, but Proskauer informed them that while he sympathized with them and urged them to keep up the good work, he could not commit direct backing by the AJC.[38]

It was then William Fineshriber who suggested that the presidency of the Council be offered to a prominent lay leader of his congregation, Lessing Rosenwald. Rosenwald was first lobbied by Fineshriber together with Morris Wolf, another prominent member of Keneseth Israel and the most vocal Council member in the AJC. Rosenwald was initially noncommittal, concerned mostly about the impact of such a position on his family—his brother William was a leading Zionist voice in the AJC. Several days later Fineshriber returned, leading a delegation consisting of Rabbis Berger, Reichert, and Lazaron to urge Rosenwald's support. Rosenwald then agreed on the condition that he receive satisfactory assurance that the Council was in no way acting counter to the foreign policy of the United States. Lazaron, who had earned Rosenwald's trust after they had been comrades in arms fighting to save the Joint Distribution Committee, immediately arranged for Rosenwald to meet in Washington with Sumner Welles, who assured him that a national organization of Jewish anti-Zionists would be most welcomed by the State Department.[39]

Lazaron also immediately began to reach out to the most likely sympathizer of the ACJ in Palestine and old friend to many of its founders, Judah Magnes. Born in 1877 in San Francisco, Magnes was ordained by Hebrew Union College in 1900 and served various pulpits in New York, where he was involved in the founding of the American Jewish Committee and married the daughter of its legendary first president, Louis Marshall, a committed anti-Zionist. After the First World War, it was only natural that Lazaron, a confirmed pacifist and the most politically precocious of the AJC founders, would settle in Palestine. He became the first chancellor of the Hebrew University in Jerusalem in 1919 and then president in 1935. Ever since the first serious outbreak of violence between the Jews and Arabs in 1929, Magnes had vigorously advocated the establishment of a binational state, in which the two communities would be federated on the model of Switzerland.

Almost simultaneously with the formation of the ACJ in the second half of 1942 was the founding by Magnes of the Ihud organization, which formally organized Jewish opposition to the Biltmore Program in Palestine in favor of the binationalist plan. But just as at least a half-dozen signers of the Atlantic City statement died within the following year, and a good many more before 1948, Ihud was nearly paralyzed with the death in 1942 of its other two most prominent leaders—Henrietta Szold, the founder of Hadassah, and Pinhas Rutenberg, who first brought electricity to Palestine—though it would also gain the auspicious support of Albert Einstein and the theologian Martin Buber. Magnes wrote to Lazaron in November of that year endorsing the Atlantic City statement, stating: "It is true that Jewish nationalism tends to confuse people, not because it is secular and not religious, but because this nationalism is unhappily chauvinistic and narrow and terroristic in the best style of Eastern European nationalisms."[40]

On August 30, 1943, the ACJ released its platform, the full text of which was included in a feature article in the next day's *New York Times*. The statement read in part:

> Racist theories and nationalist philosophies, that have become prevalent in recent years, have caused untold suffering to the world and particularly to Jews. Long ago they became obsolete as realities in Jewish history, they remain only as a reaction to discrimination and persecution. In the former crises of Israel in ancient Palestine, the Prophets placed God and the moral law above land, race, nation, royal prerogatives and political arrangements. Now, as then, we cherish the same religious values which emphasize the dignity of man and the obligations to deal justly with man no matter what his status. . . . Palestine is a part of Israel's religious heritage, as it is a part of the heritage of two other religions of the world. We look forward to the ultimate establishment of a democratic, autonomous government in Palestine, wherein Jews, Muslims and Christians shall be justly represented, every man enjoying equal rights and sharing equal responsibilities, a democratic government in which our fellow Jews shall be free Palestinians whose religion is Judaism, even as we are Americans whose religion is Judaism.[41]

It was on that very day that the American Zionist Emergency Council was able to convene under its auspices an American Jewish Conference along the lines that had been plotted but never brought to effective fruition by Stephen Wise. This was the turning point in the displacement of Wise in the American Zionist leadership by Abba Hillel Silver. Gathering in New York, the event can only be described as having been organized along the lines of a Soviet politburo, with delegates who ostensibly were democratically elected but with an agenda completely set by the Zionists.[42] The high point of the conference was the electrifying speech in which Silver declared: "If we surrender our national and historic claims to Palestine and rely solely on the refugee philanthropic appeal, we shall lose our case as well as do violence to the historic hopes of our people."[43]

On September 1, the last day of the conference, the Biltmore Program was endorsed by a vote of 478 to 4, at last codifying the existence of an "official" American Jewish community devoted to Zionism. Outraged at the temerity of the ACJ to release its platform during the Conference, the American Jewish Conference also passed a resolution denouncing the Council, in shockingly totalitarian language, for "attempting to sabotage the collective Jewish will to achieve a united program."[44] The Conference also authorized the formation of the darkly named "Committee on Unity for Palestine" to combat the Council in the media and elsewhere, which by 1948 grew to have numerous local branches. The ramifications of this can hardly be overstated, as this Conference would in the 1950s become known as the National Community Relations Advisory Council, and by the 1960s would change its name once more to the Conference of Presidents of Major Jewish Organizations, which would, however fancifully at times but nevertheless with enormous political power, act as the governing body of "the Jewish people" in the United States, effectively functioning, at least in theory, as the mythical "elders of Zion."

Naturally, the anti-Zionist reaction to these developments was swift and uncompromising. Lessing Rosenwald urgently wrote to his colleagues on the executive committee of the AJC, pressing immediate action and pleading, "The Conference Resolution threatens to do incalculable injury to the surviving Jews of Europe. The foundation upon which the Conference Resolution is built is 'Jewish homelessness', a mystic belief of Jews that they do not belong to their present countries but yearn for a home of their own."[45] The AJC, which had participated in the Conference in hopes of being a moderating influence, withdrew by October by a vote of 52 to 13, prompting several Zionist members of the executive committee to resign. This raised the hopes of the Council once more that it could align itself with the AJC, but this came to naught when their executive director, John Slawson, began implementing plans for mass membership in the AJC. Slawson would be the key Zionist mole in the AJC, checking the anti-Zionist sympathies of its leaders for the next decade.[46]

Also coming to a head as a result of the American Jewish Conference were the outspoken sympathies for the ACJ of Arthur Sulzberger. Sulzberger had given an adamantly anti-Zionist speech to the Baltimore Hebrew Congregation Men's Club in October 1942, and by the time of the Conference and its aftermath he was already conferring with Lazaron, Judah Magnes, and Nelson Glueck about publishing a magazine to advance the views of Ihud.[47] Then, on October 28, at the annual banquet of Hadassah, Abba Hillel Silver gave a speech furiously denouncing the growing anti-Zionist backlash, singling out Sulzberger for making the *Times* into "a mouthpiece for the American Jewish Committee and the channel for anti-Zionist propaganda."[48] In a publicized letter to Silver, Sulzberger responded forcefully:

> You are inaccurate when you associate me with the American Jewish Committee. I have never been a member of it, nor have I any influence upon its policies. If I had, the Committee would never have sent delegates to the American Jewish Conference, for it was obvious to me from the beginning that the Conference was a Zionist maneuver— and I have no lack of respect for your political astuteness. Believing, as I do, that Judaism is a faith and a faith only, it was with real regret that I tendered my resignation as a member of the executive committee of the Union of American Hebrew Congregations when they, too, agreed to send delegates.[49]

Though he was offered the vice presidency of the ACJ, Sulzberger never formally associated with it, though he did give several speeches as a free agent on behalf of his views until 1948, and the *Times* would make a point of giving significant publicity to the Council as late as the 1960s. This would result in a curious assignment of villainy to the *Times* in the Zionist imagination to this very day. A bizarre accusation that Sulzberger's views led to the *Times* giving insufficient real-time coverage to the Holocaust would find currency in the last decades of the twentieth century. Sulzberger's legacy would continue to generate Zionist hostility to the paper ever after, regardless of its long and varying record of Middle East coverage, which even helped inspire the quixotic and short-lived ultra-Zionist daily *New York Sun* in the first decade of the twenty-first century.[50]

Having been galvanized by the ominous shadow cast by the American Jewish Conference, the High Holiday season of 1943 would see some of the boldest moves by the rabbis of the ACJ. In San Francisco, Irving Reichert began a decade of uncompromising anti-Zionist agitation with his Kol Nidre sermon, in which he urged his congregants that they could no longer stand on the sidelines of the debate over Zionism and that they must either join the American Council for Judaism or the Zionist Organization of America. Titling his sermon with the simple question "Where do you stand?" and addressing generations

to come, Reichert urged as Yom Kippur began that "God does not judge us col-
lectively. Before His tribunal, every man is lifted out of the protective
anonymity of the group and held to strict accountability for his decisions and
actions. This holy day reminds us that we are responsible as individuals, not
only for our personal behavior, but for the conduct of the group of which we
are a part."[51] True to form, Reichert threw down the gauntlet:

> I do not believe that the 67,000 members of the Zionist Organization
> are qualified to declare that they represent the settled and responsible
> convictions of the five million Jews of America. I challenge the claim
> that the American Jewish Conference, which displayed the Zionist flag
> at equal size and prominence as the American flag, which conducted
> much of its proceedings in Yiddish, with hardly a word of prayer or a
> religious reference, and very little concern for any problems besetting
> world Jewry other than a Jewish political state in Palestine, mirrored
> the true sentiments of the five million Jews of America. I protest as a
> misleading and dangerous distortion of truth the implication that
> American Jews are fighting and dying, not so much to secure a just
> and lasting peace under the Four Freedoms for all men everywhere,
> not so much for love of America and devotion to it as their home-
> land, as for special rights and favors and privileges for Jews that go
> beyond the elementary principles of democracy.[52]

The sermon garnered Reichert national attention, and it electrified the
whole following of the ACJ in the wake of the American Jewish Conference.
Even Berger would give his own version of the same sermon two years later
when he led auxiliary High Holiday services at Rodef Shalom, Louis Wolsey's
Philadelphia congregation. Although Reichert was able to use the sermon to
kick off a membership drive in San Francisco, which would become a
Council stronghold with the support, financial and otherwise, of the San
Francisco aristocracy, the sermon did cause serious dissension at Emanu-El.
Several members of the temple board resigned in protest, and heated arguments among the worshipers followed the service. The wife of Emanu-El's
distinguished cantor and well-known Zionist Reuben Rinder even compared
the rabbi to Hitler within earshot of the congregation.[53] But even the
prophetic call that rang out from San Francisco could not be matched in
boldness by the events that began to transpire at Congregation Beth Israel of
Houston when pledges to the principles of the Pittsburgh Platform were circulated to all the High Holiday worshipers.

The president of Beth Israel, Israel Friedlander, had been one of the most vocal laymen in registering his solidarity with the Atlantic City conference and had even issued a long letter on behalf of his board repeating its grievances to James Heller. During the momentous High Holidays of 1943, the leading Reform pulpit in Houston passed from aging ACJ supporter Henry Barnston to Hyman Judah Schachtel, who had been a close friend of Berger, though a year ahead of him, at Hebrew Union College. Schachtel, who as rabbi of New York's West End Synagogue was openly denied the presidency of the New York Board of Rabbis because of his association with the Council,[54] infused a youthful militancy into the already militant Houston congregation. Despite a reported 142 resignations from the temple from outrage over the pledge, which among other things could have been interpreted as expressly forbidding members from keeping kosher, the board of Beth Israel formally adopted it as a statement of principles that would be binding on the membership on November 23.[55]

That very day Berger gave one of the highlight performances of his early years with the Council in a public debate in Richmond, Virginia, with Maurice Samuel, who had published an article attacking the ACJ at its formation, and Lessing Rosenwald in particular in *American Mercury*. In this debate, Berger forthrightly stated the fundamental position he would champion for his entire career to come:

> I oppose Zionism because I deny that Jews are a nation. We were a nation for perhaps two hundred years in a history of four thousand years. Before that we were a group of warring Semitic tribes whose only tenuous bond of unity was a national deity—a religious unity. After Solomon, we were never better than two nations, frequently at war with one another, disappearing at different times, leaving discernibly different cultures and even religions recorded in even the Biblical records. Certainly, since the Dispersion we have not been a nation. We have belonged to every nation of the world. We have mixed our blood with all peoples. Jewish nationalism is a fabrication woven from the thinnest kind of threads and strengthened only in those eras of human history in which reaction has been dominant and anti-Semites in full cry.[56]

On the heels of this speech, Berger would excitedly write to Schachtel:

> I happened to be with Rosenwald when Friedlander's wire came and we both rejoiced at the victory. As I wrote to Mr. Friedlander today, I am forever amazed and bewildered at the fact that institutions like

the Union are afraid of the principles of Reform Judaism. They are obsessed with a mania that all Jews must be one happy family—and imagine that that won't be the death of Reform![57]

Indeed, the mood of the ACJ cadre was, despite all their early successes, turning toward one of apocalypse. In contrast to the optimism he typically exuded throughout the years leading up to 1948, Berger would declare in more personal correspondence that the ACJ was "the last of the Mohicans."[58] This surely helped propel the disillusionment of Louis Wolsey, whose own sympathies toward the preservation of Classical Reform Judaism over the battle with Zionism were no doubt steeled by his increasing alienation from the movement he had birthed.

As much, apparently, to satiate his own ego as to advance the cause, throughout 1944 Wolsey reportedly floated plans for the Council to establish a "College for Reform Judaism," which would serve as an alternative seminary to Hebrew Union College, the last Reform institution of which non-Zionists continued to hold even the most tenuous grasp. Most of his anger would be directed at Rosenwald—the person most able to fund and least inclined to support such an endeavor—whom Wolsey would accuse of turning the ACJ into an "instrument of assimilation by atheistic Jews."[59] Presumably the founding of a new college would have led, sooner or later, to the founding of a new denomination, to which there did indeed take place the most perfunctory stirrings.

Inspired and perhaps encouraged by the leaders of Beth Israel in Houston, Bernard Gradwohl, a zealous Council supporter in Lincoln, Nebraska, led a small group of the members of the Reform temple in that city to establish an "American Reform Congregation" that would be constitutionally committed to the Beth Israel statement of principles. This action, however, would be particularly reckless, since the rabbi in Lincoln, Meyer Marx, was at least a nominal supporter of the ACJ. Gradwohl received at least one letter of encouragement from Abraham Cronbach, who declared himself firmly committed to "the Judaism of Emil Hirsch, Joseph Krauskopf, and Moses Gries," that is, the most radical wing of the early Reform movement in America, stating that "I emphasize not Zionism but Americanism."[60] A furious letter on the matter came to Wolsey, however, from Hebrew Union College president Julian Morgenstern, who, though a signer of the Atlantic City statement, had begun to distance himself ever further from anti-Zionism. While appealing to Wolsey's sense of what was in the best interests of the anti-Zionist cause, Morgenstern expressed the belief that Hyman

Schachtel was leading a conspiracy to form a new denomination on the basis of the Beth Israel pledge.[61]

Any prospect for leaving the Reform movement and forming a new denomination was almost certainly crushed in the first week of 1945. Against the impassioned pleas of his heretofore devoted disciple Elmer Berger, Louis Wolsey resigned from the executive committee of the Council, disheartened by the whole controversy and accusing Rosenwald of fascism.[62] Nevertheless, a meeting to discuss options had taken place in Chicago in late 1944, convened by Bernard Gradwohl and attracting a modest group of ACJ lay supporters, including some of the leading members of the Council in San Francisco such as Marcus and Hattie Sloss, a former California Supreme Court justice and his wife, a leading San Francisco socialite. Wolsey apparently had some sympathy for the gathering, as did Irving Reichert, who also confided to Wolsey sympathy for his reasons for disengaging from the Council.[63]

The question of why the profound divide over Zionism within American Reform Judaism did not lead to the formation of a new religious movement by the anti-Zionist heretics cannot go unaddressed. It is telling, to be sure, that the initiative, such as it was, to this end came from clearly unsophisticated laymen. For example, one participant in the discussions, Isaac Bernheim of Santa Monica, California, proposed a vision for a "Reformed Church of American Israelites," which would have scarcely been countenanced by even the most radical early reformers.[64] The rabbis who might have leaned in this direction were not much of an improvement either. Berger, for his part, felt that what truly drove Wolsey in his disaffection was that he did not become the guru of the Council—in other words, that he was not sought out for advice, his intellect widely considered inferior to many of the other rabbis.[65] Schachtel, for that matter, proved himself to be the ultimate flake, renouncing the Council by the early 1950s and all but feigning amnesia in his notably Zionist career to come.[66]

Nevertheless, the question is an urgent one when we consider what might have been. Even assuming it would have been lucky to hold on to a quarter million adherents, a liberal Jewish denomination standing outside of, and completely rejecting the official Jewish community (as constituted in the Conference of Presidents and its instrument, the Israel lobby) as a matter of first principle, could have been a powerful living testimony to the enduring spirit of prophetic Judaism. It might have taken its place in the constellation of progressive American religions in the postwar era and indeed the whole era of the American Empire and the outrages of the State of Israel. Constituted

along these lines, such a denomination would surely have been able to re-
plenish its ranks in the age of the New Left, to say nothing of the disillusionment of the present generation of Jews with Zionism.

In considering why all this was completely lost on the founders of the
American Council for Judaism, at least one factor can be identified that distorted their perspective, which was their taking for granted the supremacy of
the Reform movement in American Jewish life. The appearance to this effect in
the first half of the twentieth century was maintained largely by the anomalous
commitments of the Eastern European immigrants, whether away from the
Jewish religion altogether in socialism or with the amorphous and fragmented
nature of Orthodoxy until the middle of the century. Indeed, only after the
Second World War did the Conservative movement truly develop a distinct character of its own and thus quickly overtake Reform in numbers, in part as a consequence of Reform's anti-Zionist legacy. Reform managed to hold its own for
a variety of reasons thereafter, to where it would be in a position of significance
as the tide turned back in its favor at the dawn of the twenty-first century.

During this time, the Council had also begun to assert itself in the U.S.
political conversation over the future of Palestine. In February 1944 hearings
were held for pro-Zionist congressional resolutions in both the House and
Senate. Wolsey, Rosenwald, Lazaron, and Fineshriber all testified against the
resolutions, while supporting testimony came from Abba Hillel Silver,
James Heller, Stephen Wise, and Israel Goldstein, president of the Zionist
Organization of America.[67] Though the resolutions would be tabled as a result of the united opposition of the secretary of state, secretary of war, and
army chief of staff, the hearings did significantly allow an airing of the fundamental questions of Zionism's claims on Jewish identity and the definition
of "Jew," which naturally provoked Zionist outrage.[68]

In Congress statements of support for the Council's position came from
Frances Bolton of Ohio, Charles Eaton of New Jersey, James Curley of
Massachusetts, William Lemke of North Dakota, James Wadsworth of New
York, and Jerry Voorhis of California.[69] The Council was also encouraged in
1944 by the platform statement of the Republican Party that year, upholding
the Balfour Declaration and the 1922 Resolutions but calling for a "free and
democratic commonwealth" in Palestine, as implicitly opposed to a "Jewish
commonwealth."[70] The congressmen, consisting of two Democrats and four
Republicans, were politically mixed but fell mostly outside the wartime consensus, and in that spirit other leaders of progressive opinion were declaring
their support of the ACJ as well. Norman Thomas, the venerable leader of the

Socialist Party of America, responded favorably to a solicitation from Elmer Berger early in 1944, declaring, "I think that if I were a Jew I should belong to your organization, but as a gentile I hesitate to dogmatize."[71]

Arthur Sulzberger had been among those who had urged the Council to reach out aggressively to Jewish socialists who had a tradition of anti-Zionism, no doubt moved by the Jewish Labor Committee in its vocal opposition to the American Jewish Conference. Around this time, Berger and Rosenwald made a personal appeal to David Dubinsky, president of the International Ladies Garment Workers Union and icon of the Jewish labor movement in America, who confided his sympathy with the Council but feared a backlash from his membership.[72] Probably the most prominent figure in the Jewish socialist milieu to become active with the ACJ was Jack Altman, who excitedly wrote to Berger that he could "use my name in any way you see fit" and served on the national board of the Council into the 1950s.[73] A veteran activist in the Socialist Party who was then serving as president of the New York District Council of the Retail, Wholesale, and Department Store Workers, Altman had been active in the purging of Trotskyist interlopers from the party, many of whom would go on to be founders of neoconservatism. Significantly, their enablers in the Socialist Party, whom Altman bitterly opposed, included such later mainstays of the Israel lobby as the journalist Gus Tyler and future AJC leader Hyman Bookbinder.

The ACJ held its first annual conference in Philadelphia on January 13–14, 1945, which definitively set the tone for the organization for the next twenty years. While including a religious service and other such trappings, the discussions of the conference focused solely on Zionism. The main addresses were given by Berger, Rosenwald, and Sidney Wallach, with Rosenwald giving the clearest statement of purpose to the group, meeting as an organization for the first time:

> We did not organize to fight the Zionists. We did organize to express those tenets and ideas which are fundamental, in our opinion, to the position of the Jew in the modern world and which clash fundamentally with the Zionist doctrine. We had to oppose them as undemocratic in conception and in operation, as archaic, attuned to medieval times rather than to the aspirations of the 20th century. We had to oppose them because their doctrines constituted a danger to the courageous settlers who have built up Palestine, a menace to the desperate remnants of European Jewry and a barrier to the integration and secure future of those of Jewish faith in other countries. We had to oppose

those as doctrines which would create a self-imposed ghetto for Jews in Palestine to which the vast majority of Jews in the rest of the world would be tied by the silver cord of religion.[74]

The conference also took in an address from Hans Kohn, a onetime German Zionist associated with the University in Exile in New York who would remain a friend of the Council for years to come. Kohn declared unequivocally, "The Jewish nationalist philosophy has developed entirely under German influence, the German romantic nationalism with its emphasis on blood, race, and descent as the most determining factor in human life, its historicizing attempt to connect with a legendary past 2,000 or so years ago, its emphasis on folk as a mystical body, the source of civilization."[75] For Berger, the conference and the year would mark his unambiguous arrival as the public face of American Jewish anti-Zionism, for in 1945 he would publish what would remain the definitive statement of his—and the Council's— abiding doctrine of an emancipated Jewish existence, *The Jewish Dilemma*.

Berger immediately struck out against the rising phenomenon of "secular Jewish" identity, which was so critical to the efficacy of Zionist propaganda:

> Some people will point to this kind of man to prove that since he is not religious, but still claims to be a Jew, Jews must therefore be something more than a religious group. Some are just, religiously speaking, bad Jews, as there are, religiously speaking, bad Catholics or Protestants. But if these men never turn to Judaism, then what makes them Jews? Their contributions to Jewish charity? Do their contributions to Chinese War Relief make them Chinese, or to a policeman's ball make them policemen?[76]

Berger then prefaced a long examination of the history of Zionist intrigues through the Second World War with a discussion of its nineteenth-century roots, emphasizing the movement's paradoxical dependence on Herzl's emancipated existence, whereas the founders of the Eastern European movements who preceded him, Leo Pinsker and Ahad Ha'am, with their bizarre mystical doctrines, were in his judgment little more than medieval messianic pretenders.

In one of his most insightful passages, Berger commented on why Herzl felt a special kinship with the kaiser, for his methods of indoctrinating his own people and all Europe toward his imperial ambitions:

> I do not condemn Herzl nor Zionism for these attitudes and plans. If he was desperate and deluded, he was never evasive. Zionists, by and

large, have announced their designs to the world. They are fighting with desperation against all of the forces of history and freedom, hoping to keep Jews compressed within a pre-emancipation formula for Jewish life. They have announced their goal as the political restoration of a nation long, long dead. And to achieve that goal, small and impotent as they are, they have never been able to create world policies. They have had to move on the tide already in motion.[77]

These words remain as incisive today in addressing the modern Israel lobby and its enablers in U.S. politics.

As in all of his earlier writings and pronouncements, Berger emphasized the alternative of "emancipation," meaning that Jews should everywhere be full, equal, and active citizens of the nations in which they reside, and that the destiny of the Jews was of a part with liberal Western civilization, whose values were ultimately the most basic of Jewish values. This led Berger to betray an embarrassing set of premises about that liberal world: he heralded the French Revolution as the beginning of Jewish emancipation and even had nice things to say about the degree of emancipation enjoyed by Soviet Jews. Moreover, he identified the best hopes for an emancipated Jewish future in postwar Europe in Czechoslovakia and Yugoslavia, two states that were at least as artificial as the future State of Israel, and even regarded the ostensible peace of the Balkans as a sign for hope in Palestine.[78]

Indeed, on one level, this faith in the new world order would not be very different from that of the Zionists. But in one respect, and perhaps the most unlikely, Berger would be salient in answering the most obvious objection to the philosophy of emancipation: its failure in Germany. Berger would argue quite convincingly, contrary to Zionist propaganda, that emancipation did not fail in Germany, but in reality had never been tried. In sharp contrast to the reality in the United States, Britain, and France, according to Berger, the German Jews merely obtained degrees of privilege and prosperity that went by the name of emancipation. Significantly, the Jewish religion, whether liberal or orthodox, could never have been said to prosper in Germany throughout the pre-Nazi era, certainly not since the time of unification. The high levels of avowed atheism and outright apostasy to Christianity among German Jews could not have been more different from the flourishing of a liberal Judaism in the U.S. that inspired the ACJ.

The Jewish Dilemma was published by the Devin-Adair Company in the fall of 1945, a major clearinghouse for isolationist and revisionist works on U.S. foreign policy. Much of the advance praise came from leaders of Christian opinion—many of whom were close friends with many leaders of the Council through the National Conference of Christians—and Jews, such as Richard Niebuhr, Morris Ernst, Samuel McCrea Cavert, and Conrad Hoffman.[79] The publication of the book also occasioned a rare exchange between Elmer and his brother Melvin, who ran a five-and-dime store in Chicago, thanking him for the education given him by the book and bragging about utilizing it in argument against his wife's Zionist family.[80] All in all, the book was a sober, if polemical, expression of the views of Berger and the Council, noticeably free of the ad hominem attacks that characterize so much of Zionist propaganda. But as the Second World War came to an end and the full extent of the Final Solution became known, an emotional avalanche, such that the Zionists had awaited for fifty years and indeed any nationalist demagogue would envy, doomed any just or rational solution to the postwar Jewish crisis.

4

THE RIGHTEOUS STAND

By the end of 1945, the American Council for Judaism (ACJ) had established itself as a functioning national organization with committed lay leadership. In New York the most prominent leaders were Admiral Lewis Strauss; the financiers Arthur Goldsmith, Leo Gottlieb, and Isaac Witkin; and Jerome Frank, a prominent jurist who was a protégé of Louis Brandeis. The most active lay leaders in Philadelphia were Morris Wolf, his law partner Stanley Sundheim, and Jane Blum, a mainstay of the sisterhood of William Fineshriber's congregation. Also hailing from Philadelphia was D. Hays Solis-Cohen, an Orthodox Jew from one of Philadelphia's oldest Sephardic families. Serving many years as the national treasurer of the Council, Solis-Cohen was deeply influenced by his friendship with Judah Magnes as a young man, perhaps making him ahead of his time in anticipating the predominance of more religiously observant Jews in contemporary "post-Zionist" movements against Israeli militarism, if not Zionism itself.

In San Francisco the prestigious list of lay leaders included Marcus and Hattie Sloss, University of California–Berkeley provost Monroe Deutsch, and such leading men of the San Francisco aristocracy as Grover Magnin, James Zellerbach, Walter Haas, and Daniel Koshland, the latter two then serving as the chief executives of the Levi Strauss Company. In Dallas, the largest Council stronghold of the South, the leading laymen were the banker Fred Florence, the brothers Herbert and Stanley Marcus of Neiman-Marcus fame, and I. Edward Tonkon, a successful hat manufacturer who would be among the

71

most loyal of all lay leaders of the ACJ. Other significant lay leaders of the pre-1948 years included Ralph W. Mack of Cincinnati; David Stern of Chicago; Milton Binswanger of Memphis; Henry Moyer of Youngstown, Ohio; Irving Feist of Newark, New Jersey; and Joseph Kaufman of Washington, D.C.

Early in 1946 the Council moved its national headquarters from Philadelphia, where the organization had largely been founded in spirit if not in actual fact, to New York in anticipation of the need to be close to the United Nations, where the future of Palestine would in great measure be decided. Coinciding with this move for Elmer Berger to the city where he would spend most of the rest of his life was an auspicious donnybrook. Ruth Winegarden, the woman with whom he had an affair in Flint, decided to take this opportunity to join Elmer in New York and left her husband, who was just returning to Michigan from the war. Within a year Berger had filed for divorce from his wife, Seville, though not without having to pay her monthly alimony for the rest of his life. Elmer and Ruth were married in the fall of 1946 in New York and would remain devoted to each other for the next thirty-three years.

In autumn 1945 President Truman's special envoy on the crisis of European displaced persons, Earl G. Harrison, released his report recommending that 100,000 displaced Jews be immediately allowed to immigrate into Palestine. While the Zionists were at this time only becoming more extreme in their demands, the Council praised the report for being "concerned with the humanitarian needs of human beings, and not with the fifty year old political ideology of Zionism."[1] The British government, mindful of the history of violence that led them to restrict Jewish immigration in the first place, was reluctant to accept the report, but by November the British and U.S. governments agreed to create an Anglo American Committee of Inquiry to examine the Jewish crisis in Europe and the question of Palestine. In announcing the agreement to Parliament, the new British Foreign Secretary Ernest Bevin roundly condemned Zionist propaganda on both Palestine and Jewish identity. Singling out Bevin for praise in endorsing the Committee of Inquiry, Lessing Rosenwald declared on behalf of the Council that "this organization stands ready to help you in every possible way in furthering the objectives of your policy."[2]

On December 4, hours after his first meeting with Chaim Weizmann, Harry Truman received Rosenwald in the Oval Office. Stressing that he could speak only for the 10,000 members of the "ACJ" and that no one could speak for all American Jews, Rosenwald asked the president for the opportunity for representatives of the Council to testify before the Committee of Inquiry and urged the admission of both Jewish and gentile displaced persons into the United States. Rosenwald also left with Truman a memorandum that proposed a seven-point plan for Palestine and the displaced persons. It urged that "Palestine shall not be a Muslim, Christian, or a Jewish state but a country in which people of all faiths can play their full and equal part," and that the United States take the lead in coordinating with the United Nations a cooperative policy of many nations in absorbing Jewish refugees.[3]

The Committee of Inquiry consisted of twelve members, six of which were appointed by the United States and Britain, and held hearings between January and April 1946 in Washington and London, as well as at displaced persons camps across Europe and in several Middle Eastern capitals. Rosenwald testified before the Committee of Inquiry on January 10 and urged that large numbers of Jews be admitted into Palestine on the condition that "the claim that Jews possess unlimited national rights to the land, and that the country shall take the form of a racial or theocratic state, were renounced once and for all."[4] He concluded with the assertion that the idea that the Jews could not remain in Europe and had to be resettled in a state of their own was an insult to all that the war had been fought to achieve. When Rosenwald was finally excused, an enraged Stephen Wise strong-armed his way from the spectators' gallery into being allowed to give a hysterical rebuttal testimony, wagging his finger in the face of the U.S. co-chairman of the Committee of Inquiry, Judge Joseph Hutcheson, for his apparent sympathy for Rosenwald's testimony.[5]

The ultimate report of the Committee of Inquiry was released in May after great lengths were taken to reach a consensus, based on three guiding principles: "That Jew shall not dominate Arab and Arab shall not dominate Jew in Palestine; That Palestine shall be neither a Jewish state nor an Arab state; That the form of government ultimately to be established shall, under international guarantees, fully protect and preserve the interests in the Holy Land of Christendom and of Muslim and Jewish faiths." Also recommending the admission of 100,000 displaced Jews into Palestine, the report was endorsed in full by the ACJ, who urged "the adoption of the report as a whole, as a humanitarian proposal designed to save and to safeguard Jews of Palestine and of Europe."[6] The State Department endorsed the report as well, but British prime minister Clement Attlee would only agree on two conditions. One was that the United States would share the cost of enforcing the recommendations of the report. The other was that the Zionist militias would be dismantled before new Jewish immigration would be allowed—the *Haganah* of the Jewish Agency as well as the more radical militias, the *Irgun* and the *Lehi*, also known as the "Stern Gang."

The ACJ was thus growing increasingly close to the State Department, having won the grateful friendship of Assistant Secretary for Near Eastern Affairs Loy Henderson, a veteran of the Foreign Service who had been a protégé of George Kennan in the Soviet Embassy. The Council's major link to the State Department was George Levison, a member of the Foreign Service from a leading family of the San Francisco aristocracy. Levison served in Cairo during the war, answering directly to Dean Acheson, then assistant secretary for economic development. When Acheson was promoted to undersecretary of state after the war, Levison had not only his and Henderson's ears but also that of his old roommate in Cairo, Kermit Roosevelt, grandson of Theodore Roosevelt and an architect of the Office of Strategic Services and its successor, the Central Intelligence Agency. Also serving with Levison in Cairo was Alfred Lilienthal, a young State Department lawyer and a descendant of Max Lilienthal, the mentor of Isaac Mayer Wise. Coming from the New York branch of perhaps the leading family of the San Francisco aristocracy, Lilienthal would be an energetic and able assistant to George Levison as he emerged as the foreign policy guru of the ACJ.

For all its success in gaining the favor of the State Department, however, the Council could count on virtually no support from elected politicians, especially in Congress. The Democratic Party, with a tradition of ethnic politics almost as old as the party itself, could be counted on to endorse the Zionist program to the hilt. In the case of the Republicans, the party's then-dominant liberal wing practiced a consistent strategy of trying to compete with Democratic ethnic politics. The bloc that was most consistently opposed to the emerging foreign policy consensus during and after the Second World War—the mostly Republican isolationists—would alas, with some notable exceptions, be thoroughly pro-Zionist.[7] Indeed, probably none was more so than the titular leader of the isolationists Senator Robert Taft of Ohio, a friend of Abba Hillel Silver, who reportedly worked directly with Taft in ensuring consistent support for Zionism in successive Republican platforms.[8] The Zionists could also count on the support of such isolationist opinion leaders as Robert McCormick, publisher of the *Chicago Tribune*.

A number of factors seem to have converged in ensuring isolationist support for Zionism: it was an easy way to deflect charges of anti-Semitism by their opponents; it allowed them to score political points against the much-resented

British; it allowed them to score points against their antagonists in the State Department, many of whom went on to become significant hate objects during the McCarthy period; and it also was viewed as a component of a conciliatory reconstruction policy in Europe and Germany in particular, the policy in which the isolationists would be most successful in the early Cold War years.[9] One point, however, must be made in the isolationists' defense, which is that for all the aspects of the "special relationship" that could have been anticipated in these years, one that clearly was not was the massive amount of foreign aid to Israel in the last generation, which, if contemplated then, would likely have dramatically changed the isolationist position. Ironically, this would be a legacy of the president widely regarded as the most successful in Middle East diplomacy, Jimmy Carter; indeed it has been the price paid for that success.

The contrast between the politically shrewd Silver, who was able to pull off the alliance with the isolationist bloc, and the consistently polarizing figure of Stephen Wise no doubt played a role in the former's ultimate displacement of the latter as the Zionist movement regrouped after the war. When the British began to crack down on armed Jewish resistance in July 1946, Chaim Weizmann, Wise's patron, threatened to resign from the World Zionist Organization in favor of a more cooperative policy with the British, which ultimately led to his displacement in the leadership of the Jewish Agency by David Ben-Gurion, who with Silver dominated the Twenty-Second Zionist Congress in December 1946. At that Congress, formal approval was granted to the scheme hatched by Ben-Gurion and Nahum Goldmann at a rump session of the Jewish Agency executive in Paris the previous August—to reply to the British proposal of a federal state along similar lines to the Ihud position with a counteroffer of "the establishment of a viable Jewish state in an adequate area of Palestine." This, the policy of partition, would be at the center of Zionist agitation right up to the moment of statehood.[10]

The mood of the ACJ rapidly grew into alarm. Immediately after the Paris meeting, Goldmann was able to not only secure the approval of the Truman administration "in principle" for partition but also score a major coup in gaining the endorsement of Joseph Proskauer, with the assurance that the partitioned state would "be Jewish only in the sense that Jews would comprise the majority of its population" and that all citizens would enjoy equal rights.[11] Then, in their last attempt to resolve the problem of Palestine before referring the question to the United Nations, the British held a conference with representatives of the Jewish Agency, prompting a vigorous protest from

the Council against the Jewish Agency's claim to be the governing body of
world Jewry. This prompted from Berger a shrewd legalistic argument that
would inform much of his writing for years to come—that a Jewish state
would in fact be a violation of the Balfour Declaration, which expressly safe-
guarded "the rights and status enjoyed by Jews in any country other than
Palestine," as well as those of its non-Jewish inhabitants. The Council also
sent an official letter to Dean Acheson protesting that the Jewish Agency had
"no right to speak for Jews who are not supporters of the Jewish nationalist
philosophy of Zionism."[12]

It was also in the fall of 1946 that Lessing Rosenwald took the lead in establishing the Citizens Committee on Displaced Persons, a nondenomina-
tional group to lobby for the liberalization of U.S. immigration laws to allow
for the absorption of large numbers of European displaced persons into the
United States. Rosenwald even convinced Earl G. Harrison, who had been
Truman's original special envoy on the displaced persons problem after first
coming into office, to accept the chairmanship of the committee. So great was
Harrison's admiration for Rosenwald that he declared "such is my regard for
him and what he has done that I have modified a hymn I sometimes sing—
Praise God from whom all Lessings flow."[13] In 2003 a minor controversy
erupted when the following excerpt was published from the personal diary of
Harry Truman: "The Jews, I find, are very selfish. They care not how many
Estonians, Latvians, Finns, Poles, Yugoslavs, or Greeks are being murdered or
mistreated as long as the Jews get special treatment."[14] However intemper-
ately stated, this was precisely the position of Lessing Rosenwald, so deeply
committed to the cause of European rescue since before the Second World
War, in his outrage over its brazen neglect and exploitation by the Zionists.

As the ACJ became increasingly embroiled in the intrigue of great power
politics, it was rapidly losing what little ground it could still claim within
American Reform Judaism. In March 1946 Irving Reichert addressed a symposium at the biennial gathering of the Union of American Hebrew
Congregations, beginning with an exhortation to remember, in approaching the postwar world, the tale of God's scolding of the Israelites for rejoic-
ing at the drowning of the Egyptians. Reichert pleaded in vain:

> This Union of American Hebrew Congregations has a commitment to
> an historic task which transcends the claims of secular political na-
> tionalism. It has a tradition of loyalty to America which cannot be rec-
> onciled with any philosophy of Jewish homelessness. It has an
> obligation to relieve distress which dare not yield priority to Zionist

politics. Our task today is to salvage human lives, to heal the hurt that cruelty has inflicted, to hold high in a world tragically confused a light for all mankind to steer by. Israel's voice today should not be an echo of that ancient cry "make us a king that we may be like other nations," but a strong and solemn affirmation of that nobler truth—"not by virtue of material strength and political power shall ye prevail, but by my spirit, sayeth the Lord."[15]

Finally, in 1947, Julian Morgenstern, who had managed to maintain a sense of ambiguity about his views since the founding of the ACJ, stepped down as president of Hebrew Union College. Only the intercession of Morgenstern himself, along with major donor Arthur Sulzberger, prevented a partisan Zionist from winning the post, with even Abba Hillel Silver under consideration.[16] Thus was the position awarded to Nelson Glueck, who remained an active supporter of the Ihud; indeed he only accepted the post at the urging of Magnes himself.[17] Like many Zionists who embraced binationalism, however, Glueck was enrapt to the illusory idea of "Jewish unity," with which his student Elmer Berger had been so totally disillusioned. Though Glueck would remain friendly with many of the anti-Zionists, including Berger, and likely remained a Magnes Zionist in his heart,[18] he would allow the premises of cultural Zionism to promote his assent to the direction of Reform Judaism. This included, first and foremost, the merger of Hebrew Union College with the Jewish Institute of Religion of Stephen Wise, just before Wise's death in 1949, and, just before Glueck's death in 1971, the requirement that all students for the rabbinate spend a year of study in Israel.

On February 18, 1947, Ernest Bevin announced before Parliament that the question of Palestine was being deferred to the United Nations. Within a matter of days, Berger urged the immediate preparation of a brief to the United Nations against recognition of the Jewish Agency, arguing that it could speak only for Zionists and would be more properly named the Zionist Agency.[19] George Levison went immediately to Washington to confer with his contacts at the State Department and wrote to Rosenwald as he left Washington, reporting that the mood of the State Department was pessimistic, now favoring a plebiscite along the lines of Ihud in which neither the Jewish Agency nor the Arab League would be represented. Levison also took the opportunity to urge Kermit Roosevelt, then leaving for the Middle East, to arrange to meet there with Judah Magnes.[20] Rosenwald was then able to meet in Washington with Loy Henderson on February 26, at which time he frankly offered the services of the ACJ to the State Department to advocate for its positions.[21]

Berger, for his part, spent most of March on a speaking tour for the Council, visiting St. Louis, Dallas, Houston, Galveston, New Orleans, Baton Rouge, Shreveport, Cincinnati, Lexington, Evansville, and Dayton. The tour was generally considered to be a success, having generated extensive coverage in all the relevant local papers and ensuring that the Council would continue to gain membership, even after 1948.[22] By May the United Nations had set up its Special Committee on Palestine (UNSCOP), where, after Abba Hillel Silver testified as the representative of the Jewish Agency that he spoke for "the Jewish people of the world," Berger naturally lodged a vigorous protest, which moved the American ambassador to the United Nations, Warren Austin, to publicly reject the claims of the Jewish Agency.[23]

On May 31 written testimony was submitted on behalf of the American Jewish Committee, which backed off of Proskauer's earlier endorsement of partition, seemingly at the urging of Judah Magnes, who continued to have close ties to the AJC.[24] The AJC presented to the United Nations a seven-point plan basically mirroring that of the Ihud and signed by Proskauer and Jacob Blaustein, who would soon succeed Proskauer as president of the AJC and maintain the organization's anti-Zionist sympathies into the early 1950s.[25] Days later the State Department submitted to the UN general secretary on behalf of the ACJ a formal memorandum written and signed by Lessing Rosenwald, outlining the Council's long-established position and urging "a worldwide humanitarian solution for the problem of displaced persons of all faiths, preventing the creation of a Jewish state, and assuring the guaranteed rights of Jews everywhere."[26] Alfred Lilienthal, Levison's erstwhile protégé, personally lobbied most of the permanent UN delegations throughout the summer.[27]

After completing its report on August 31, UNSCOP was divided on the question of partition. A majority of seven of eleven members supported partition—Canada, Czechoslovakia, Guatemala, the Netherlands, Peru, Sweden, and Uruguay. The minority of India, Iran, and Yugoslavia supported a federal plebiscite, inspired by Ihud and now supported by both the State Department and the American Jewish Committee. The eleventh member of UNSCOP, Australia, abstained from the question of partition. The majority report proposed that two barely contiguous pieces of the British Mandate of Palestine, comprising 56 percent for the Jews and 44 percent for the Arabs, be recognized as independent states within two years of the report's release, and that Jerusalem, Bethlehem, and their outlying areas be governed by a permanent UN trusteeship. The majority report also called for a ten-year treaty between the two states that would provide for common customs, currency, and communications.[28]

It must be remembered, when considering the original UN partition plan along with the various federal and binationalist schemes, that none of them stood any realistic chance of success. As the events of 1948 made abundantly clear, the bottom line was always that the *Yishuv* had the guns it needed and was prepared to use them to get what it wanted. Nor can the Arab leadership in Palestine be taken for granted, which, though unfairly tarred by the Axis sympathies that naturally existed among nearly all subject peoples of the British Empire, certainly could not have helped matters by their intransigence toward compromise. Lack of responsible or even competent leadership certainly does not excuse the horrible human tragedy that has befallen the Palestinian Arabs, but the latter cannot excuse the former either. Indeed it bears acknowledgment that the ten-year treaty proposed in the majority report stands as an early recognition of the problems that remain inherent in any "two-state solution."

Finally, the designs of the United Nations and its dominant powers for Palestine betrayed an extraordinary degree of hubris in the wake of victory in the Second World War. The idea that the United Nations could ever have occupied Palestine, to say nothing of directly governing it, is laughable when we consider the haplessness of the organization in living memory and the determination of its member states to make it so. Indeed, the insistence of the British and others, including much of the United Nations and even some in the State Department, that they must stay in Palestine until there was a political solution bears a marked resemblance to those who currently insist that the United States must stay in Iraq and Afghanistan until there is a political solution to the conflicts of those countries. In the best-case scenario, Palestine would have become like its neighbor Lebanon, with equally matched ethnic and sectarian factions constantly on the brink of civil war and likely needing a relatively benign occupier, such as Syria in the case of Lebanon historically, to keep the peace along with any degree of normalcy.

On September 9 the National Executive Committee of the Council met in New York to discuss its response to the UNSCOP report. Berger and Levison urged an endorsement of the minority report, but ultimately the only statement to come out of the meeting praised UNSCOP for its work and suspended judgment on the conclusions of the majority report.[29] Sensing what was to come, Berger wrote in a letter to Levison that "should the majority report of the UNSCOP be adopted, it becomes many times more important for us to continue our work of making it clear that we are Americans, completely dissociated in any ideological or organic way with such a Jewish political entity as is recommended."[30] Largely at Berger's instigation, the Council did by the end of the month issue a formal response in the form of a memorandum to Secretary of State George Marshall outlining the most fantastic federal proposal for Palestine yet and calling for an immediate UN trusteeship and interceding on behalf of "land reform laws" and "establishing educational and economic equality between the Jewish and Arab groups."[31]

The State Department, for its part, remained sympathetic to the opposition to partition and let it be known through Levison that as far as they were concerned, partition was not a fait accompli. Kermit Roosevelt was especially impressed by the Council's position and as a private citizen became one of their most aggressive champions in Washington.[32] But even at this early date, the ACJ knew it was only registering a record of dissent, however prophetic, and that the organization's rank-and-file were increasingly restive and demoralized. By November Berger was able to outline his vision for the Council in the increasingly likely event of Jewish statehood. "Zionists will continue to seek control of the lives and institutions of Americans of Jewish faith," he warned. "They will attempt to solidify support for their principle that Jews are members of that 'nationality' and that the homeland of members of that nationality is in their 'Jewish state.' Against this certain, continued drive of Jewish nationalism, in our opinion, the work of the Council will be of even greater importance and necessity than in the past."[33]

On November 29, 1947, by a vote of 33 to 13 with 10 abstentions, the UN General Assembly approved the UNSCOP majority report, thereby approving partition and giving the stamp of international law to the existence of a Jewish state. Violence immediately erupted across Palestine, with 450 dead and 1,000 wounded in December alone.[34] Both the United States and Britain were very quickly chastened by the violence instigated by the vote for partition. Within a week the United States imposed an embargo on arms sales to the region, and within another week the Attlee government announced that it was relinquishing the Mandate on May 15, absolving itself of any responsibility to enforce partition. On December 5 the ACJ executive committee met and decided that though it would withhold for the time being from making a public statement, it would accept the principle of partition and move to what it regarded as its "second line of defense"—combating the Zionist influences, which were bound to increase dramatically after statehood, on Jewish life in the United States.[35]

Meanwhile, as the bloodshed of the year to come was commencing, a grave prophetic warning was issued by Judah Magnes in his address that opened the academic year at the Hebrew University of Jerusalem. After warning that "if there was one victory as a result of the last war, that was the victory of totalitarianism, even among the democracies which were once liberal," like the Prophet Samuel before him, he warned of where the ominous path the Jewish people were once again setting out upon would lead:

> This strange phenomenon, a kind of Zionist assimilation, has been pointed to long since, and it is this which has led not only large sections of the *Yishuv* but also myriads of Jews throughout the world, particularly in America, to yield to that Zionist totalitarianism which seeks to subject to its discipline the entire Jewish people and every individual therein, and, if necessary, by force and violence. Woe to those of us whom this totalitarianism is to cast into the Hebrew Latrun. It is now harder and harder to be a Jew and be faithful to the spirit of Israel among these new-fashioned Hebrews. This totalitarianism is on the way to converting us from that people of whom it was said "who is like thy people Israel, a unique nation on earth," to that people of whom it was said "House of Judah—like all the nations."[36]

The address marked the beginning of the end for Magnes, particularly in Palestine, where he quite naturally became a marked man. The ACJ immediately began distributing the speech along with press clippings of the coverage it received in America. Rosenwald, who would soon personally finance Magnes's sojourn to New York, wrote personally to Magnes, praising him for the address. Rosenwald confided to Magnes:

> I humbly admire your courage and moral statesmanship. You may be able to better realize how sincerely I mean that when I tell you that everything you have said to your Palestinian audience is applicable here. Only your courage in saying these things in Palestine surpasses anything I have seen anywhere else. Whatever the result of all this, you have made a notable and historic pronouncement. I thank you for it and I only pray that Jews may heed your logic and your challenge.[37]

In January the Council held its fourth annual conference in St. Louis. The conference formally accepted partition and thus ended its official opposition to Jewish statehood, declaring that it wished the new state well. Rabbis Berger and Lazaron, along with Lessing Rosenwald and Sidney Wallach, all addressed the consequences of partition. Other speakers at the conference included Paul Hutchinson, the sympathetic editor of *Christian Century*, and William Bernard from the Citizens Committee on Displaced Persons.[38] After passing a resolution calling on the United Jewish Appeal to once again separate its political and humanitarian funds, the conference adopted the following statement of principles, which would define its purpose with the existence of a Zionist state:

1. Nationality and religion are separate and distinct. Our nationality is American. Our religion is Judaism. Our homeland is the United States of America. We reject any concept that Jews are at home only in Palestine.

2. The United Nations Assembly has recommended the partition of Palestine. We hope that it will bring peace to that long troubled land and that each of the proposed states will be a peace loving, democratic nation. The nationalism of the proposed Zionist state must be confined to the boundaries of that state. Its spokesmen, representatives, agencies, and instrumentalities in no way represent us.

3. We are dedicated to extend the fullest philanthropic aid to our coreligionists and to suffering humanity everywhere.

4. No Jew or group of Jews can speak for, or represent, all the Jews of America.[39]

By the time of the St. Louis conference, however, the ACJ was more isolated in the American Jewish community than ever before. In addition to relying on sympathetic Christian clergy for any outside speakers at their conference, the Council's leading rabbis were increasingly outside of the congregational rabbinate. Lazaron had retired from Baltimore Hebrew Congregation as early as 1946, though he continued to be an honored rabbi emeritus, despite several years of tension over his refusal to divorce his activities there from those with the Council. Both William Fineshriber and Samuel Goldenson retired from their respective congregations in 1948, though the culture of each remained decidedly non-Zionist for years to come. But the most acrimonious case, as one might expect, was that of Irving Reichert, a strong-willed man whose illustrious temple, despite its association with the San Francisco aristocracy, was never as uniformly Classical Reform or non-Zionist as Emanu-El of New York or Keneseth Israel in Philadelphia. A leader in the San Francisco aristocracy, Harold Zellerbach, rallied the board of Temple Emanu-El to give Reichert the boot by 1947, replacing him with a militant Zionist, Alvin Fine.[40]

As the ACJ was already beginning to look ahead in St. Louis, the partition plan was falling apart. Beginning in January multiple Arab militias began to challenge the Zionists on the ground and all through February appeared to have the upper hand. The British, for their part, were determined to wash their hands of the whole sorry mess and even had to be dragged into providing even the most minimal assistance to the UN fact-finding teams commissioned by the vote for partition. In short, the single British priority was to simply be out of Palestine by May 14. Indeed, as early as December, similar attitudes were reigning at the State Department, with Loy Henderson concluding in a report coauthored with his illustrious mentor, George Kennan, that partition was "impossible of implementation."[41] On February 21 Lessing Rosenwald wrote to George Marshall, with the Council's blessing, stating that events since November 29 had shown the assumptions underlying partition to have been completely fallacious and that a UN trusteeship was necessary.[42]

Late in February Kermit Roosevelt gathered together a group of distinguished Christian clergy to form the Committee for Peace and Justice in the Holy Land, with himself acting as the group's executive director and with the chairmanship going to Virginia Gildersleeve, the dean of Barnard College. Morris Lazaron was immediately on board at Roosevelt's invitation, and he served with Gildersleeve and Roosevelt in the committee's top leadership along with Henry Sloane Coffin, president of Union Theological Seminary.[43] Other supporters of the committee included Harry Emerson Fosdick of New York's Riverside Church, Bayard Dodge of the American University of Beirut, historian Garland Evans Hopkins, and Paul Hutchinson of *Christian Century*. Though Lazaron was the only representative of the Council on the committee, Berger was intimately involved, attending almost every meeting and assisting with publicity and recruitment.[44] At once culminating the record of Congress in the years leading up to statehood and beginning a new record of congressional calumny for generations to come, the committee was endorsed by a mere two members of Congress—Lawrence Smith of Wisconsin and Karl Mundt of South Dakota, both Republicans.

Within a week of the Committee for Peace and Justice in the Holy Land announcing itself publicly, Judah Magnes registered his enthusiastic endorsement of the committee in a letter to Virginia Gildersleeve.[45] Almost simultaneously, however, Magnes received a note of protest from Leon Simon, head of the American Friends of the Hebrew University, who said of the committee: "They notoriously represent missionary and pro-Arab interests. They

are bitterly anti-Zionist, and I think it would not be entirely unjust to call
some of them anti-Semitic. Such people may be fit company for Rabbi
Lazaron, but it seems strange that Dr. Magnes can allow his name to be associated with theirs."[46] Magnes replied to his American friend: "You use
rather strong expressions concerning Miss Gildersleeve and her friends. Even
though all you say were true, that would be all the more reason for encouraging my efforts to persuade them to advocate the justice and practicability
of our program. Or is everyone who has opposed the official Zionist program since the fatal Biltmore resolutions and could foresee the catastrophe
to which they would eventually lead an anti-Zionist?"[47]

On March 19 Ambassador Warren Austin announced before the UN
Security Council that the United States was suspending its support for partition and proposed a UN trusteeship. There would be controversy over
whether President Truman specifically endorsed the policy, which he did as
a matter of last resort but continued to reassure Chaim Weizmann, his main
contact with the *Yishuv*, that it did not change his administration's support
for partition as a long-term goal. What did catch Truman off guard was the
timing of Austin's announcement, which put him in the worst of all possible worlds politically, both in his dealings with the Zionists and in terms of
public perception.[48] The Council, of course, was thrilled. Rosenwald immediately sent letters of support to the president, Secretary of State Marshall,
and Ambassador Austin, and the State Department was now coordinating
its efforts with both the Council and the Committee for Peace and Justice in
the Holy Land.

Much mythology surrounds the decision of Harry Truman to recognize
the State of Israel. To this day, a great deal of it remains grounded in the story
of his onetime Jewish business partner, Eddie Jacobson, and the apocryphal
tale of his persuasion. A non-Zionist most of his life, whatever role Jacobson
played was as the well-directed tool of Chaim Weizmann.[49] A number of recent revisionist accounts stress the role of Truman's urgent need for Zionist-
connected money to fund his reelection campaign, an idea that carries
considerable weight. In any event, the legend is most dramatically illustrated
by the opposition of the giant George Marshall being overcome by two mere
political advisers to the president, Clark Clifford and David Niles. Indeed it
does not take much imagination in this case to uncover cynical political cal-
culation beneath the veneer of idealism.

There is, however, one factor that has rarely been discussed, which was the
threat plainly in evidence of a loss of Jewish support in 1948. In February the

quixotic Progressive Party, an explicitly pro-Soviet outfit running the disaffected former Vice President Henry Wallace for president, won a special congressional election in an overwhelmingly Jewish district in the Bronx solely on the strength of the Zionist issue. The candidate, Leo Isaacson, declared in his literature that "it is part of the Truman Doctrine and the Marshall Plan to sacrifice Jewish blood for Arab oil," and his loss in the general election the following November illustrates plainly that his congressional victory was based solely in the passions of the moment.[50] Indeed the early endorsement of the Biltmore program by Stalin could not have been more convenient for the American Communists as they sought to hold on to significant voting strength, as well as the loyalty of their Jewish base in their desperation to recover from the debacle of the Hitler-Stalin pact. In short, the threat of Jewish voters and money defecting to a viable pro-Soviet political party was a most ominous one to the Truman administration.

The Committee for Peace and Justice in the Holy Land released a statement of principles on April 5, declaring, "The articulate, highly organized lobbying of those who, for a variety of partisan reasons, favor the partition of Palestine must not steamroller us into an action that may have the most serious consequences for our national security, our foreign policy, our friendship with the Near East peoples, and the cause of world peace."[51] Two days later, Rosenwald gave an address over CBS radio in rebuttal to one given the previous week by Abba Hillel Silver, painting an idealistic picture of what could be accomplished under a UN trusteeship, claiming that "the people of Palestine would learn to exhibit statesmanship, understanding, and conciliation."[52] Kermit Roosevelt attempted to broaden public support by recruiting a "Citizens Committee," hoping to recruit such household names as Bernard Baruch, Dwight Eisenhower, and Herbert Hoover.[53]

On April 16 a secret telegram was sent from the State Department to the American consul in Jerusalem urging Judah Magnes to immediately leave Palestine for America, extending the invitation of Rosenwald, Lewis Strauss, and Jerome Frank. Having been warned for over a year by British authorities that his life was in danger, Magnes arrived in New York six days later with his travel and living expenses personally provided by Rosenwald out of his own pocket. Though addressing a group of his supporters four days after his arrival and meeting with George Marshall on May 4, all Magnes could accomplish by that time was to make known in the United States that there was dissent among the Jews of Palestine.[54] Throughout April the military position of the *Yishuv* vastly improved, largely with money and arms from the

Communist regime that had just come to power in Czechoslovakia in a
brazen coup d'état. The consequent Zionist routing of the Arab militias led
to a massive flight by the civilian Arab population, whose subjection to continued Zionist terror as they fled would be known ever after as the *nakba*.

With few illusions, the ACJ courageously took its last stand in the days
and weeks leading up to the expiration of the Mandate. Irving Reichert made
an impassioned speaking tour of multiple cities between April 30 and May
18, visiting New York; Philadelphia; Baltimore; Washington; Pittsburgh;
Cincinnati; Youngstown, Ohio; Wheeling, West Virginia; Richmond, Virginia;
and New Haven, Connecticut, giving several radio addresses over the course
of his sojourn. Also visiting America at this time was Israel Mattuck, the
Hebrew Union College–ordained rabbi of the largest Reform congregation
in London, who led a sister organization to the ACJ in the mother country,
the Jewish Fellowship, founded by the philanthropist Basil Henriques.[55]
On May 6 an audience of 400 came to a rally in Washington addressed by
Kermit Roosevelt along with Rabbis Reichert and Lazaron. On May 11 nearly
a thousand came to the annual meeting of the New York chapter of the
Council, addressed by Rosenwald, Mattuck, and Paul Hutchinson.[56]

On May 14, 1948, as the British completed their evacuation of Palestine
and the forced removal of Arab civilians was beginning to wrap up, the executive committee of the Jewish Agency gathered in the Tel Aviv Museum to
approve and sign a declaration of independence, which was then read aloud
by David Ben-Gurion, who as leader of the Jewish Agency was now the new
head of state. The new State of Israel was granted de facto recognition by the
United States nine hours after the reading of the declaration and full recognition by the Soviet Union the next day. Though an incredible mythology
surrounds the routing by Israel of the invading regular armies of its Arab
neighbors and how the recognition of the state by Truman saved Israel from
certain doom at the hands of those armies, the fact is that the Zionist forces
never lost the upper hand after the aid from Czechoslovakia arrived.
Moreover, while the U.S. arms embargo remained in effect for the rest of the
year, the announcement of recognition by Truman served only the most symbolic significance.

The Council did not even have time to formulate its response to the historic events of May 14 when the very next day, Louis Wolsey, who had
scarcely been heard from since he resigned from the leadership of the
Council three years earlier, announced in a speech to the Rodef Shalom
Men's Club in Philadelphia that he was resigning his membership in the ACJ

altogether. After reiterating his view that the tragedies of the past six years and the crisis unfolding as he spoke could have been prevented were it not for the passage of the Biltmore Program, he recounted the whole saga that unfolded in the intervening years before declaring: "I am today neither a Zionist nor an anti-Zionist, but an objective student of the whole situation. That Jews have set up and proclaimed a government on the land partitioned by a decision of the United Nations, that to date six nations have recognized that government, chief among them Russia and our own United States, that Jews defend it with their lives and with great courage, should move every Jew whether he be nationalist or anti-nationalist to support Israel."[57]

Wolsey did not, however, formally notify the Council of his action until doing the courtesy of writing to Rosenwald weeks after the fact on June 1.[58] The Council did go on to issue a lengthy press release stating:

> More important than the misrepresentations of the Council contained in Dr. Wolsey's attack is his underestimation of the very realities which he claims moved him to speak. The first of his unreal realities is his call to the Zionist Organization to dissolve. Dr. Wolsey should know that the ZOA made it plain, following the UN recommendation of November 29, 1947, that the creation of a Zionist state could not be considered the occasion for an end of Zionist-nationalist pressures and activities in the United States. The Zionist Organization is on record that it intends to continue its program of Zionist nationalism in America in connection with problems that it foresees as inevitable following the proclamation of a Zionist state.[59]

It was clear, therefore, that the ACJ was unbowed in sticking to the "second line of defense" that it had already begun eight months earlier.

Few could have been more convinced of this imperative than Elmer Berger, the firebrand whom Wolsey had been in so many ways responsible for unleashing onto the American Jewish scene. In his own response to his mentor, Berger declared on behalf of the organization that Wolsey had conceived and practically given to him:

> We shall continue to seek the integration of Jews into American life. We are convinced that this necessary integration cannot be accomplished as members of a separatistic national group with national interests in a foreign state. Therefore, we shall continue to reject concepts and programs for Jews that derive from national or racial theories. We pray that the State of Israel may also construct itself upon

that basis, granting full equality of rights and obligations, in all aspects of life, to all of its people. But for ourselves, and our relationships in the American scene, we entertain no question as to our determination in these matters.[60]

Indeed, Wolsey had to have been conscious of the hopelessness of his stated position, that both the ACJ and the Zionist Organization of America should disband and that a united Jewish community could simply move on. He died a virtual recluse in 1953.

Morris Lazaron issued his own statement within a week of statehood, insisting:

> The declaration of a Zionist State and the United States' recognition of its de facto status does [sic] not change the basic issues in the Palestine question. Let us pray that the things that many of us have feared—the destruction of much that has been built in Palestine, unnecessary loss of Christian, Muslim, and Jewish life in a useless civil war, the stopping of orderly immigration, difficulties for our own country, international complications—will not come to pass. Surely the truth of our Council position has been revealed beyond doubt, this is not a fight for homes for the homeless, this is a fight for a state. The first qualification for any immigrant to Palestine is that he must be a fighter.[61]

Ever the optimist, Lazaron concluded: "I call upon my friends all over the country to rally with eager enthusiasm and persistent unflagging determination under the banner of the one living God. Let us go forward together in the struggle for that democracy under which Jews and all men will be free."[62]

As early as May 21, Abraham Cronbach affirmed his continuing solidarity with the Council and immediately began consulting with Berger on what would be the most immediately pressing problem after statehood, the refusal of the United Jewish Appeal to separate the funds for its Zionist and humanitarian efforts, and directed Cronbach to the efforts already under way of numerous Council members through the American Friends Service Committee.[63] Edward Tonkon, Rosenwald's loyal friend in Dallas, also registered his determination to go forward and helped rally the leaders of the Council in San Francisco on a personal visit there. In a letter to Tonkon, Berger outlined four clear short-term objectives: keeping the events in Palestine out of the presidential election, preparing legal briefs on the question of safeguarding the interests of American Jews in relation to Israel, granting a scholarship for a young Polish refugee to Hebrew Union College, and addressing the problem of the United Jewish Appeal.[64]

There could be no question that the ACJ was now more determined than ever in what it regarded its fundamental purpose to have always been, to challenge Zionist objectives in America. The Council responded vigorously to a speech before a Union of American Hebrew Congregations (UAHC) gathering by Abba Hillel Silver that declared there could be no further debate of Zionism, as anti-Zionism would now be "fighting an established state."[65] Charging that the Zionists sought to quash all open debate of their activities in America, a letter was also drafted to the *New York Times* protesting a report of the Anti-Defamation League (ADL) charging that anti-Semitism was rising with the "vilification of Jews because they favored establishment of a Jewish state in Palestine." The letter, likely written by Berger, countered that "those who seek to identify political Zionism with religious Judaism work a profound and dangerous injustice to Americans of all faiths. If support for political Zionism is dangerous to our national interests, it endangers the interests of American Jews more, not less, than those of citizens of other faiths."[66]

The ADL, which had been founded in 1913 and was until now generally aligned with the American Jewish Committee, turned almost on a dime in the months leading up to statehood into a stalwart Zionist outfit, despite the involvement of ACJ members into the early 1950s, developing the stock-in-trade method of directly equating anti-Zionism with anti-Semitism. This, of course, is the ADL's modus vivendi to this very day.

One of the earliest targets of the anti-anti-Zionist crusade of the ADL was the Committee for Peace and Justice in the Holy Land, which also was persisting beyond May 14. The committee remained active in calling attention to the plight of the Arab refugees and also expressed particular outrage at reports of American Jews in Israel whom the Israeli government was not allowing to return home.[67] The committee was also calling attention to the relentless push of the Israeli forces beyond the lines of the UN Partition and quoted the foreign minister of the new state, Moshe Sharett, to the effect of admitting openly that the Zionist support for partition had been nothing but a ploy to buy time for the conquest by force of the whole of Palestine. Indeed, by the end of 1948, the Israelis controlled a full 78 percent of the territory of the Mandate, and thereafter all discussions of an eventual "two-state solution" have been along that armistice line, not along the lines of the original partition.

In August a special edition of the *Council News* was distributed, consisting entirely of an extended essay by Berger that outlined "the challenge to all Americans who are Jews by religion presented by Zionist plans to foster an 'Israel-centered' Jewish life in the United States." Setting the tone for his work of the next twenty years, Elmer Berger wrote:

> The creation of a sovereign state, embodying the principles of Zionism, far from relieving American Jews of the urgency of making that choice, makes it more compelling. Each day of drift and evasion, in the face of overwhelming Zionist-nationalist propaganda makes extrication from the web that is being spun more difficult and lends strength to the relentless Zionist effort to endow all Jews with the nationalism that derives from Israel. That way leads to the fastening upon American Jews who determine to remain Jews the status of a permanent national minority in America.[68]

But for all the tragedy of 1948, probably none came as a more crushing blow to the ACJ and to the cause of peace and justice in Palestine generally than the sudden death of Judah Magnes on October 28. Days earlier, in a final act of prophetic witness, he had resigned from the American Jewish Committee after it refused to give any money to help the Arab refugees in Palestine. Rosenwald, in a telegram extending condolences to Magnes's widow, declared, "His fearless convictions and high-minded idealism in the cause of human brotherhood place him in the tradition of our great Prophets. The cause of peace and friendship among peoples to which he was dedicated will always be inspired by the memory of his services."[69] Berger, who visited Magnes many times in New York, recalled that his family insisted that Magnes had died of a broken heart, adding, "I don't really know what that means."[70] As Magnes had warned in his final speech at the Hebrew University, the world was now irreversibly on an advance to barbarism, and in their assent to Zionism, the Jewish people would tragically prove themselves only the most eager to join.

5

A COUNCIL FOR JUDAISM?

All told, May 14, 1948, did not turn out to be an especially significant date in the rise and fall of the American Council for Judaism. Undoubtedly this was because of the preparations for the "second line of defense," which Berger had insisted begin as early as nine months prior to the founding of the State of Israel when the United Nations first received the recommendation in favor of partition. In the five years between beginning formal solicitation of lay membership and statehood, the ACJ would accumulate just over 14,000 dues-paying members. This number leveled off, but did not decrease, after 1948. Within another few years, the Council was claiming a member-ship of 16,000 and claimed close to 20,000 before the end of the 1950s. As late as that time, it would not be unreasonable to speculate that the ACJ con-tinued to give voice to a silent majority of Reform Jews (as opposed, that is, to all of American Jewry).

As Berger saw it, "We could afford to lose, as we did, the battle against Jewish nationalism in far off Palestine. Having lost it, our task here is, in many ways, more difficult. But we cannot afford to lose the battle against Jewish nationalism in America."[1] But this had always been the more hopeless battle. One way or another, the great majority of American Jews at the midpoint of the twentieth century were emphatically determined not to be "Americans of Jewish faith," the identity that had meant so much to those who formed the Council. Zionism would give the most compelling answer to the anxieties of that generation, as it was inevitably becoming more Americanized, however much perhaps in spite of themselves. As the "official" Jewish community that had begun to coalesce in the Zionist agitation of the 1940s emerged after statehood, it would presume to govern the American Jewish community in a manner not unlike that of medieval rabbis over their respective communities. This, at any rate, was the analogy that set off alarm bells for American Jews who, in the Council's telling, still believed in the promise of enlightenment and emancipation.

The headline of the December 1949 issue of the *Council News* announced "Zionists Reveal Plan to Control U.S. Jewry," referring to a report published by Zionist Organization of America President Daniel Frisch titled "Democratization of the American Jewish Community." The article quoted Frisch as saying that "the slogan of capturing the communities which Herzl in his day coined has now become a must of the hour for American Zionism."[2] It went on to warn: "Reorganization of Jewish community life along the lines of the Frisch plan would rapidly enable Jewish nationalists to gain the ascendancy they require for effecting their 'revolution' in the lives of Americans. Such a supreme authority as Frisch proposes would provide the most favorable framework for directing the activities of religious institutions, schools, community centers, and welfare funds into Zionist channels."[3] The report, which directly led the American Jewish Conference to reconstitute itself as the National Community Relations Advisory Council (NCRAC), helped move the ACJ to establish a Committee on Religious and Synagogue programs and to combat the reach of this Zionist encroachment into the most intimate and fundamental aspects of their lives as Jews, the most notable of which would be religious education.

Throughout 1949 the Council, led by Rosenwald, continued to plead for consideration of the plight of Palestinian Arab refugees, sending letters to both the American Jewish Committee and the Synagogue Council of America, a representative body of the leaders of the three major branches of Judaism. The Synagogue Council was thus moved to make a statement intoning that

> the deep concern of the American Council for Judaism for the Arab "refugees" stands in sharp contrast to its long record of callous indifference to the plight of millions of refugees who happened to be Jews. This attitude was highlighted by alleged statements of some of the leaders of the ACJ throughout the bitter years of the Nazi destruction and the cruel aftermath of the postwar years, that they would not contribute to the United Jewish Appeal because part of its funds were

going to Palestine. Evidently they are determined, now that their campaign to prevent the establishment of the State of Israel had failed, to undermine it with every means at their disposal.[4]

In January 1950 the Synagogue Council proceeded, based on its statement, to move within the new NCRAC that a public denunciation of the ACJ be issued, which in the spirit and theory of the Frisch report effectively amounted to a *herem*, or writ of excommunication. The statement by the NCRAC, which easily passed, read in part:

> The small but highly vocal group of Jewish individuals known as the American Council for Judaism has been responsible for the publication in the nation's press of reiterated statements casting doubts on the loyalty of American Jews who have demonstrated their sympathies with Israel. The overwhelming majority of American Jews, Zionist and non-Zionist alike, recognizing their obligation to help Israel in the huge task of resettling and absorbing hundreds of thousands of homeless Jews, and conscious of their deep religious and cultural affinity with the Jews of Israel, are abiding in the upbuilding of that land.[5]

In replying to a letter of protest from Rosenwald, NCRAC Chairman Irving Kane was unbowed, declaring that "what is shocking and distressing is the fact that the ACJ has expressed views so strikingly similar to those disseminated by professional anti-Semites as to provide them with a sanction for their attacks against Jews."[6] Rosenwald also sent letters urging a protest against the statement to each of the constituent organizations of the NCRAC, including the members of the Synagogue Council, the American Jewish Committee, the Anti-Defamation League, the Jewish Labor Committee, and the Jewish War Veterans of America. The Council itself issued a defiant press release, stating that "Nothing exemplifies the totalitarian-like tactics of the NCRAC more clearly than its relations with the Council. We were never invited to submit evidence. We were condemned in ex-parte hearings and in absentia. Only thereafter were we invited to attend a conference for the purpose of hearing the verdict."[7]

This banishment of the ACJ also occasioned their endorsement by the accomplished Yiddish journalist William Zukerman, a stalwart of the Jewish socialist tradition who would all but singlehandedly keep its anti-Zionist tradition alive in the years ahead. Born in Brest-Litovsk, Lithuania, he arrived in the United States during the heyday of the Socialist Party and immediately went to work as the Chicago correspondent of *The Forward*, the party-aligned Yiddish paper based in New York, which was the highest-circulating Yiddish newspaper in the world. After serving in the First World War, he remained in Europe as the Amsterdam-based European correspondent of *Der Tag*, the Orthodox competitor of *The Forward*. In London during the Second World War, his earlier contacts enabled him to announce to the world the news of the Warsaw Ghetto uprising, at which time he already received the accolades of Council leaders for his emphasis on the decidedly anti-Zionist aims of the uprising, that is, their determination to have a future in Poland.[8] Returning to New York after the war, Zukerman served briefly on the editorial board of *Der Tag* before resigning in early 1948 to devote his full energy to the publication of his *Jewish Newsletter*.

As early as April 1949 Zukerman was seconding his dear old comrade Norman Thomas, who said, "We shall pay a price we can ill afford if Judaism should become merely an extension of Israeli nationalism, and if American Jews should consciously or unconsciously consider themselves exiles and strangers in the lands of their citizenship because their affection turns largely to physical Jerusalem."[9] No sooner had he also begun to praise the Council itself as "the party of opposition in American Jewry." As Zukerman would lament:

> The fiercely anti-Zionist Jewish Labor Committee goes on a pilgrimage of worship to Tel Aviv. The non-Zionist American Jewish Committee is likewise worshipping at the shrine. And the Agudath has capitulated to the political-orthodox Mizrachi. All vie with each other and with the Zionists in voicing their patriotism, loyalty, and devotion to the Jewish State. All except the American Council for Judaism. It seems that the emergence of the Jewish State has had a reverse effect on the people of the Council than on most other Jews.[10]

After the NCRAC pronouncement, Zukerman wrote glowingly to Rosenwald that "you have strengthened my faith in man and in the worthwhileness of fighting for what I believe to be right."[11] Zukerman himself would write of the episode:

> It is shocking to realize how much of that morbid psychology which had long disappeared even in Eastern Europe, where the ghetto fears were transformed into courage and isolationism into a desire for equality and fraternity with the non-Jewish world, has been transferred to and retained in this country by American Jews who were born and bred

here. The entire NCRAC incident is based on the ghetto premise—that the Christian world in America is potentially the same sworn enemy of the Jews as were the Russian and Polish anti-Semites, that Jews have some kinds of secrets to hide from non-Jews, and that those Jews who reveal those secrets are to be held up as informers and traitors.[12]

By June Zukerman and the Council were exchanging mailing lists, with the Council getting Zukerman into their network of libraries around the country, and Zukerman distributing Council literature to his friends in the Jewish labor movement and among students.[13]

In 1949 there would be two other auspicious beginnings for the cause of the ACJ. In September, *Reader's Digest* carried an article by Alfred Lilienthal titled "Israel's Flag Is Not Mine," thus beginning for the idealistic young lawyer a long public career as a Jewish anti-Zionist that would at times even rival that of Berger. In declaring emphatically that "the plain fact is that we Jews are not a race and we should not let the Zionists persuade us that we are," he went on to recall an event from during the war: "One evening I went to see an opera performance in Jerusalem. In that theater lobby you could distinguish almost at a glance the Yiddish-speaking Jew from Poland, the Spanish-speaking Jew from North Africa or Turkey, the German Jew, Jews from scores of different countries all differing in dress, language, manners, and attitudes. I had visual proof of the arguments of anthropologists, who laugh at the notion of a distinct Jewish race."[14] He went on to say of the founding of the State of Israel: "There was no holiday in my heart, nor in that of the late Rabbi Magnes, who said sadly 'we had always thought that Zionism would diminish anti-Semitism in the world, we are witness to the opposite.'"[15] The consummate publicist, Lilienthal hoped to succeed Sidney Wallach, who left the Council in 1950, as their public relations adviser,[16] but even then the ACJ felt a need to distance itself from a talk Lilienthal gave at a New York synagogue.[17]

But the ACJ would still make an auspicious hire, in autumn 1949, of the man who would keep the organization running for virtually the whole period until the momentous war of 1967. Leonard Sussman, who had been active at Temple Emanu-El in New York since he was a schoolboy, walked in the door of the New York office unannounced asking for a job. As much a product of "our crowd" as any leading figure of the Council would ever truly be—all eight of his great-grandparents had fled Germany after the 1848 revolution—Sussman was enrolled at the religious school of Emanu-El by his agnostic parents and prospered there through his adolescence. At New York University in the late 1930s, he was a prize student of philosophy professor Sidney Hook, who awakened his political consciousness and would remain a lifelong friend. After graduating from the Columbia University Graduate School of Journalism in 1941, he served as an army press officer in Puerto Rico and, when he returned to New York, was hired as the youth director of Temple Emanu-El. Upon meeting him, Berger immediately knew he had to snap up this hot young talent, and he hired him on the spot as eastern regional director. Sussman rose through the ranks to become the Council's executive director within five years.

In the summer of 1951, in his capacity as youth director of Emanu-El, Sussman attended at Haverford College, a summer institute of the National Federation of Temple Youth, an organization he had helped found. He wrote of his culture shock for the *Council News*, declaring earnestly that "Isaac Mayer Wise would revolt anew!"[18] After describing the use of Hebrew greetings, which were frankly described in Zionist literature as "Zionese," and the accompaniment of meals with Hebrew Zionist anthems, he related a bizarre ceremony to mark Tisha b'Av, the day of mourning for the destruction of the biblical Temple, which even today is not typically observed by Reform Jews. The ceremony took place in a dark hall with the telling of tales from the recent Holocaust, which suddenly culminated with the proclamation that Tisha b'Av "now has its happy side because the state of Israel has been refounded," at which point the lights were suddenly turned on and the group broke out into Israeli dances. Feeling that the youth of the conference did indeed need to be consciously indoctrinated by these means, Sussman prophetically warned "there is no telling how many Haverford experiences our young people can withstand."[19]

While the article galvanized the Council, it created a serious uproar in the Reform movement, prompting direct attacks by the new president of the Union of American Hebrew Congregations (UAHC), Maurice Eisendrath, as well as from Arthur Lelyveld, who had been a leader of the "Committee on Unity for Palestine," which was committed exclusively to combating the Council in the 1940s. In a memo written to several Council leaders to assist them in responding to the attacks that resulted from the article, Sussman declared: "If it is blasphemous in Judaism to inquire into the changing of religious practices, if it is blasphemous to criticize the officials of the UAHC, if it is blasphemous to report to members of Reform congregations on one's views of an important program in the Reform movement—if, in brief,

Reform Judaism has become a closed corporation, then indeed I have blasphemed."[20] Whatever else may have been at work, what this controversy did reflect was the fact, however much so many Jews did not want to admit it, that they ultimately needed to reconcile such a thoroughgoing ideological Zionism with the reality of their lives in postwar America.

On September 10, 1950, American Jewish Committee president Jacob Blaustein returned from a meeting in Israel with David Ben-Gurion, declaring that they had reached an agreement about the status of American Jews in connection with the State of Israel. After a series of aggressive appeals by Ben-Gurion in the preceding two years that alarmed the Council, among others, for American Jews to emigrate to Israel, including for children to be sent away by their parents, the AJC decided it had to take the task of addressing this upon itself, knowing that the Israeli government continued to put as great a premium on the friendliness of the AJC as it had since the time of the Biltmore Conference. Basically a reiteration of the "Cos Cob formula" by which the Zionists had sought the committee's assent to Zionism a full decade earlier, Blaustein could confidently declare that "The Prime Minister's statement makes clear, among other things, that without any reservations the State of Israel speaks only on behalf of its own citizens and in no way presumes to represent or speak in the name of Jews who are citizens of any other country, and that the Jews of the United States, as a community of individuals, have no political attachment to Israel."[21]

Officially, the Council welcomed these developments, and for his part, Blaustein would insist as long as he remained at the head of the AJC that the two organizations sought the same ends by different means. But there was cause for deep concern about those means, as the AJC was now seeking to build on the agreement with Ben-Gurion by trying to influence the increasingly Zionist-directed institutions of the American Jewish community from within. As early as November, an extremely wary Berger gave a speech in Denver, Colorado, in which he welcomed the statement "from a purely public relations angle, but it doesn't cover the problems arising today out of Israel-U.S. Jewish relationships," which he identified as being the continued Zionist domination of the UJA, its growing drive to promote the sale of Israel Bonds, and the "transplantation of Israeli culture into American Jewish life."[22] Rosenwald, meanwhile, was still a member of the AJC and continued to urge Blaustein to take a less conciliatory posture, warning that Ben-Gurion was merely seeking to effect a repeat of the acquiescence of elite "non-Zionists" that occurred after the First World War.[23]

By 1952, however, the Council was abandoning whatever illusions it ever had about what the reaffirmation of "non-Zionism" by the AJC could lead to. At an executive committee meeting that January, Frank Sulzberger, a Council leader from Chicago who also remained active with the AJC, expressed his pessimism and reported that financial pressure as well as a wave of public denunciation was being exerted by the Zionists.[24] Some hope remained, however, as long as the AJC, along with its allies in the Anti-Defamation League, were increasingly at odds with the increasingly powerful National Community Relations Advisory Council. But Berger himself remained deeply distrustful of the self-proclaimed "non-Zionists," warning his colleagues in the Council that the AJC was seeking to intervene in Israeli policy and compete with Zionist organizations, as opposed to the Council, for the support of American Jews.[25]

Curiously, the Reform movement also seemed to be hedging its bets around this time, electing the non-Zionist Jacob Marcus to a term as president of the Central Conference of American Rabbis in 1951. Marcus had hoped, along with Solomon Freehof, that the founding of the ACJ could have been prevented, and that the anti-Zionists could have continued to advocate for their views inside the CCAR, though he would welcome the Council when it held its annual conference in Cincinnati in 1950. Rosenwald had reached out to Marcus upon his election and felt that he shared many of the Council's views as they extended beyond the issue of Zionism, specifically with regard to religious education.[26] Nelson Glueck also sought out both Rosenwald and Berger for their views on excising Zionist influences from Reform religious schools, expressing sympathy for their position as well as the hope that the rift between the Council and its adversaries could be healed.[27] But by then, the Zionists had simply achieved too great a domination of the rank-and-file Reform rabbinate for any meaningful resistance.

The AJC also had its own Zionist specter from below to contend with, in the form of a plucky little magazine they had sponsored since 1945 called *Commentary*. Founded by Eliot Cohen and Irving Kristol, two disaffected writers from the avant-garde *Partisan Review*, they managed to secure an unrestricted grant from the AJC largely on the initiative of their Zionist Executive Director John Slawson.[28] As early as 1947, Lewis Strauss lamented after a direct attack on the "Americanism" of Classical Reform Judaism that "we are expending a very substantial sum of money which does positive harm, and frequently offends by affording a forum for writers to work off personal grudges or indulge in deliberate misrepresentation."[29] *Commentary* would thus become the natural sounding board for a momentous exchange of polemics with Elmer Berger that would capture this turning point in the history of American Judaism.

This came with the publication of Berger's second book, *A Partisan History of Judaism*, in 1951, again published by the Devin-Adair Company and with an introduction by Paul Hutchinson of *Christian Century*. The book was based on a series of lectures on Jewish history Berger had given throughout 1949 at Hunter College and took the form of an extended pamphlet. The title referred to Berger's declaration that the views he was advocating were "openly partisan," that is, of the party of universalism as opposed to the party of Jewish nationalism. The biblical history he related was based mostly on the theories that were in vogue and had deeply influenced him during his time at Hebrew Union College, essentially arguing that the Prophets conceived of this party of universalism and that the party of nationalism began to rise against it with the restoration of Ezra and Nehemiah under Cyrus the Great, the event that concludes the Old Testament and is thus traditionally regarded as the dawn of rabbinic Judaism. Indeed the book was striking for how neatly it fit into the Classical Reform narrative of the controversy of Zionism. In analogizing between the rabbinical despotism of the ghetto and the rising "professional Jewish class," he would more often denounce the former for being comparable to the latter.[30]

Though Berger continued to hold many of the problematic assumptions about revolutionary liberalism that plagued *The Jewish Dilemma*, at the same time he concluded *A Partisan History of Judaism* by grounding himself in unusually political terms in the classical liberalism of Moses Mendelssohn and Isaac Mayer Wise, boldly proclaiming a vision for the good society for all of liberal civilization, which should be the goal of prophetic Judaism:

> We may save capitalism, if that is our objective, by saving human freedom. And we should be mature enough to know also that, if we save human freedom, it may follow that some other economic reflection of that freedom will evolve for our day. It means that cooperation should be free, voluntary, a joining of hands with other men, who are also individuals, in compacts that transcend race or creed and which are founded on the deeply personal cornerstones of conviction, likeness of spirit, and mutuality of ideas. Anything less is a relapse to tribalism—this goes for capital, labor, government, and religion.[31]

The man who would rally to the defense of the new Jewish counter-Enlightenment against Berger was Milton Himmelfarb, a staffer of the American

Jewish Committee under John Slawson and brother-in-law of Irving Kristol, who, as a student at the Jewish Theological Seminary, would combine his deeply Orthodox background with the generally secular authoritarian philosophy of the Zionist German émigré Leo Strauss to forge the peculiar brand of neo-Orthodoxy that has been *Commentary*'s consistent editorial line in regard to theology. Indeed the very first iteration of this neo-Orthodoxy appears to have been in Himmelfarb's review of *A Partisan History of Judaism* for *Commentary* in February 1952. Seizing upon the extreme view articulated by Berger most clearly in this most recent work, that there was "no such thing as the Jewish people," Himmelfarb inferred from this that Berger was now advocating a species of secular humanism, as opposed to the "seamless web" of the universal and particular by which Himmelfarb defined his neo-Orthodoxy and portrayed it, somewhat duplicitously, as a big tent welcoming Reform Zionists.[32]

Berger's response to the review, and a reply from Himmelfarb, were published in the April issue. After posing the question directly "or is Judaism, after all, a tribalism, in which the worship of God without the worship of peoplehood is heresy?," Berger challenged "Mr. Himmelfarb to the contrary notwithstanding, Judaism is not now and never has been one 'seamless web.' If it has not been a constant struggle between 'the universal and the particular,' then Mr. Himmelfarb owes the world a new interpretation of the conflict between the Prophets and Priests, between the Pharisees and Sadducees, between the Maimunists and anti-Maimunists, between Orthodox and Reform."[33] Himmelfarb rejoined with the mocking response: "Rabbi Berger gives a long list of pairs of controversialists in Jewish history. It would have been even longer if he had added Hillel and Shammai, Saadia and Ben Meir, Eybeschutz and Emden, Hasidim and Mitnagdim, Wise and Einhorn— longer, but equally irrelevant."[34]

This was a disingenuous response from Himmelfarb, for most of the controversies cited by both men resulted in the definitive triumph of one and the stamp of heresy upon the other, and just such a result was the aim of this latest addition to the list of "Berger and Himmelfarb." Himmelfarb was correct to point out that Berger's unequivocal rejection of Jewish peoplehood was an extreme not broached by early Reform—even the Pittsburgh Platform spoke of "the Jewish people." But in the context that clearly haunted Berger—the original Reform movement's kinship with the German Romanticism that had birthed both Zionism and Nazism—this was not an unreasonable extreme. Indeed, it was all but unavoidable in the face of Zionism's elevation of "the Jewish people" to a political entity.

What Himmelfarb represented was the attempt to not merely banish as heretics those who rejected Jewish peoplehood as a political concept, but to brand them as outright enemies of the Jews. In other words, it was to equate anti-Zionism with anti-Semitism and thus radically alter the nature of Jewish identity and forever brand the views of the ACJ as anti-Semitic. This was by no means the first time that what would become known as anti-Semitism was a product of specifically Jewish controversies. The logical extension of this position was to brand the fiercely antirabbinic classical *haskalah* itself as a species of Jewish anti-Semitism, as befell its reiteration by the Israeli author Israel Shahak in the past generation. Indeed, this was the historic position of Zionism, as the nineteenth-century European anti-Semitism it held up as evincing the failure of emancipation was largely an adoption of *haskalah* rhetoric by unsophisticated gentiles. Even the infamous *Protocols of the Elders of Zion* may be little more than a Russian retelling of the tall tales of the anti-Talmudist Karaite sect that gained the favor of the czar in the nineteenth century.[35]

In any event, Himmelfarb would win this round, as he would help make *Commentary* an entryist wedge, no doubt partly inspired by his Leninist brother-in-law Irving Kristol, by which the Zionists would clear away whatever resistance remained to their objectives in the American Jewish Committee. The final nail in the coffin of "non-Zionism" came in 1954 when Blaustein stepped down as president of the AJC in favor of the Zionist Irving Engel. The AJC would thereafter be led by such impeccably Zionist partisans of Cold War liberalism as Arthur Goldberg and Hyman Bookbinder and by the 1990s would be as militantly neoconservative as *Commentary* itself. Whether for political purposes it was felt necessary to include some acceptable variety of Reform Judaism into Himmelfarb's "seamless web," the rigid neo-Orthodoxy that *Commentary* began to set down in taking on Berger would have a far-reaching impact on the politics of American Jewish identity in the years to come.

The early 1950s was the peak of Berger's personal involvement in the day-to-day operations of the ACJ. The mainstays of the national office staff beginning in the decade included Leonard Sussman; Victor Raphals, a New York University graduate and former marine; Alfred Russell, a Brooklyn College graduate and active socialist; Charlotte Condell, Berger's personal secretary, believed by Sussman to carry a torch for her boss; and Gerald Blank, a former staff writer for the short-lived New York daily *PM*, as public relations director. Probably the most colorful character was David

Goldberg, the research director, a product of an Old World yeshiva who reluctantly entered the Reform rabbinate after a brief stint as a biblical Hebrew professor at Texas Christian University upon first arriving in America; Goldberg was notably useful as a reliable translator of both the Hebrew and Yiddish press.[36]

Berger's management style was harsh and could even border on abusive. After giving his staff members denigrating nicknames, he would typically demand that they join him for lunch each day and usually begin the conversation with a hostile question along the lines of "So what are you geniuses up to today?"[37] At one point he felt compelled to severely micromanage the staff, demanding each member give him reports of his or her tasks undertaken that week in an open staff meeting every Friday morning.[38] This prompted the exasperated resignation of at least one secretary, Barbara Levine, who protested, "I will no longer work in an office where the work is not appreciated and where workers are spied on constantly and every minute of the time spent in the office is questioned, where one is supposed to feel guilty when 5:30 comes and it is time to go home, and where the employees are told daily that they are doing nothing and getting paid for nothing."[39]

These impasses were largely responsible for Berger being replaced as executive director by Sussman, with Berger being given the title of executive vice president to continue in his central advisory role in the Council. Though Berger continued to draw a salary, by this time the Council was never his primary source of income, allowing him to be less and less involved in day-to-day operations as time went on. Berger also had another significant source of income in these years: he was widely reputed to be the only rabbi in New York who would officiate at an intermarriage wedding.[40] His wife, Ruth, was able to draw on her large family fortune, so they were able to afford a nine-room apartment on Park Avenue. In addition to frequently traveling together, Ruth was also active in the liberal social circles of the Upper East Side and was even active in the first senatorial campaign of Jacob Javits.[41]

In April 1952 the ACJ held its annual conference in Washington and was invited to have its religious services at Washington Hebrew Congregation, where Rabbi Norman Gerstenfeld remained, what in a more overtly political context might have been called a "fellow traveler" of the Council. The sermon that Friday evening was given by Irving Reichert, easily the most talented orator among the rabbis of the Council, in what would prove to be his last major address on their behalf, but which would bear his prophetic witness

forever after. In words that could be downright inflammatory in the context
of later generations, Reichert thundered:

> Racism can never be a substitute for Judaism. Racism is a boorish im-
> poster. At best it is bigotry wearing a mortarboard, at worst it is the res-
> urrected ghost of Hitler. Nationalism is no substitute for Judaism. It
> has attempted to counterfeit the currency of Judaism, and so many
> Jewish eyes, tear dimmed by tragedy, have not detected the fraud, that
> this bogus specie has gained wide circulation. "Jewish culture" is no
> substitute for Judaism. Emptied of religious content, it is either a
> phrase or a fetish, dependent on kitchen recipes, musicians, painters,
> and story tellers, but not on God.[42]

Indeed, the sermon, however moving, had a quite surreal quality, which
neatly summed up the dilemma of Classical Reform Judaism and indeed
all of liberal American religion in the postwar era. To the modern Jewish
reader it can be no less than shockingly surreal to read a fire-and-brimstone
Jewish preacher identifying superficial Jewish identity with the trend to "put
a *tallit* and a *yarmulke* on the rabbi as they do in Tel Aviv, and teach the children to speak Hebrew and plant trees on Israeli Arbor Day."[43] The declaration that underlay this, that the social justice committee of the UAHC had
been surpassed in importance by the committee on customs and ceremonies, elicited a vigorous response from the chairman of the former committee, Roland Gittelsohn, a combative Zionist who held the pulpit of
Boston's prestigious Temple Israel, to which Reichert would reply: "[I]s rabbinical good will and good manners to be limited strictly to dealings with
Christians on public occasions?"[44]

But Reichert was no doubt also shaken by the resignation of his brother
Victor from the Council that August. Continuing to serve in the pulpit of the
historic Rockdale Avenue Temple in Cincinnati, the younger Reichert happened to run into Lessing Rosenwald in Rome on his way back from Israel
and would formally write in a letter of resignation to Rosenwald the most
flowery Zionist rhetoric:

> I do not know of any other Jewry in the wide world where the sacred
> Scriptures, and the sacred Tongue, and the sacred Soil combine to evoke
> magnificent sacrifice, and miraculous enterprise. The commanding task,
> therefore, of our day, for us who through no act of our own have the
> great good fortune to be Americans, is to use this Heaven-sent blessing
> as did our biblical forebear Joseph and to seek to help our brethren.[45]

A year earlier, Reichert himself had given a remarkably muted speech on Israel in the familiar surroundings of San Francisco's Commonwealth Club, praising the country's economic success three years after declaring independence.

The 1952 conference also took in a stirring address from Morris Lazaron, who warned:

> So long as the State of Israel is unsound economically, so long as it is dependent for its very life upon the Jewish communities of the world and particularly upon the Jews of America, there will continue year after year these giant drives of the United Jewish Appeal and the bond drives with their attendant pressures—all our attention, all our energy, all our resources will be tied for an unforeseeable period of years to Israel. There will be no security for Israel so long as it is surrounded by hostile peoples and subject to economic boycott or the threat of war from them. Let us pray that some generous proposal will be made by the state of Israel to the Arab and Muslim peoples to help solve their refugee problem.[46]

Also making his first appearance at that conference as a notable gentile friend of the Council was Vincent Sheean, the accomplished foreign correspondent and novelist probably best known for his friendship with Mahatma Gandhi.[47]

Norman Thomas continued to grow close to the ACJ in this period, as early as 1949 singling out Rosenwald for praise in a syndicated column on the Arab refugee crisis,[48] and speaking frequently at Council functions not only in New York but in cities as far as Cincinnati and Dallas.[49] Many years later after Thomas's death, Berger would recall: "I needed him, for our basic agreement about the Middle East and Palestine reassured me in the many moments of self-doubt, not of our fundamental principles, but of my continuing ability to see those principles in the broad vision of a world which we hoped, somehow, to leave a little better than we found it."[50] Thomas also had his own reasons for deep spiritual identification with the Council, as an ordained Presbyterian minister from a prominent family in that ministry. Rooted in the Scottish Enlightenment, the Presbyterian Church was probably most like Classical Reform Judaism among Protestant denominations for its rationalism and foreswearing of political messianism as a matter of first principle, and Thomas had become a socialist out of his disillusionment with the church upon being swept up in its elder Woodrow Wilson's crusade to make the world safe for democracy. In Zionism's capture of Reform Judaism, Thomas no doubt saw an echo of his own church's fate, which haunted him his whole adult life.[51] In 1952 Thomas would write for the *Council News*:

> An Arab, without too much exaggeration, could complain that the Jews were practicing Hitlerism in reverse. He could certainly maintain that the volume of Jewish criticism of the McCarran Immigration Bill comes with extraordinary bad grace from such American Zionists as might support or apologize for Ben-Gurion's law of nationalism. Our fight against the mood of reaction in America is made far more difficult when Jewish papers have to spend time apologizing for their double standard of nationalist ethics—one for Israel, where Jews are a majority, and another for America, where they are a minority. But not all the evil of Israeli chauvinism is its ill effect on the struggle for equality in America. Even more dangerous will be the consequences of this new law in fanning the flames of Arab chauvinism and Muslim fanaticism.[52]

After the founding of the State of Israel, the major institutions of the Jewish socialist milieu in America split three ways. *The Forward*—whose legendary founder and editor, Abraham Cahan, had begun to lean toward Zionism as early as 1925—was firmly in the Zionist camp by the end of the Second World War and became its major enforcer in the aging Yiddish-speaking community. The Workmen's Circle, the historic Yiddish "language federation" of the Socialist Party, adopted a version of non-Zionism that easily proved more resilient than that of the American Jewish Committee. The Workmen's Circle's two most prominent leaders, Nathan Chanin and William Stern, would be supporters of both Norman Thomas and William Zukerman. This left the Jewish Socialist Bund, the U.S. branch of the original party in Eastern Europe, decidedly anti-Zionist. What remained by the 1950s of the larger Socialist Party, however, was badly split on the issue. One of their major leaders, Samuel Friedman, was an employee of the UJA and advocated aggressively for Ben-Gurion and his party in the Socialist International.[53]

Among the Council's rabbinical supporters in these years, the most remarkable for his political activities outside the ACJ was undoubtedly Abraham Cronbach, who continued to lead the Jewish Peace Fellowship, though it never grew beyond a small circle of activists. Nominally a Norman

Thomas socialist, Cronbach was no doubt also highly sympathetic to the anti–Cold War presidential campaigns of his fellow Cincinnatian Robert Taft, whom he had publicly praised when they were both speaking out against the Nuremberg Trials.[54] Cronbach probably remains best remembered, however, for his involvement in the case of Julius and Ethel Rosenberg, campaigning after the conviction of the atomic spies against their execution, even being received by President Eisenhower to hear him out. Most memorable of all though was the eulogy he gave at the rally protesting their execution in June 1953, when the Communist crowd in New York's Union Square booed him off the stage for urging that "we who befriended the Rosenbergs should show the entire world that we are loyal among the loyal in our allegiance to America."[55] Cronbach's true sympathies would reassert themselves a few years later when he became active with the Committee for the Return of Confiscated German and Japanese Property, joining forces with such champions of Second World War revisionism as Harry Elmer Barnes, Austin J. App, and Henry Regnery.

Late in 1952, as Harry Truman prepared to leave office, the president who would have few friends in the years ahead besides the Zionists who were forever grateful to him, left an unusual parting gift for the ACJ in appointing a new assistant secretary of state for Near East Affairs, Henry Byroade. A West Point graduate who after the Second World War joined the Foreign Service in order to run the Office of German Reconstruction and thus became a key implementer of the Marshall Plan, Byroade would prove to be the best friend the ACJ ever had in the U.S. government. By the end of the Truman administration, Berger was naturally pessimistic about any future impact of the Council on U.S. foreign policy, especially since no benefits had been forthcoming from the elevation of George Levison's friend Dean Acheson to secretary of state.[56] But when word got out that Eisenhower planned to keep Byroade on at the Near East desk, the Council's mood turned to optimism. In the earliest days of 1953, Berger, Levison, and Rosenwald were closely collaborating on a memorandum to be presented to the new administration, with Levison stating that "my guess is that one of the few areas of the world where there may be a really changed policy is in the Middle East."[57]

Eisenhower received Rosenwald and Levison at the White House on April 8 and accepted their memorandum outlining the issues they had earlier tried in vain to call to the attention of the second Truman administration, namely the "confusion of Judaism with the nationalism of Israel" as it impacted matters of international law, such as Israel's "Law of Return" enacted in 1951, which could be interpreted as granting de facto Israeli citizenship to all the world's Jews.[58] The new secretary of state, John Foster Dulles, took the memorandum with him on his first trip to the Middle East the following month and, partly at Byroade's urging, echoed many of its points in a radio address at the end of the trip on June 1. Dulles urged in that radio address that Israel "become a part of the Near East community and cease to look upon itself as alien to that community" and warned that "the Arabs fear expansionist Zionism more than they do Communism."[59] The Council immediately praised the speech, in particular that Dulles stated "the need for the United States to allay the deep resentment against it that has resulted from the creation of Israel."[60]

The Zionist response was not immediate, but within a few weeks the American Zionist Council did issue a statement opposing the plans for arms sales to several Arab states, which was a result of the Dulles trip.[61] The substance of the new Eisenhower-Dulles policy was that the Arab states should recognize Israel in exchange for a settlement of the refugee problem, perhaps combined with reduced Jewish immigration, and that Israel could therefore be a part of a regional coalition against Soviet expansionism, as would come to fruition excluding Israel in the short-lived Baghdad Pact. As had been the case in the years leading up to statehood, the State Department would find in the ACJ a refreshing voice of agreeable moderation against both Zionist and extreme Arab demands. Shortly after the speech, Dulles would even engage in a lengthy correspondence with Henry Moyer, a vice president of the Council, over his concerns about particulars of the rhetoric Dulles reportedly employed about the domestic Jewish scene.[62]

Here it is necessary to examine the Cold War context of the activities of the ACJ over the next decade, which was beset then and in future rhetoric by much confusion. The bulk of American Zionist rhetoric in this era argued, largely on account of the overwhelming Democratic affiliation of Jewish voters, that Republican oil interests wanted to secure Arab friendship at Israel's expense. To the contrary, the anti-Zionism in the foreign policy establishment came overwhelmingly from architects of Cold War liberal policy such as George Marshall, Loy Henderson, and Henry Byroade.[63] Dulles, the only significant Republican official to ever be notably "Arabist," had established himself in the 1940s as the architect of Republican assent to the foreign policies of Roosevelt and Truman. Their policies were equally concerned with containing the Soviet Union as with ensuring access to Middle Eastern oil, two goals that were not mutually exclusive.

The linchpin of this policy was never found, as some Zionists would claim, in the Egyptian regime of Gamal Abdel Nasser, but rather in Saudi Arabia, where an alliance with the monarchy was first established by Franklin Roosevelt at the close of the Second World War. Eisenhower and Dulles had hoped to extend this alliance beyond convenience, to build up and use the religious influence of the House of Saud to battle both communism and pan-Arab nationalism throughout the Muslim world.[64] Under these circumstances, a creative Israeli statesman might have called upon U.S. mediation to resolve the refugee problem and other outstanding issues to create the sort of bloc anchored in Saudi Arabia and welcoming of Israel, which America then desired, thus securing for Israel both peace with its neighbors and the protection of a great power. But alas, in this case Israel would not miss the opportunity to miss an opportunity.

Nevertheless, it is true that the Cold War policies in the Middle East that the Council embraced were detrimental to the true interests and aspirations of the Arab world and bear great responsibility, along with that of Israel, for the crisis that began with the attacks of September 11, 2001. Kermit Roosevelt, who remained close to the Council and a personal friend of Berger well into the 1950s, would achieve certain infamy in recent years as the mastermind of the CIA overthrow of Mohammed Mossadegh in Iran in 1953 (Loy Henderson was also a participant), regarded by many scholars as the beginning of U.S. calumny in the Muslim world. Even today, the taboo around discussion of the Israel lobby utterly pales in comparison to that which surrounds the proposition that the Muslim world has legitimate grievances against the United States. Still, it would be foolish to ascribe sinister motives or even active abetting to the Council in these policies, as they had no reason to believe them to be anything more than what was in the best interests of their country and of the cause of peace.

By 1954 the Council hoped that a corollary speech could be given to clarify the general principles that had been outlined by Dulles, and Berger went to work persuading Byroade, who increasingly looked upon him as his unofficial adviser on Jewish affairs. Berger was now consulting with Byroade on a first-name basis, and Byroade would affectionately call him "mad rabbi." After inviting Byroade to address the annual conference of the Council, Berger agreed that the speech would best be given on neutral territory, and thus it was given to a foreign policy association in Dayton, Ohio, on April 9. In Dayton, Byroade called on the Arabs to "accept the state of Israel as an accomplished fact" and also on the Israelis to "drop your conqueror attitude and see your future as a Middle Eastern state and not as a headquarters of worldwide groupings of people of a particular religious faith who must have special rights within and obligations to the Israeli state."[65]

The general response of the Zionists was to accuse Byroade of interfering in the religious beliefs of Americans and in internal Israeli affairs. Berger recalled that when he called him to see how he was handling the blowback, Byroade immediately replied, "[M]ad rabbi, if the invitation to speak at your conference still stands I will here and now accept."[66] When Berger asked how Dulles had reacted to the speech, Byroade reported that he was supportive but still less than pleased, and that he approved of speaking to the ACJ to give a "clarification." The day before Byroade was due to speak in Philadelphia, he called Berger, already at the conference, telling him that he was about to receive a Zionist delegation led by Louis Lipsky, but before letting them in, he wanted to review his remarks for the next day.[67]

The second speech created a firestorm of protest, including that from Moshe Sharett from the floor of the Knesset. This only delighted Berger, who could not help but issue a boastful press release, declaring, "The Israeli Prime Minister, other Israeli officials and leading American Zionists have properly evaluated as high policy pronouncements two recent addresses of Assistant Secretary of State Henry Byroade. Such proper recognition of the importance of these statements by our Assistant Secretary of State is a first, constructive step in a clarification of the important issues involved."[68] As late as July, Dulles received a letter of protest from Louis Lipsky on behalf of the American Zionist Council over Byroade's speech to the ACJ being circulated by the State Department as an official policy statement.[69] By the following year, however, at least partly as a consequence of the whole episode, Byroade was reassigned as ambassador to Egypt, where he served for four years and held later posts in countries as varied as Afghanistan and South Africa. Late in his life Byroade would lament: "I was played as pro-Arab and anti-Semitic. I really don't consider that any of that is fair. Even today, I don't think I ever did anything except try to go down the middle on a very tough problem."[70]

But the Byroade episode did not mark the end of the Council's intrigues in American foreign policy. In 1951 the supporters of the Committee for Peace and Justice in the Holy Land reconvened in a new organization, American Friends of the Middle East (AFME), with the stated objective of combating communism in the Arab world. Instigated by Kermit Roosevelt from his perch at the CIA and likely directing it from behind the scenes, AFME was generously funded by members of the Saudi royal family and the

Arabian-American Oil Company (ARAMCO), along with money coming from numerous CIA backchannels. Garland Evans Hopkins, who had been active with the Committee for Peace and Justice, was the new group's executive director, with other carryovers including Harry Emerson Fosdick, Virginia Gildersleeve, and William A. Eddy. Other notable members included Vincent Sheean and FDR's political fixer-turned-critic James Farley.

The chairman and most visible public advocate of AFME was Dorothy Thompson, the journalist who achieved great fame as one of the first to cover the unfolding of Hitler's rise to absolute power in Germany. Thompson had been notably Zionist in her public pronouncements during and immediately after the Second World War, even addressing a Zionist rally at Madison Square Garden in 1944 before becoming deeply alarmed by the plight of the Palestinian Arabs. Thompson had begun corresponding with Berger as early as 1949, and in his memoirs he would vividly describe the imperious and neurotic manner in which she demanded his company one evening to pour her heart out to him, lamenting that "my Zionist friends do not seem to understand the universality of simple moral principles."[71] Berger told her that he would be "delighted to have so eloquent and formidable an ally," but that he "could not, in all honesty, recommend the strategy as a prudent course or even one, for all of her talent, which would provide early vindication or efficacy."[72]

Thompson would speak at many Council functions in the years ahead, and she would continue to string Berger along on her insufferable whims, most memorably forcing him to come along once as she stormed into the offices of the *New York Times* to berate a Middle East correspondent whom Berger actually respected, for what Thompson perceived to be his campaign to vilify Nasser.[73] Still, the Council was delighted to collaborate with AFME, and both Berger and Morris Lazaron served on its board. In fact, Berger urged Lazaron to become active with AFME out of a desperate seeking for respectable Jewish representation in the organization, warning that "the Protestant churches have embarked upon a program of considerable scope and intensity on behalf of the Arab refugees. This is almost certain to lead them into rather bitter anti-Zionism and unless it is apparent, in such an organization, that there are some Jews who share a sense of general humanitarian responsibility for these people, the transition from such anti-Zionism to anti-Semitism could be very easy."[74]

AFME would even sponsor a trip to the Middle East in 1954 consisting of Lazaron, a rabbi; John Cogley, editor of the lay-Catholic magazine *Commonweal*;

and Harold Fey, a Protestant minister, with Lazaron writing a book on the trip, *Olive Trees in Storm*, which would be published by AFME the following year. The three had a cordial meeting with Moshe Sharett shortly after the incident known as the Kibya massacre (involving the killing of sixty-nine Arab civilians in an operation led by future Israeli prime minister Ariel Sharon), and in the book Lazaron upheld as a beacon of hope the still active Ihud, which issued a statement with thirty-three signatures, led by Martin Buber, condemning the massacre.[75] In discussing the rise of the Orthodox establishment of religion in Israel, which was granted a monopoly of all marriage and civil affairs in Israel unheard of even in explicitly theocratic states, Lazaron even quoted Mordecai Kaplan, the early prophet of Jewish nationalism in America who now increasingly found himself in the narrow confines of his own Reconstructionist movement, as saying, "By maintaining the Orthodox rabbinate at the expense of the State and permitting it to define the qualifications for the rabbinate, the State virtually stamps all other understandings of Jewish religion as illegitimate and subversive."[76]

Coinciding with the rise of AFME was the publication of a book by Alfred Lilienthal, *What Price Israel?*, in 1953.[77] Though he could not hold a candle to Berger in intellect, Lilienthal's talents as a natural publicist nonetheless made his book a more effective articulation of the positions and perspective of the ACJ than any of Berger's books, which tended to take on high concepts in a short and brisk fashion at the expense of directness and clarity. The book comprehensively covered the dark intrigues surrounding the rise of Zionism, the Zionist encroachment upon U.S. politics through the specter of "the Jewish vote," the tragedy that unfolded with the founding of the State of Israel, and the Zionist transfiguration of the Jewish religion, all grounded in the Classical Reform critique. At the same time, however, Lilienthal suffered a grating lack of nuance, embracing the most reactionary "our crowd" nostrums about Yiddish-speaking immigrants and First World War–era "Americanism," recklessly attacking Council-friendly members of the American Jewish Committee such as Joseph Proskauer and adopting the term "Judaist" to describe a follower of Judaism as opposed to an ethnic "Jew," a term many Zionists would later adopt as a slur toward the ACJ.[78]

What Price Israel? was published by Henry Regnery, whose eponymous publishing house was rooted in the progressive-isolationist milieu but was now the rising star of the slowly emerging "conservative movement." Along with Devin-Adair, Regnery affirmed that even if the rapidly declining isolationist politicians were going to assent to the Zionist tide in U.S. politics, the still-vibrant intellectual wing of the movement would embrace its kindred spirits of the Jewish faith. Impressed by Lilienthal's original *Reader's Digest* article, Henry Regnery commissioned the book, believing him to be "an honorable man and that his position deserved a hearing," though subjecting the manuscript to the review of both Berger and his friend Willi Schlamm, an ex-communist Austrian-Jewish émigré.[79] Though Berger strongly urged the publication of the book, he and other Council leaders began to view Lilienthal as a loose cannon at best and were compelled to distance themselves from their flawed yet talented advocate. More than thirty years later Regnery would say, looking back on the extensive publicity Lilienthal received, "Much blood has been spilled in the Middle East and peace seems more remote than ever, but his position still has much to be said for it."[80]

It was, however, in the peak years of the Cold War intrigues of the ACJ that it would make its most earnest effort to prove itself to be, in fact, a Council *for Judaism.* The most ambitious tasks undertaken by the Council's Committee on Religious and Synagogue Programs were to survey religious school textbooks for their Zionist content or lack thereof and to potentially undertake the publication of Classical Reform textbooks for wide distribution. As this was taking place, however, many parents affiliated with or otherwise sympathetic to the Council and disturbed by the growing domination of Zionist propaganda in Reform religious schools began appealing to the Council for assistance in establishing their own religious schools for their children. In the forefront pushing for these "Council schools" was Clarence Coleman, a successful flooring salesman who had grown up attending Chicago Sinai Congregation and risen through the ranks of the Council from its earliest days to be its most active leader from Chicago by the early 1950s.

Coleman founded the first of what became known as "Schools for Judaism" in 1952 in the Chicago suburb of Highland Park. The following year there were two more schools in White Plains, New York, and in Milwaukee, and by 1955 as many as ten schools had been established across the country.[81] The ACJ responded to this growing demand early on by appointing a full-time director of religious and synagogue activities, Samuel Halevi Baron, a native of Austria ordained by Hebrew Union College in 1927. As a stalwart Council supporter, Baron had accepted the Reform pulpit in Lincoln, Nebraska, in 1947 to end the schism initiated by Bernard Gradwohl. Previously ministering to congregations as far flung as Fort Lauderdale; Austin, Texas; Leavenworth, Kansas; and Sedalia, Missouri, Rabbi Baron would administer, with nominal input from Berger, an extremely detailed

Elmer Berger's class photo at Hebrew Union College.
(American Jewish Archives)

Louis Wolsey, Berger's boyhood rabbi who initiated the founding of the
American Council for Judaism. (American Jewish Archives)

Isaac Mayer Wise, the father of American Reform Judaism, may well have foreseen the modern Israel lobby when he denounced the antics of Theodor Herzl as "a prostitution of Israel's holy cause to a madman's dance of unsound politicians." (American Jewish Archives)

Joseph Proskauer, old New York political hand who was the leading anti-Zionist in the officially "non-Zionist" American Jewish Committee. (American Jewish Archives)

Elmer Berger with ACJ President Lessing Rosenwald (seated) and his associate
I. Edward Tonkon, 1945. (Wisconsin Historical Society)

Lessing and Edith Rosenwald at an ACJ conference, 1940s.
(Wisconsin Historical Society)

ACJ RABBIS

Samuel Goldenson of New York, a vociferous opponent of the various schemes to have an official governing body of American Jewry. (American Jewish Archives)

Morris Lazaron of Baltimore, disillusioned Zionist who maintained close ties to the binationalist movement. (American Jewish Archives)

Irving Reichert of San
Francisco, known for his
political radicalism before
becoming an outspoken
anti-Zionist.
(American Jewish Archives)

Abraham Cronbach of
Cincinnati, outspoken
pacifist and beloved Hebrew
Union College professor.
(American Jewish Archives)

Berger (third from right) at a Rosh Hashana gathering near Chicago, 1955. To his immediate left are longtime ACJ staff member Alfred Russell and Henry Moyer, an ACJ vice president. At far left is Clarence Coleman, Berger's eventual nemesis within the ACJ. (Courtesy of Lakeside Congregation)

Philip Bernstein, Berger's archnemesis and a founder of AIPAC. (American Jewish Archives)

William Zukerman, whose *Jewish Newsletter* spread the ACJ message to the Jewish labor and socialist communities. (American Jewish Archives)

Leonard Sussman, day-to-day manager of the ACJ for virtually the whole era following the battle against Jewish statehood. (Wisconsin Historical Society)

George Levison, the well-connected Foreign Service officer who became the ACJ foreign policy guru. (Wisconsin Historical Society)

Alfred Lilienthal, Levison's protégé who would eventually rival Berger as the face of American Jewish anti-Zionism. (Wisconsin Historical Society)

Henry Byroade, who closely consulted Berger as Assistant Secretary of State for the Near East and affectionately called him "mad rabbi." (Official State Department Photo, National Archives)

Lessing Rosenwald and John Foster Dulles, 1953. (Wisconsin Historical Society)

Elmer and Ruth Berger on their tour of the Middle East, 1955.
(Courtesy of Leonard Sussman)

Berger (center) at an interfaith gathering led by famed pastor Norman Vincent
Peale (far left), 1968. Also pictured (left to right) are Muhammad Abdul Rauf,
Lowell Russell Ditzen, and Isabelle Bacon. (Wisconsin Historical Society)

William Thomas Mallison, Berger's
collaborator on studies of international
law beginning in the 1960s. (Gelman
Library, George Washington University)

Norton Mezvinsky, Berger's protégé
after leaving the ACJ. (Courtesy of
Leonard Sussman)

Elmer Berger in his final years. (Courtesy of Leonard Sussman)

curriculum designed by Leonard Sussman. Virtually without exception, the classes were taught and administered by the parents, sometimes with the assistance of a rabbi, if a sympathetic one was available. As early as November 1952, the rise of the Schools for Judaism was noted in *Time* magazine.[82]

Sussman outlined the Council's draft curriculum in an article for the *Council News* in March 1953. The article stated that "the guiding aim of our curriculum is to make the child's association with Judaism pleasant and to keep it on the level of a spiritual experience" and declared as cardinal principles that "Jews have not gone through history with the mark of martyrdom and suffering, as a hunted and wandering people, except as there were basic forces in the world, at any given time, that made for basic insecurities for all men" and that "the only collective concept we recognize as valid for them as individual Americans and as Jews is Judaism."[83] The curriculum also restricted itself to the teaching of liturgical Hebrew, as opposed to conversational or modern Hebrew, and explicitly taught a rational interpretation of the Bible with emphasis on the prophets and, as was common in the Classical Reform tradition, placed Jesus in that illustrious pantheon. Of Zionism, they merely taught "that it exists and why we reject it, just as we teach that Orthodoxy exists and why we reject it."[84]

The Council published an impressive array of textbooks through a small New York publisher, Bookman Associates. They included Samuel Baron's *Children's Devotions*, Abraham Cronbach's *Judaism for Today*, the primer on the fundamentals of Jewish belief *Tell Me Why* by Dorothy Bobrow, and *Not By Power* by Allan Tarshish, a close friend and HUC classmate of Berger who held the pulpit of the founding Reform congregation of America in Charleston, South Carolina. David Goldberg, the Council's learned research director, wrote a total of three textbooks: *Meet the Prophets*, *Stories about Judaism*, and *Holidays for American Judaism*. For a number of years, the Council even published a children's magazine titled *Growing Up*. The Council enjoyed considerable success, selling its textbooks to Reform religious schools beyond its own orbit. In at least one case—at a newly formed congregation in Bethesda, Maryland—the textbooks led to active interest in the Council by the lay leadership.[85]

It would indeed be difficult to dispute the assertion by Thomas Kolsky in his study of the ACJ that the religious education program was "undoubtedly the most successful Council activity."[86] Naturally, therefore, it was viewed only with alarm and suspicion by the leadership of the Reform movement. In 1954 the president of the CCAR, Joseph Fink, attacked the Council schools

in his address to the annual convention, charging that "recognizing as they
do that Judaism must be taught, they propose to teach it in diluted form."[87]
The chief organizer of the Indianapolis School for Reform Judaism, Ernest
Lee, wrote an impassioned letter of protest to Fink, insisting, "Only as a last
resort did we form our own school. Outsiders did not come to us—rather
we went to them—actively seeking their aid and assistance which had been
refused in our own congregations."[88]

But the CCAR moved quickly to establish a commission to investigate
the schools, as Fink recommended. The committee of ten was chaired by a
determined Roland Gittelsohn of Boston and also included the equally outspoken Alvin Fine, who had succeeded Irving Reichert in San Francisco. Two
Council supporters were named to the committee for the appearance of fairness, Samuel Baron and Allan Tarshish. The committee released its report in
June 1955, asserting that "for the most part the children in Council Schools
come from marginal Jewish families whose affiliation with existing Reform
congregations has been at best nominal" and that "there is a strong feeling
on the part of several members of the committee that actually these religious
schools have served a useful function in that they have drained off a small
group of malcontents."[89]

Baron blasted the report in a long letter to Gittelsohn, credibly charging
him with having written it singlehandedly without any regard for input:

> One of the most revealing sentences in the entire report is the final
> one, as it places the role of Reform Judaism on the auction block of
> organizational prerogative. For, despite the earlier concession, some-
> what gratuitous, that every Jew has the right to devise and teach a
> Judaism that suits him, the report concludes with the "confidence"
> and "assurance" that the Schools for Judaism and the men, women,
> and children who practice Judaism therein, will, in the words of Rabbi
> Gittelsohn, "of their own accord disappear."[90]

This cavalier view taken by the Reform leadership, that the ACJ would simply disappear like all other heresies before it, would define their position ever
after. Many Reform rabbis would even have the chutzpah, in the name of a
movement whose most recent platform had declared the "upbuilding of
Palestine" to be its "messianic goal," to compare the ACJ to the messianic sects
of the seventeenth and eighteenth centuries. This was especially ironic since the
case could easily be made that the figure in Jewish history to whom Elmer Berger
was most comparable was the adversary of Shabtai Tzvi, Jacob Sasportas.[91]

No fewer than five of the Schools for Judaism would serve as the foundation for new congregations: Lakeside Congregation for Reform Judaism in Highland Park, Illinois; the Congregation for Reform Judaism in White Plains, New York; Temple Sinai in Milwaukee; Temple Micah in Denver; and the Houston Congregation for Reform Judaism in Texas. In White Plains, Samuel Baron ministered to the congregation after leaving Nebraska to work out of the Council's national office. The congregations in Highland Park and Milwaukee were fortunate enough to find young rabbis sympathetic to the Council to serve their pulpits devotedly: Jay Brickman, who came to Milwaukee from a pulpit on Staten Island, and Richard Singer, who came to Highland Park from a pulpit in West Palm Beach. All of the congregations were able to affiliate with the UAHC with little or no controversy, the Reform leadership having apparently judged, as Lyndon Johnson would memorably put it in another context, that it was better to have them inside the tent pissing out rather than outside pissing in.

The Lakeside Congregation, with Clarence Coleman serving as its president, was easily both the largest and most directly aligned with the Council. Berger even ghosted for the Lakeside Congregation a lengthy statement of principles, which provides an indispensable window into his evolving view of the Jewish religion as he increasingly grew into an iconoclast.[92] The statement read in part:

> The distinguishing criterion of a living faith is its historic ability to meet, with new forms and emphases, man's spiritual requirements at any time. The mark of a universal faith is its ability to meet such contemporary spiritual needs in any place. The Old Testament Prophets wrote the most significant pages in the development of Judaism. They first conceived and articulated a religion dependent upon inner, moral strength, rather than upon land, nation or ritual. . . . In Prophetic Judaism, as well as in the noblest conceptions of the American dream, God is conceived as "indwelling" within man. The most cherished manifestation of Divinity is to be found in the aspiring human spirit, regardless of race, faith or nationality.[93]

This statement is interesting in a number of respects. Perhaps most striking is its highly humanistic conception of God, while not expressly denying the existence of a personal God, leaving the statement open to that interpretation.[94] Although Reichert and Lazaron, for instance, clearly had a very God-centered outlook, Berger seemed to take most of his cues from Cronbach, whose commitment to the most radical interpretation of Reform Judaism nearly matched his legendary pacifist convictions. In this spirit, Berger was also known to speak favorably of Sunday Sabbath worship, which in the 1950s was still not unheard of in the most committed Classical Reform settings.[95] It should be noted though that while it has gained vogue in recent generations as a position of quasi-agnosticism, the concept of the "indwelling God" has an ancient pedigree in Judaism, originating as the *shekhina* of kabbalah.

Berger's friend Justus Doenecke even believes that, had he grown up in a more culturally Jewish setting, Berger could have easily found his way into a more cutting-edge stream of progressive Judaism such as Reconstructionism, for which he actually had a peculiar abiding respect.[96] In this connection, even Cronbach seemed to have some anticipation of the worship practices of contemporary progressive Judaism, which could hardly be more different from Classical Reform, when he advised the Council's committee on religious and synagogue programs: "Let the service consist of well chosen, frequently varied, and appealing music and of a conscientiously prepared discourse. If there is to be any audible prayer at all, let it be spontaneous and original or let it, varying from service, be chosen from a wide range of devotional literature."[97] In his own words, however, Berger pledged himself to "the Judaism of Isaiah, Jeremiah, Jesus, and Magnes."[98]

The ACJ also sought to assert its positive program in these years through philanthropy. In particular, the deep displeasure of the Council with the United Jewish Appeal and the means by which it ensured Zionist domination of all aspects of Jewish community life instilled in the Council a special sympathy for those Jews in need who had been left behind by the Zionist juggernaut. Lessing Rosenwald had a particular commitment to Fohrenwald, the last displaced-persons camp in Germany, and visited there, giving generously many times. Berger himself would visit the camp in 1952, bringing toys and other items that had been collected by the children of the Schools for Judaism.[99] Rosenwald was also deeply alarmed by the implications of the "anti-Zionist" turn by Stalin at this same time, seeing it as the fulfillment of Stalin's cynical strategy in supporting the creation of Israel, only to create an intractable obstacle for the West in opposing his designs on the region.[100] In 2008 Sergei Khrushchev, son of the former Soviet premier, would admit as much in an interview with the *Block Island Times*.[101]

Rosenwald was further alarmed by how the Zionists were seizing on this, salivating at the prospect of as many as two-and-a-half million Jews in the Warsaw Pact countries immigrating to Israel. A generation before the elaborate campaign for Soviet Jewry by which the Zionist apparatus desperately sought to preserve Israel's Jewish majority toward the end of the Cold War, it was thus decided that the primary objective of a philanthropic fund of the Council should be for the assistance of Jewish refugees anywhere in the world in search of options other than Israel. The American Council for Judaism Philanthropic Fund was formally incorporated in 1955 under the management of Rosenwald's son-in-law, Harry Snellenburg. Regular recipients from the Philanthropic Fund included the American Council for Emigres in the Professions, the American Friends Service Committee, the International Rescue Committee, the Relief Committee of the General Jewish Workers Union of Poland, and the Shaare Tzedek Hospital in Jerusalem.[102]

At the urging of Kermit Roosevelt and American Friends of the Middle East, Berger traveled in the Middle East for two months in 1955 and was one of the first Jews to set foot in both Israel and its Arab neighbors since 1948.[103] Elmer and Ruth sailed to Rome aboard the SS *Constitution* and began their Middle East sojourn by flying from there to Cairo. At sea during Passover, Berger led a seder for the Jewish passengers, among them a Sephardic Israeli family. As part of the seder, Berger had given a dollar bill to the family's young son as a reward for his participation, but the dollar was returned with an angry note from his father after learning who Berger was.[104] In Cairo, Berger met with the chief rabbi of the community, which still then numbered 50,000, who had been a close friend of the old non-Zionist leaders of the Joint Distribution Committee. Berger went on to emphasize that, contrary to the Zionist propaganda line of police-state–style repression of Arab Jewry, the meeting consisted only of himself, Ruth, the rabbi, and his son in the rabbi's home, with no regime minders present.[105]

From Cairo they flew to Baghdad, where Berger had a long meeting with the chief rabbi, who likened the violence against Iraqi Jews after the 1948 war to the fate of Japanese Americans during the Second World War, proclaiming the loyalty of Iraqi Jews to their government during the war. As in Egypt, where a Jewish journalist had been able to speak frankly with Berger about the Nasser regime but spoke with dread about the negative impact of Israel and its American enablers on their situation, the rabbi in Baghdad was critical of all the actors in 1948 and repeated a point made by an Iraqi official echoing Irving Reichert twenty years earlier: Judaism as we know it was chiefly conceived not in Palestine but in Babylon.[106] Berger observed:

> Once a government which legislated expulsion of the Jews was accused
> of anti-Semitism. Now it is a government which seeks to reassure its

Jewish citizens and may even take steps to protect them against foreign Zionist nationalism which is so denigrated. By modern Zionist standards, Torquemada would be a friend of the Jews and Henry Byroade is slandered as an anti-Semite.[107]

After a largely relaxing stay in Beirut, where Berger met with representatives of the city's 8,000-strong Jewish community, he finally arrived in Arab Jerusalem, writing, "I met people who used to cross this tiny area and go to their homes. Tonight they can only look and remember. It is utter nonsense to argue whose fault it is that they are here. The fact that the showcase glass separates the candy from the child is not changed by the further fact that there is disagreement over the name of the glazier who put in the glass."[108] Of the Old City he wrote: "I am affected as negatively by the ostentatious potentates of Christianity as I am by the ostentatious members of my own profession. There have always been money-changers here, and they are here now. But there have been prophets also, and they are still here. And those of the past are still here also."[109] The Jordanians even presented Berger with a Torah scroll they had salvaged from the Old City during the 1948 war, which he went on to present to Temple Emanu-El in New York. Of his visit to a Palestinian refugee camp, Berger movingly wrote:

> I say to you, friends and people with whom I am honored to be associated, that Judaism is on trial out here, and Jews too. And the judges are not only these poor refugees but are business people of all nationalities, government officials of many countries, simple tourists from the four corners of the earth. All of these do not stop and haggle over legalities and proprieties. They just see the problem and find no rationalizations good enough.[110]

Through Berger's contacts with American Friends of the Middle East, an American consular car was arranged to escort him and his wife across the border into Israel. After a hastily arranged propaganda tour by the Jewish Agency, Berger was able to meet in Jerusalem with several members of the Ihud, whose magazine, *Ner*, was sometimes circulated in America by the ACJ. Of the editor of *Ner*, who was simply known as Rabbi Benjamin, Berger proclaimed him "a prophet who might well fill Magnes' shoes if he were not some 77 years old."[111] Of the prospects for peace as Ihud saw them, Berger reported:

> Benjamin is frank to say there can be no peace here while Ben-Gurion is alive. The country certainly has the political machinery of freedom,

but the machinery is so well lubricated by the economic stranglehold which the Histadrut[112] maintains that the freedom offers little opportunity to test its fiber with a real challenge to Mapai.[113] Ben-Gurion also adeptly feeds the activist spirit in his own and other parties and so, in addition to the economic control, he provides the psychology of the strongman who is closely linked to the military and who has never really renounced claims to all of Palestine.[114]

Upon Berger's return, the ACJ published a small booklet of his letters to America over the course of the trip with the provocative title *Who Knows Better Must Say So*. Berger concluded the book with the following assessment of the Arab-Israeli conflict:

> The Arab countries will not negotiate with a political entity in Israel which regards itself, and which is regarded by non-Israeli Jews, as the spearhead in the Middle East for "Jewish" national aspirations. I return firmly convinced, however, that there is hope for peaceful negotiations of outstanding issues if the Arab countries are convinced the other party is just another, normal state in the area, prepared to share the vicissitudes and to contribute to the progress of the whole area on a basis of respect and equality. Therefore, I do not shut my eyes to the material progress in Israel. The important point is that this progress is not at issue.[115]

The day after leaving Israel, however, Israel Radio carried a fictive report worthy of *Pravda* that declared among other things that "Dr. Berger expressed admiration for the statesmanship of Israel's leaders."[116]

This no doubt served to prompt Berger's telegram to his friend Isaac Witkin that "you will never appreciate your exile until you have been in and out of the homeland."[117] The publication of Berger's travel letters occasioned vigorous attacks on the Council as never before, including a lengthy letter of denunciation to the *New York Times* by Berger's old nemesis Philip Bernstein as well as a long rebuttal to the book by the Anti-Defamation League, which declared: "Berger's recent activities in the Middle East must be viewed against the background of a serious situation involving Jews which is now developing in the United States. Arab propagandists in this country, acting on orders from their home ministries, are helping to foster a new growth of anti-Semitism."[118] For his part, Berger was unbowed as always: "I am more than ever convinced of the absolute necessity for Jews outside of Israel to divorce themselves completely from a situation of moral degradation apparent in the Arab refugee problem."[119]

Also in the spring of 1955, Clarence Coleman was rewarded for his spearheading of the Council's successes in religious education by being elected to succeed Rosenwald as the president of the ACJ, with Rosenwald being given the new title of chairman of the board. For another decade he would remain as active in the leadership of the Council as before. In a move that would prove ironic on multiple levels, Coleman inaugurated this new era for the Council by backing away from the strides toward developing a positive program and beginning the campaign that would arguably be the Council's greatest success but would prove its undoing. In his first official address as president of the Council, Coleman called for a federal investigation of the United Jewish Appeal for its long-standing lack of transparency, which had aggrieved the Council and its leaders for so long, as well as the possibility that it was acting as a foreign agent of the State of Israel. A consummate social climber, which had led him to his new office in the first place, Coleman was no doubt partly motivated by the desire to ingratiate himself with Rosenwald and Berger, but at the same time he remained a player in "official" Jewish affairs around Chicago, for which the Council would ultimately pay a heavy price.

But for now this was the least of the blowback. The National Community Relations Advisory Council passed a whole new edict against the ACJ, declaring, "Such organizations as the American Friends of the Middle East and the American Council for Judaism appear to have accepted and integrated into their own propaganda some of the most extreme and dangerous falsehoods and distortions put forth by the Arab propaganda apparatus. The tone and content of the Arab propaganda has grown in virulence and become increasingly anti-Semitic."[120] The Reform movement would also be moved by the Coleman statement to issue the closest thing it ever would (or could) to a *herem* against the ACJ, in the form of a resolution by the CCAR in June 1956 charging them to have "impaired the vital work of the UJA in a time of dire emergency, injected damaging divisiveness within some of our own Reform congregations, reinforced the efforts of Arabs and others to incite prejudice and enmity against the State of Israel and Jewish people throughout the world, and distorted and misrepresented the nature and meaning of Judaism." The resolution concluded by declaring in the affirmative that the Council "does not represent liberal, Reform Judaism or any other valid interpretation of Judaism."[121] The following year, virtually the same resolution was adopted by the Union of American Hebrew Congregations.

The firestorm Coleman initiated would also, however, occasion the resignation from the Council of Irving Reichert, who had scarcely been heard from since the annual conference of the Council was held in San Francisco in 1953. In a long and publicized letter to Coleman, Reichert denounced the Council for having "attempted to influence the policies of our government in precisely the same fashion as have the Zionists," affirming, "I have consistently endorsed and contributed to the United Jewish Appeal, even though I have disagreed with some of its policies and practices," though also insisting, "No one knows better than I how wicked and unfair has been the vilification heaped upon the members of the American Council for Judaism."[122] Among those who wrote letters of sympathy to Reichert was Sidney Wallach, who expressed his own disillusionment with the Council in saying of Berger: "But what can one do, when the liberal spirit of constant inquiry and self-searching is smothered by the megalomania and messianic postures of a self-proclaimed martyr?"[123]

Reichert's decision to resign from the Council remains an enigmatic one. On the one hand, part of him had clearly come to admire the accomplishments of Israel and was moreover sensitive enough to anti-Semitism to be deeply disturbed by the turn of the debate over Zionism. On the other hand, his fundamental convictions remained intact, and he was under no illusions that militarist Israel was a horrible affront to his values. No doubt also was a man of Reichert's political radicalism upset by the Council's service to Cold War propaganda, with his onetime congregant George Levison at every annual conference, giving the latest message on high from the State Department. Berger, for his part, had simply written him off as a prima donna, a conclusion for which he could hardly have been alone.[124] In this, as in his stated reasons for leaving the Council and apparent emotional fragility, Reichert had much in common with Louis Wolsey, whose own dilemma he had expressed much sympathy for years earlier. In the first week of 1968, no doubt partly in response to the euphoria that followed Israel's triumph in war seven months earlier, Reichert died from a hospital drug overdose, widely believed to have been suicide. His son would always blame the Zionists for his death.[125]

For all the setbacks occasioned by the Council's call for an investigation of the UJA (probably all of which could have been predicted anyway), the Suez Crisis of 1956 would give it considerable hope of vindication. Morris Lazaron set the tone for the Council in its response:

> No little nation can long endure, surrounded by hostile people, unless it makes sincere efforts to dissipate the suspicions and fear of its neighbors and unless it makes sacrifices to win the friendship of its

neighbors. No nation can live long in the shadow of catastrophe. Our American Jewish leadership, lay and rabbinical, did nothing to bring home this truth to the Israelis. On the contrary, it has given unquestioning and unreserved support to Israel's foreign policy. It has encouraged chauvinism in Israel, where it should have fostered generosity and an appreciation of other points of view. Indeed American Jewish leadership has been far less critical of Israel than many important groups in Israel itself.[126]

As it happened, Elmer and Ruth were vacationing at a mostly Jewish resort in Key West when Eisenhower announced his demand that Israel retreat from the Sinai. Berger recalled a large crowd gathering in the hotel lobby to watch the president's address on the resort's only television, and after the speech he perused the crowd quietly with Ruth to hear the reactions of the other guests, which he would describe as "slightly less than full approval," with characteristic remarks like "what else could he do?" and "not so bad."[127] This was no doubt encouraging to Berger. He recalled that as far as he knew, no one at the hotel knew who he was, revealing much about his impact and legacy that at the very peak of his infamy, he could go unrecognized in the lobby of a Jewish resort. In any event, after the Suez Crisis and the ultimate dénouement of the British and French Empires it represented, it was clear to Israel that its future fortunes lay with the United States, and that extraordinary measures would be necessary to secure them there.

6

PYRRHIC VICTORIES

The year 1957 began with the climax of the bitter split over Zionism in the rapidly declining world of Jewish socialism. Deeply alarmed by the events in the Suez and the attacks it occasioned on him by his former comrades at *The Forward*, Norman Thomas began to make plans for a trip to the Middle East. Thomas's friend with the Jewish Socialist Bund, Morris Polin (who was also on the editorial board of *The Forward*), urged Thomas to write an open letter expressing his concerns about the Middle East in anticipation of his trip to the region. Thomas agreed but was skeptical, knowing the editor of *The Forward*, Harry Rogoff, to be a committed Zionist and even suspecting his wife intended for them to eventually relocate to Israel.[1] As anticipated, Thomas received an angry reply from Rogoff:

> *The Forward* is a Jewish newspaper and cannot be used as a platform for anti-Israel and pro-Arab propaganda, such as the manuscript you have submitted for publication. Your article is a resume of all the prejudices and false accusations and insinuations made by the enemies of Israel and by the Arab leaders who seek its annihilation. Not a single charge against Israel contained in your article is new to our readers. They have heard them repeatedly on the radio and television delivered by Arab hatemongers.[2]

Thomas immediately distributed the harsh letter from Rogoff to several friends. Polin himself said that it gave him a sleepless night, and he urged the

like-minded members of the Forward Association to take action, even offering to come all the way from Chicago for a relevant board meeting in New
York.[3] William Zukerman, of course, was especially galvanized, contending
that "I have never read anything more crude and contrary to the principles
of the freedom of the press by any reactionary editor, let alone a socialist."[4]
Zukerman would distribute Thomas's article, which the *Jewish Newsletter* only
had the space to print in excerpts, as a special supplement, with the Bund
agreeing to distribute 200 copies to both Jewish and gentile labor leaders.[5]
Thomas also received letters of support and encouragement from several
members of the press, including Arthur Sulzberger and the distinguished
New York Post columnist James Wechsler.[6]

   Thomas had been a dear friend and kindred spirit of Judah Magnes since
their days protesting U.S. involvement in the First World War together and
had even made Berger's acquaintance decades before during the Flint sit-
down strike. Thomas was a vocal advocate for his friend during his trying advocacy for binationalism, so it was auspicious that he would have a leading
acolyte of Magnes as his young companion when he finally went to the
Middle East that November. Don Peretz, the son of a Jewish immigrant from
Ottoman Palestine, was active with the Socialist Party as an adolescent and
became an outspoken Magnes Zionist while also active with the Jewish Peace
Fellowship, founded by Abraham Cronbach. He was hired as a researcher by the
American Jewish Committee in 1955 after completing a doctoral dissertation on the Arab refugee problem, which Thomas often distributed to friends
and also earned him the friendship of the ACJ, which he reciprocated by
speaking at many of their functions.

   After being well received in several Arab countries, Thomas and Peretz were
received in Israel by Golda Meir, the new foreign minister who had her own
political consciousness forged in Socialist Party–dominated Milwaukee before
fatefully immigrating to Palestine, who turned hostile toward them when asked
about Israeli expansionism.[7] For his part, however, Thomas had more than an
equal share of criticism for the Arab regimes he visited and returned extremely
critical of the Eisenhower-Dulles policies, warning that they would "add oil to
the smoldering fires of the area."[8] He hoped to be able to meet with President
Eisenhower to discuss the findings of his trip but was instead politely received
by Loy Henderson, who was now back at the Near East Desk. Peretz would resign from the AJC soon after the trip, citing the new demand that all his statements on the Middle East had to be cleared by the Israeli embassy.[9] He entered
academia and became an accomplished and well-regarded scholar of the

Middle East, was long a mainstay of the Middle East Institute in Washington, and not infrequently contributed to Berger's publications and those of the ACJ.

The peak of Norman Thomas's engagement with the Middle East conflict also came when the culture of Jewish socialist anti-Zionism fostered by William Zukerman and the *Jewish Newsletter* was at its zenith. The newsletter flourished with the generous support of several Council members, including the Rabbis Morris Lazaron, Samuel Goldenson, and Abraham Cronbach. Lay leaders of the Council who rallied to the *Jewish Newsletter* included I. Edward Tonkon, D. Hays Solis-Cohen, Moses Lasky of San Francisco, Philip Sachs of Baltimore, Robert Gries of Cleveland, and Berger's loyal friend from Pontiac, Norman Buckner. Other notable Jewish intellectuals on Zukerman's masthead included Hans Kohn, Don Peretz, the sociologist David Riesman, and the philosopher Erich Fromm. Gentiles with the distinct privilege of being included on the masthead were Norman Thomas, American Civil Liberties Union founder Roger Baldwin, Alford Carleton of American Friends of the Middle East, and the writer Dwight Macdonald, a loyal friend of Zukerman who would passionately lament in writing of a young Norman Podhoretz: "What was always strange to me was that all these people that were leftists and Marxists together with me suddenly turned out to be Jewish nationalists. We wouldn't have spit on that position when we were Marxists."[10]

Not to be outshone by the others, the *Jewish Newsletter* enjoyed the enthusiastic support of a distinguished list of stalwarts of Jewish socialism. They included the revered founder of the Jewish Labor Committee Adolph Held, a onetime Socialist alderman in New York who along with David Dubinsky had been active in resisting Zionist pressures on the American Jewish Committee and Joint Distribution Committee before the Second World War.[11] In addition to the Workmen's Circle leaders Nathan Chanin and William Stern was the leader of the Jewish Socialist Bund, Emanuel Scherer, a leading member of the Polish government-in-exile during the Second World War. From the International Ladies' Garment Workers Union (ILGWU) was Louis Nelson, who led their Knitgood Workers Local, fondly remembered by the radical memoirist William Herrick as "the most democratic labor leader in America."[12] From the rival Amalgamated Clothing Workers came Elias Rabkin, who had served as the first president of the Amalgamated Bank, and Louis Hollander, then president of the New York Council of the Congress of Industrial Organizations (CIO). Rounding out the list were Jacob Panken, a onetime Socialist candidate for mayor of New York and prominent judge, and J. B. S. Hardman, a pioneering scholar of the U.S. labor movement.

Paradoxically, while the neoconservatives, in the central narrative of their existence, would associate anti-Zionism with the new left and with "anti-anticommunism," the most resilient anti-Zionist forces on the Jewish old left would come from its most stubbornly anticommunist wing. Jacob Panken had a generation earlier chaired the Socialist Party committee that expelled the founders of the Communist Party. Both Elias Rabkin and Louis Hollander remained fierce anticommunists in the Amalgamated Clothing Workers, as its president, Sidney Hillman, began to tilt toward the Communists by the eve of the Second World War. As for their anti-Zionist counterparts in the ILGWU, Louis Nelson and Will Herberg, they had both been disciples of Jay Lovestone, the founding member of the Communist Party who would go on to a notable career with the CIA. These right-wing socialists likely saw in David Ben-Gurion's Israel the fulfillment of what they always feared from their fellow traveling left-wing socialist comrades. Indeed, as a left-wing strongman who led a constitutional democracy while zealously committed to a nationalist revolution of his imagination, Ben-Gurion resembles no one as much as Hugo Chavez on the contemporary world scene.

But if the *Jewish Newsletter* represented the death throes of one tradition, the ACJ would be fortunate enough to be present at the birth of another. In the late 1950s, a number of young Israelis who had been in the orbit of the Ihud published a "Hebrew Manifesto." The authors of this manifesto adopted the label of Canaanites, or *k'nanim* in Hebrew, to affirm their ethnic identity in Palestine in a manner divorced from Zionist ideology, declaring that they were a "Semitic people" and sought reintegration with the other "Semitic peoples" of the region. Of Zionist ideology, the manifesto declared:

> This inheritance, a product of a different social entity and a bygone reality, is an obstacle in the way of the Hebrew Nation. It subjected the State to the fallacious Zionist myth, dug an abyss between the country's two nations, caused the dismemberment of Palestine, isolated the State within the Semitic region and the community of Asian and African peoples, caused the State's subjugation to imperialism, turned the state into a pawn in the game of the world power blocks, established a parasitical economy, erected a corrupt and communal regime of authoritarian parties, and atrophied Hebrew cultural creativity.[13]

Like the spiritual leader of Ihud Martin Buber, the authors of this manifesto were followers of Ahad Ha'am, the father of "cultural Zionism," who bitterly opposed Theodor Herzl and his Zionist Congress, declaring that "the salvation of Israel will come through prophets, not through diplomats."[14] The ACJ had an organic connection to this new movement in Moshe Menuhin, who as a follower of Ahad Ha'am was so totally disheartened by the issuance of the Balfour Declaration that he left Palestine altogether and spent the rest of his life in northern California, where he would be in touch with the Council as early as 1949. Menuhin would convincingly argue that "Ahad Ha'am's spiritual Zionism became synonymous with classical, prophetic Judaism," thus affirming the fundamental kinship of the so-called Zionism of Ha'am, Buber, and Magnes with Classical Reform Judaism.[15] In calling for a "de-Zionized" Israel, the Hebrew Manifesto was echoing almost perfectly the position of the Council and its State Department allies since 1948, and that of Elmer Berger especially.

The rising star of this movement was Uri Avnery, a disillusioned *Irgun* fighter who would go on into his old age as the indomitable champion of the Israeli peace camp. Avnery came to America in search of support for the new movement among American Jews around this time and received a warm welcome from Berger but a cold shoulder in most other quarters, only to be attacked by the Israeli press on returning home for embracing the ACJ.[16] In 1965 Menuhin would follow up on the Hebrew Manifesto with the publication of his own epic tome, *The Decadence of Judaism in Our Time*. The book was glowingly reviewed for the Council by Morris Lazaron, who was so moved by it to proclaim: "In the face of the brutalizing nationalism of our times, we must cry out the universal message of Israel. Not the blood cult, state cult, hate cult, war cult of nationalism, but one humanity on earth as there is one God in heaven."[17]

The Council also had a significant lifeline to the world of Jewish religious thought in these years, chiefly through the *Menorah Journal*, the last remnant of the old Menorah Society, the collegiate Jewish society generally aligned with the Reform movement that prospered in the early twentieth century before being displaced by the pro-Zionist Hillel. In a speech to the ACJ annual conference in 1958, the editor of the journal, Henry Hurwitz, implored his audience: "We can harmonize our broadest and most universal ethics, which we may well be proud of as Jews, so that we may enjoy the spiritual culture that should properly go with our religious faith, and so that we may be the instruments for advancing the knowledge of that great faith and culture not only among ourselves, but also as an integral part of the culture, the philosophy, and the religion of America and of free mankind."[18] Among the frequent contributors to *Menorah Journal* was Jacob Petuchowski, a professor at

Hebrew Union College who was sympathetic to the Council, who along with Jacob Marcus would keep alive a certain stealth non-Zionism at the college.

The other great scholar of Judaism who would have at least some affinity with the Council was Will Herberg. One of many who left the Communist Party with Jay Lovestone and thereby obtained gainful employment with the ILGWU as its education director, Herberg befriended the theologian Reinhold Niebuhr and was about to convert to Christianity when Niebuhr urged him to first consider returning to Judaism. After a period of study at the Jewish Theological Seminary, he became the earliest and most thorough interpreter of Martin Buber, seeing in him the Jewish manifestation of Christian, particularly Catholic, social teaching. Though tending toward the orthodox in theology, Herberg owed his enduring anti-Zionism more to the Reform than the Orthodox expression, considering Zionism a form of idolatry. While critical of Classical Reform theology, he nevertheless recognized its indispensability to the application of Judaism to the modern world, declaring before an ACJ annual conference in 1961: "The American Jew cannot see himself as an alien in a strange land, he sees himself as thoroughly and entirely an American, whose Jewishness itself is really an aspect of his Americanness."[19]

But perhaps the most fascinating aspect of the engagement of the ACJ with the larger intellectual community was its presence at the creation of the postwar American right. In 1999 the preeminent historian of American conservatism George Nash would publish an article on the "premature Jewish conservatives" of the 1950s, who, in contrast to the then-ascendant neoconservatives, were confirmed individualists, being for the most part disillusioned ex-communists and therefore finding equally distasteful the self-described "collective" that was the Zionist-inspired political conception of the Jewish people. Nash, however, made the serious error of associating this fact with a rejection of Judaism altogether, notwithstanding his discussion of the alignment with the ACJ of two of his major subjects, Frank Chodorov and Morrie Ryskind. Significantly, they were the only two of Nash's seven Jewish subjects who even faintly identified with the Jewish religion.[20]

Chodorov is perhaps the most unlikely subject in this discussion, as a man who famously threatened to punch in the nose anyone who called him a conservative. The product of a middle-class immigrant family in turn-of-the-century New York, Chodorov gave his best years as an evangelist of the social theorist Henry George but grew disillusioned as the movement increasingly entered the tent of New Deal liberalism. As he began to develop his own philosophy of individualism, he abandoned his earlier atheism for a deistic conception of God that lent itself quite naturally to Classical Reform Judaism. In March 1948 Chodorov began an autobiographical essay by declaring, "I am a Jew, not that anyone cares, least of all myself," and emphatically threw down the gauntlet against Zionism in saying that "the ideology of the proposed restoration smacks too much of Hitlerian nationalism based on racial purity, reinforced with claims of divine selection. It defies the record and is decidedly dangerous."[21]

Chodorov's collaborator in developing his new individualism was Albert Jay Nock, a lapsed Episcopal priest who took on eccentric aristocratic airs as a writer, lamenting the rise of totalitarianism by proclaiming the duty of individualists against the horror of the twentieth century to be "Isaiah's job," that is, to stand for the quiet remnant of justice and righteousness as did the Prophet Isaiah. The echo here of prophetic Judaism is undeniable, as was surely evident to Nock as a onetime man of the cloth. In discovering the American Council for Judaism, Chodorov was undoubtedly overjoyed to find that there yet remained a hardy band of liberal Jews committed to carrying out Isaiah's job. Chodorov wrote glowing reviews of *A Partisan History of Judaism* and *What Price Israel?* for Henry Regnery's *Human Events* and later reported on Berger's trip to the Middle East for *American Mercury*.[22] In the latter article Chodorov asserted that "Israel is only part Israel, the rest being world-wide Zionism, and it is not certain which part wags which. Until this uncertainty is resolved, peace in the Middle East will be precarious, and American foreign policy will be in a similar state of turmoil."[23]

Also notable for his association with the ACJ was Chodorov's young protégé Murray Rothbard. The son of the militantly assimilationist brother of the Labor Zionist "Pioneer Women" leader Dvorah Rothbard-Schwartz, Rothbard was a confirmed young reactionary when he discovered Chodorov as a student at Columbia University. A self-described agnostic who rarely discussed Jewish issues in his long career as the architect of the modern libertarian movement, and despite having the undeniable manners of a New York Jewish intellectual, Rothbard would be a dues-paying member of the Council as late as 1959.[24] He also carried on a lengthy correspondence with Leonard Sussman throughout the 1950s and wrote a memo on the Council's views for the libertarian think tank Volker Fund in 1956.[25] The influence of Classical Reform Judaism and its fundamentally individualist philosophy can thus be deeply felt in the foundation of modern libertarianism through its influence on both Chodorov and Rothbard, naturally repelled by the collectivist claims of Zionism.

Morrie Ryskind, the other "premature Jewish conservative" in the ranks of the ACJ, was a highly accomplished humorist of the stage and screen who would be propelled by his success as a writer for the Marx Brothers to be the highest-paid screenwriter in the golden age of Hollywood. A practicing Jew, if nominally so, his whole life, Ryskind was long active in the Socialist Party before leaving with the "old guard" faction after a brief pro-communist ascendancy in the party in the early 1930s. Horrified by the rise of the Communist Party in Hollywood, he campaigned for Wendell Willkie in 1940 and by the end of the decade was a supporter of Robert Taft. In 1948 Ryskind would help found the American Jewish League Against Communism with Rabbi Benjamin Schultz, an activist with the New York Liberal Party from his pulpit in Yonkers who would go on to be a zealous advocate for Joe McCarthy.[26] Ryskind likely made his most lasting contribution to political discourse as a key fundraiser for the launch of William F. Buckley's *National Review* in 1955. In 1958 he would also be a founder of the controversial John Birch Society.[27]

Ryskind would often write favorably of the Council in his syndicated columns and may have appeared at a couple of their functions but was never a dues-paying member. Nonetheless, he frequently lobbied on the Council's behalf to Bill Buckley, whom he hoped would meet with Berger and become a champion for Berger's views.[28] While he would assuredly have been averse to the leftist tone of Zionist activism in his youth, after the 1956 war Buckley was likely compelled to embrace Israel along with anyone else who stood with European imperialism at its last stand. It was this impulse that moved Buckley to swiftly purge from *National Review* early on such antimilitarist contributors as Murray Rothbard and John Flynn, and significantly, this process culminated with the purge of a devoted friend, Freda Utley, for her views on the Middle East after the 1967 war. It also likely set the stage, a generation later, when he would ruthlessly purge all opposition to the First Gulf War by equating it with anti-Semitism.

Perhaps the most personally extraordinary gentile friend of the Council, Freda Utley came from a prominent family of British socialists and was an active Communist journalist before being cruelly disillusioned by the "disappearance" of her Russian Jewish husband into the gulag in 1934. After resettling in America, she established herself as an expert on China and also established her enduring progressive impulses by writing one of the key early works for Henry Regnery urging a conciliatory policy toward Germany at the end of the Second World War, *The High Cost of Vengeance*. In the Arab world,

Utley saw ominous parallels to the events by which Western imperialism drove China into the arms of the Soviets and feared they were about to be repeated. She did not believe Israel or Zionism to be a major villain of this imperial great game, but she did see Zionism as a totalitarian menace that would only lead to catastrophe.

In 1957 Utley published a book on this theme with the Henry Regnery Company titled *Will the Middle East Go West?* Premised on the hope that Eisenhower's actions in Suez would lead to a new beginning for U.S. foreign policy on the side of anti-imperialism, Utley warned: "Once again the West is denying the legitimate national aspirations of a people with an ancient civilization, fallen behind in the march of technological, economic, and political progress, and humiliated by past or present subjection to alien rule."[29] Utley singled out Berger for praise throughout the book, quoting one of his more prophetic statements toward the present U.S. dilemma in the Middle East, when he said in a speech to American Friends of the Middle East that year: "If we continue to try and play God, choosing first the Arabs and then the Israelis, in frantic efforts to apply palliatives in order to avoid a policy of American fundamentals, we shall not only not help the Middle East but we shall lose our own soul."[30] The book also praised Alfred Lilienthal, who published his own book in response to Suez with Devin-Adair, *There Goes the Middle East*, but was now acting completely outside the Council as a free agent.

That same year, Berger was compelled to write a third book, *Judaism or Jewish Nationalism?*, focusing on the increasingly severe attacks against the ACJ and on a comprehensive response to them. Published by the Council's new publishing ally Bookman Associates, the book broke the typical critique of the Council down to six charges: the misrepresentation of Jews and Judaism, harming Israel by giving aid and comfort to the Arabs, accusing American Jews of dual loyalty and thereby giving aid and comfort to anti-Semites, urging complete assimilation by American Jews, not understanding that America is a pluralistic society, and having no humanitarian interest in its fellow Jews. The book began with a homiletic introduction by Morris Lazaron and was also, curiously, dedicated by Berger to his parents.[31]

With respect to the charge of dual loyalty, Berger repeated in this book the argument that had been made by the Council and by Rosenwald in particular since the 1940s: it was not they who affirmed the identity of Americans of Jewish faith, who raised any questions about dual loyalties, but that it was in fact the Zionists who raised the issue by ascribing Jewish "nationality" to

American Jews. As Berger argued in reference to internal Zionist objections to the continuation of organized Zionism after 1948: "None of the people who now, without any proof, accuse the Council of charging dual loyalty have raised as much as a whisper about the United Jewish Appeal which was accused publicly and specifically by Zionists of having forfeited its American status while enjoying American privileges. Yet the condition which evoked the charge still exists."[32] He followed up on this with this insistence: "In defining Zionism the Council invariably uses Zionist authorities, instead of relying on hearsay or the opinions of the Council itself."[33]

The ACJ continued to have certain organizational strengths heading into the 1960s. The Philanthropic Fund, though a pittance beside the United Jewish Appeal, continued to prosper, now chaired by Henry Moyer with the assistance of Richard Korn, an orchestra manager in New York. The fund was even able to employ an able executive director, Anna Walling Matson, a leading socialite of the New York literary scene. The Council also had an especially active youth group around this time whose core included Allan Brownfeld, who became active while still in high school in Brooklyn and continued to be at the College of William and Mary; the brothers Ned and Peter Hanauer, whose maternal grandfather, Elias Kaufman of Lake Charles, Louisiana, was a loyal lay leader of the Council; Eliot Bernat at Northeastern University; and Stephanie Limberg at Brandeis.

In autumn of 1958, largely due to the urging of Leonard Sussman, the Council News was converted into a serious journal that aspired to general interest, Issues. Prominent friends of the Council in American politics in these years included Senator Ralph Flanders, Republican of Vermont, and Congressman Omar Burleson, Democrat of Texas. Both men spoke at numerous Council functions, and Flanders especially was notable for several speeches on the floor of the Senate blasting the United Jewish Appeal. Flanders believed in a sort of light footprint approach to the Cold War, relying on large states as offshore balancers like Egypt and India instead of investing so heavily in small client states like Israel and Pakistan. Especially notable also among gentile friends of the Council in these years was the historian Arnold Toynbee, who became severely critical of Israeli treatment of the Arabs and was enthusiastically embraced by the ACJ.

It was also around this time that the man who would eventually be the closest thing Elmer Berger ever had to a son became seriously involved in the work of the ACJ. Norton Mezvinsky, the son of an Orthodox grocer in Ames, Iowa, first began corresponding with Berger while a student at the

University of Wisconsin, where he was earnestly studying under such champions of the progressive school of U.S. history as George Mosse, Howard Beale, and William Appleman Williams. While finishing up his PhD at Harvard University, Mezvinsky was commissioned by the Council to write a sociological study of Jewish self-segregation in America, which he would then present as a paper to an ACJ annual conference to be subsequently published.[34] After completing his PhD in 1960, Mezvinsky was hired on to the staff of the Council in New York and would go on to the thankless job of running its day-to-day affairs during the crisis of the organization occasioned by the 1967 war.

Early in 1957 Lessing Rosenwald traveled to Israel at the personal invitation of David Ben-Gurion, who wined and dined him while giving him the grandest of propaganda tours. Rosenwald returned favorably impressed with much of the economic and cultural progress that the country had made in just a decade of independence but insisted that the trip did not fundamentally alter his views of Zionist ideology and the continuing problems it posed for American Jewish life. Two years later Berger returned to the region, spending much of his time in Tunisia, writing from there to Clarence Coleman:

> The U.S. position on Algeria weakens our influence in the country and creates difficulties maintaining a high level, pro-Western orientation in the face of the deep feeling for Algeria. It is the old story. All intelligent Tunisians recognize our concerns in NATO and France. They would respect us if we frankly stood on these "national interests." But we run around the world talking about democracy and the right of people to self-determination, and consistently back off from the political decisions necessary to put legs under these ideals.[35]

In 1959, resulting in part from the protests of the ACJ and its allies such as Ralph Flanders, Undersecretary of the Treasury Fred Scribner issued a warning to the United Jewish Appeal that it needed to undergo serious restructuring and completely overhaul its fundraising operations in the United States or else face prosecution by both the Justice Department and the Internal Revenue Service. The UJA followed suit in the first quarter of 1960, effectively beginning the process by which the old organized Zionism gave way to the modern Israel lobby. This was primarily executed by transferring the functions of the American section of the Jewish Agency, which included fostering the immigration and indoctrination of young American Jews to Israel, to the American Zionist Council. The successor to the former American

Zionist Emergency Council, in theory it was a consultative body of the different American Zionist factions, but increasingly inseparable from its public affairs arm, which was now known as the American Israel Public Affairs Committee (AIPAC).

Shortly after the reorganization was announced, the Council had its annual conference in Denver. The conference passed a resolution on the UJA, protesting that "deliberations to reorganize the United Jewish Appeal were conducted between their beneficiaries and the World Zionist Organization in a manner which precluded the American donors to the UJA from participating in the discussions," and also called for "a valid and genuine separation of the United Jewish Appeal from the Jewish Agency for Israel and other Zionist organizations," as well as for an American Jewish philanthropy completely controlled by Americans and with the utmost transparency.[36] The resolution was printed as a bookend to a pamphlet personally authored by Rosenwald, who emphasized the revelations of the reorganization, that $18 million over ten years went from the UJA to Israeli political parties and $15 million returned to the United States for propaganda purposes.

After praising the concrete results of the reorganization, the end of subsidies to political parties, and the transfer of public relations and cultural undertakings to the American Zionist Council, Rosenwald asserted "these are superficial changes, a good start perhaps, but not by any means the answer to ending Zionist control over the UJA."[37] Berger also wrote a lengthy analysis of the reorganization for the *Jewish Newsletter*. After pointing out that the Israeli government-granted charter of the Jewish Agency stated its mission of "deepening Jewish consciousness and unity among the Jews of the Diaspora" and "fighting against assimilation and the denial of Jewish peoplehood," Berger insisted, "It will take, therefore, ideological anti-Zionists or independent-thinking Jews to draw contracts and supervise expenditure of funds in ways which will ensure that Jewish nation building is not fused with philanthropy."[38] It would not be long, however, before even greater scrutiny would be leveled against the reshuffled Zionist apparatus.

In the meantime, another new controversy emerged that grabbed the Council's attention: the capture and trial by Israel of Adolf Eichmann. The Council joined a broad consensus in Western opinion that Eichmann would be more properly tried by an international war crimes tribunal instead of by the Israeli government, a position that was even affirmed by the State Department in a letter to Clarence Coleman.[39] The Council was deeply alarmed by the propaganda assault that Israel seemed to be waging in its conduct of the Eichmann trial, quoting with approval in a pamphlet on the case from *Time* magazine: "In his justifiable determination to see Eichmann punished for his monstrous past, Ben-Gurion seemed to be unaware of the inverse racism implicit in his claim that Israel, as 'the only sovereign authority in Jewry,' had the right to seek out criminals guilty of offenses against 'the Jewish people' anywhere it could find them."[40]

Leonard Sussman spoke for the Council in giving a speech on the Eichmann trial to the American Humanist Association in June 1961:

> In brief, Israel wanted to try Eichmann on Israel's terms, she also wanted the world to react in ways favorable to Israeli interests and not necessarily consistent with the interest of justice. I believe it is not too early to say that the world has failed to grapple with the fundamental moral issues which the trial should have raised, it failed because the extraneous Israeli-Zionist political interests have become paramount.[41]

The Council's views on the episode were echoed by Hannah Arendt, the distinguished German émigré writer who covered the trial for the *New Yorker*. Her belief was that Eichmann was not guilty of "crimes against the Jewish people" but rather reflected "the banality of evil," meaning the unconscious development of evil out of ordinary human behavior in a state bureaucracy.

This was an extremely powerful and dangerous idea to Zionism, because it reduces evil to human nature on essentially value-neutral terms, completely obliterating the fundamental Zionist premise that anti-Semitism is a constant mystical force in history (an idea that would be increasingly essential with the rise in the years to come of the so-called "holocaust industry"), and to the whole world order of perpetual war for perpetual peace, which ultimately rests on the very same narrative. Berger was extremely moved by Arendt's reporting on the Eichmann case and invited her to speak and publish in the forums of the Council. Arendt replied with deep gratitude but explained to Berger that like their mutual friends in the Ihud, "I am not really an anti-Zionist, and when Ben-Gurion passes from the scene Zionism will revert to the kind of broad, liberal movement it was as I first knew it in Germany."[42]

Largely in response to these ominous implications of the Eichmann case, Berger felt that it was necessary to seek a formal declaration from the U.S. government as to whether or not it accepted the claims that Israel made to justify its capture and trial of Eichmann in international law; in essence, for the United States to declare once and for all, as the ACJ had in one way or another sought since it campaigned against the creation of Israel, whether or not it recognized the existence of "the Jewish people" as a matter of international law. In taking this on, Berger decided to seek out a respected scholar of international law to prepare a formal brief to be presented to the State Department. The man who ultimately took on the project was William Thomas Mallison Jr., a product of a navy family who held chairs at both George Washington University and the Naval War College. As the Eichmann trial was proceeding, Berger had a long meeting with Mallison outlining the reasoning of his legal case as it had developed since his days clashing with Abba Hillel Silver at the United Nations, updated to include the implications of such legislation as the Law of Return. Mallison told Berger that legally speaking he knew nothing of the data before him, but if Berger's account of the facts was accurate, he had a case. By 1961 Mallison was addressing the Council's annual conference.[43]

The Council would be seriously weakened by the deaths of several key supporters in the early 1960s. Within days of each other in November 1961 came the deaths of Henry Hurwitz and William Zukerman. Zukerman's death came as an especially bitter blow. The *Jewish Newsletter* had been a great success, but it was agreed by all that no one could replace him. The friends of the newsletter did, however, raise money for a memorial volume of Zukerman's work, *Voice of Dissent*, which was published by Bookman Associates in 1964. At the Council's annual conference following his death, Rabbi Cronbach gave a moving eulogy for Zukerman:

> William Zukerman was a bold dissenter. He resembled the Prophet Elijah in the Bible. Elijah stands alone confronting the 450 prophets of Baal and the 400 prophets of Astarte, vanquishing all of them in the debate. In personal appearance Zukerman was meek, mild, and unassertive. But with the pen he was a valiant fighter. Mordecai Kaplan, ardent Zionist, once wrote to Zukerman "May you continue for many years in the much needed role of gadfly in Jewish life."[44]

With the following year came the deaths of two of the few remaining rabbis who remained loyal to the ACJ from its inception: Samuel Goldenson in New York and David Marx in Atlanta. This no doubt played a part in moving Nelson Glueck in 1963 to confer honorary doctorates on the two remaining elder rabbis, Morris Lazaron and William Fineshriber. This decision was just as likely motivated by Glueck's guilt over the spurning of his onetime prize student Elmer Berger when he had been pointedly excluded from receiving the honor with the rest of his class years earlier at the twenty-fifth anniversary of their ordination. In the years ahead, he increasingly became "Dr. Berger" as opposed to "Rabbi Berger," and though he did not complain about having been so spurned, he would never object to being so called. Glueck had to give the doctorates to Lazaron and Fineshriber over the vocal objection of the head of the Union of American Hebrew Congregations, Maurice Eisendrath, with whom he had a frosty relationship for a variety of reasons.[45] Eisendrath, however, felt it necessary for the UAHC to pass a new resolution reaffirming the *herem* of 1957, asserting, "Nothing has occurred in the intervening years to modify the charges articulated in the 1957 Biennial resolution. If anything, the damage and dishonor visited upon American and world Jewry by the activities of the American Council has become more extensive."[46]

The leaders of American Zionism had good reason to be alarmed by any sudden advances by their opponents at this juncture. In 1962 the chairman of the Senate Foreign Relations Committee, J. William Fulbright of Arkansas, began to issue subpoenas to the various leaders of the Jewish Agency, the UJA, and the American Zionist Council to verify their compliance with the Treasury Department's findings that had led to their reorganization and to determine if formal registration as a foreign agent was in fact necessary. As early as 1959, Fulbright had written a reassuring letter to Berger about the activities of the congressionally mandated Institute for Mediterranean Affairs, and the following year the Council would protest vigorously the boastful suggestion by the virulent Zionist columnist Max Lerner that "the Jewish community" had successfully torpedoed the rumored appointment of Fulbright as secretary of state by the incoming Kennedy administration.[47] Fulbright and his staff even consulted Berger and a wide berth of documents in his possession in preparing evidence for the hearings.[48]

In his first hearing, Fulbright questioned two executives with the U.S. section of the Jewish Agency, Maurice Boukstein and Isadore Hamlin, who revealed a highly interconnected organizational web connecting the Jewish Agency to the American Zionist Council and the UJA. They deferred an increasingly large number of matters to AIPAC, which was taking on a growing number of public functions under the chairmanship of Philip Bernstein from his pulpit in Rochester, New York, and with the vigorous labors of its executive director in Washington, I. L. Kenen.[49] At one point in the hearings, Boukstein even implicitly threatened, with the Israel lobby's political muscle, that the laws covering foreign agent registration would have to change to accommodate the Zionist apparatus, rather than the Zionists accommodating the law.[50] By the end of 1962, the Justice Department formally opened an investigation and announced that it would require the American Zionist Council to register as a foreign agent.

In May 1963 William Fulbright addressed the annual conference of the ACJ in New York. After warning that "compromise and accommodation, which are the essence of diplomacy, have become suspect and foreign policy as a consequence is more rigid and messianic in character," Fulbright urged that President Kennedy "must lead our people to the acceptance of partial rather than complete solutions, to the acceptance of continuing responsibility, rather than a single national effort."[51] JFK came into office hoping to finally resolve the Palestinian refugee problem but was pressured even during his campaign by major Jewish donors such as Abraham Feinberg and Philip Klutznick and was denounced by Ben-Gurion himself for posing "a more serious danger to Israel's existence than all the threats of the Arab dictators."[52] Kennedy was ultimately compelled to sell arms to Israel on account of his failure to achieve rapprochement with Gamel Nasser's Egypt but firmly drew the line against Israel acquiring nuclear weapons. It is even believed by some that the Israelis tacitly approved of the Kennedy assassination on account of this opposition.[53]

The same weekend as Fulbright's speech to the Council, Philip Bernstein addressed an AIPAC gathering in Washington, where, after a long tirade against Hannah Arendt, he launched an utterly hysterical attack on the Council. After duplicitously claiming that "I have maintained through the years that the American Council for Judaism is of no consequence" and that he was speaking of them "only because the Chairman of the Senate Foreign Relations Committee chooses its convention as a platform for a policy statement," Bernstein let loose:

> Therefore, I must say this is a handful of sick Jews. They are soul sick. They are self-hating Jewish anti-Semites. They have been repudiated by every Jewish religious body, lay and rabbinical. The reaction of the entire organized Jewish community to these sick Jews who derive some distorted satisfaction from traducing their people is the fulfillment of the prophetic word in the 18th chapter of Leviticus, "all who do any of these abhorrent things, such persons shall be cut off from their people."[54]

Indeed, the Council would loom especially large in the thinking of the Zionists as they contemplated their response to the antagonism of Fulbright and the Justice Department. Berger, for his part, took on all comers in giving a major address on these developments to the New York chapter of the Council in June:

> Except for people who have something to hide, therefore, there is no need for hysterics about this situation. There is no suggestion of irresponsible prying into the affairs of unquestionably private voluntary associations of any Americans. There is nothing inherent in this situation aimed directly at Jews, or even at Zionists. The investigation should be welcomed by every American who is at all conscious of the gigantic responsibilities of our country in this era of danger in which we live and who, at the same time, is aware of the subtleties and colorations of propaganda and of the instrumentalities used for the dissemination of propaganda in today's world of mass communications.[55]

Berger went on to warn:

> And finally, American Jews this time have what may be a last opportunity to put their house in order. There is nothing illegal, per se, about being agents of a foreign power. All that is required is proper identification as prescribed by United States legislation. But it is for purposes of public identification that the requirements exist. If, in fact, the present investigations find that the Zionist-UJA structure is in the status of a foreign agent, American Jews should understand the consequences. If the institutions which they have passively permitted to claim to represent them are identified as agents of a foreign principal, the nearly two-century-old hope of American Jews to be regarded as individual, integrated citizens whose religion carries no implication of identification with a foreign nationality will be blasted. No rationalizations about cultural pluralism or superficial analogies of apologizing for a duality of loyalties will hold water. The Council has said this for twenty years. Either Zionism does not exist in any meaningful sense and we have tragically wasted our time and substance, or tragically American Jews, helped by the apologetics of non-Zionism, have ignored the mounting evidence of how profoundly right we have been. The present formidable confrontations with responsible agencies of our government suggest this second alternative.[56]

After receiving formal notification from the Justice Department that they were forthwith required to register as a foreign agent, the American Zionist Council hired as legal counsel the well-connected New York lawyer Simon Rifkind, who had just served as chairman of a special White House commission on the future of railroads. He began meeting with Justice Department representatives in search of a negotiated settlement in January 1963 but, when push came to shove, would typically stonewall with flourishes of good versus evil rhetoric and insinuations that the Zionists were owed on account of their political support to the Kennedy administration.[57] The negotiations continued well into the spring, at which time the deputy attorney general overseeing the case, Nicholas Katzenbach, offered reconsideration of the registration order itself in exchange for complete financial disclosure. Based on the leak of this offer, the *Wall Street Journal* reported that the Justice Department was about to drop the case, which prompted a flurry of letters of protest from the Council rank-and-file, led by Edward Tonkon, to Attorney General Robert F. Kennedy.[58]

As the Foreign Registration office at the Justice Department struggled to keep the case alive, Fulbright finally held his second hearing in August, and Berger sent a letter, cosigned by his new collaborator, Tom Mallison, urging that the U.S. section of the Jewish Agency be forced to disclose the totality of its relationship with the government of Israel. After new revelations emerged from the continued Fulbright hearings of Jewish Agency payments to the American Zionist Council and of AIPAC's "cultivation of editors," Katzenbach withdrew his earlier offer but allowed that a statement could be filed to indicate that their registration as a foreign agent was under protest.[59] At this point, Rifkind pleaded with Justice Department officials that the ominous danger awaiting them if they registered was the satisfaction that would accrue to the ACJ, betraying a bizarre obsession on the part of the Zionists with their modest adversary.[60]

The case essentially died with the Kennedy assassination, petering out until early 1965 as Lyndon Johnson was now beholden to the campaign dollars of a wiser and shrewder Abraham Feinberg. The U.S. section of the Jewish Agency would eventually fold into the U.S. section of the World Zionist Organization, which registered as a foreign agent in 1971. The American Zionist Council would quietly disband by this time as well, leaving behind its quixotic child AIPAC, which would for the next generation circle the square of "dual loyalty" under the wily leadership of I. L. Kenen. An entirely new form would be adopted by the Zionist apparatus, which discarded many of the more ostentatious trappings that were grist for the Council's mill and whose rise would catch the Council totally off guard.

As the drama of this ultimate reckoning for thoroughgoing Zionist ideology in America played out, the younger generation of American Jews was in the main more wrapped up in the great upheaval that was sweeping their own country—the civil rights movement. Young Jews from New York and other northern cities became "freedom riders" mostly out of deep personal conviction, but the self-appointed leadership of the American Jewish community, and the leadership of the Reform movement in particular, would have an awkward relationship to the movement. It is significant that the one Jewish figure to address the March on Washington was the virulent Zionist Joachim Prinz, then serving as chairman of the Conference of Presidents of Major Jewish Organizations, thus theoretically speaking as the ecumenical representative of all American Jewry. Insult was added to injury in light of Prinz's past as an active Zionist in Germany at the time of Hitler's accession of power. Prinz exultantly welcomed Hitler's rise in his 1934 treatise *Wir Juden*, celebrating it as "the death of liberalism."[61]

Berger himself was especially vexed by the hypocrisy he saw in his Zionist rabbinical adversaries rallying to the civil rights movement, making it a major theme of his aggressive jottings of commentary in every CCAR yearbook he received.[62] This support for the civil rights movement was especially ironic, given that it was avowedly antinationalist in its struggle for integration into U.S. society. A generation earlier, the black community had been taken by storm by an uncanny mirror image of Theodor Herzl and his movement in Marcus Garvey. In response to the horrible race riots that followed the First World War, Garvey packed Madison Square Garden in 1921 to proclaim himself "Provisional President of Africa" in a stunning echo of Herzl's declaration to have founded the Jewish State at Basel in 1897. Like Herzl, Garvey had a conspicuous taste for pompous dress and manners, mercilessly mocked by his Socialist Party adversaries as a "negro with a hat." The Garveyites, in turn, were no less fanatical than the Zionists against their adversaries, disparaging them in racially charged terms as "mulattoes" and "octoroons."[63]

Like Herzl, Garvey had little appetite for military conquest and sought to achieve his goals through colonization by a joint stock company, the gross mismanagement of which ultimately led to his conviction for mail fraud in 1925.[64] But unlike Herzl, Garvey would not have the good fortune to be succeeded by the ruthless political animal of a Chaim Weizmann, but by curious analogs to Herzl's occultist predecessors in the Zionist pantheon. The best known of these, Elijah Muhammad, preached bizarre pseudoscience eerily resembling that of Leo Pinsker, who believed that the genetically innate fear of ghosts of the Caucasian race spurred their anti-Semitism at the sight of the "ghost nation" of the Jews, thus requiring the resurrection of that nation in Palestine.[65] It could be, as historian of early America Edmund Morgan believed about the slaveholding class in Virginia entering the vanguard of the revolution against what they regarded as political slavery, that the militants of American Zionism entered the vanguard of the civil rights movement because as partisans of an apartheid system abroad they understood the nature of that system at home.

But by the mid-1960s the movement's ballyhooed black-Jewish alliance fell apart as younger black activists became disillusioned with the goal of integration and embarked on a futile search for "authenticity." Thus was the grave contradiction of Jewish support for the civil rights movement laid bare: they had served in a movement for the complete integration into U.S. society of African Americans, a goal that, at least in theory, they had rejected for themselves. The trauma of the Jewish community's betrayal by the black power movement undoubtedly led to the epiphany that they were not interested in what the civil rights movement was offering either. They would therefore embark on their own search for "authenticity," which had numerous manifestations for the future of U.S. Jewish identity, not least of which was a reinvigorated militant Zionism, but also, notably, the dramatic decline of the Classical Reform, mostly English "high church" rite, which was left largely untouched by the Reform Zionists.

In the meantime, a not-insignificant blow would be dealt to the construction of this new Jewish identity. By 1964 Tom Mallison had completed his brief that would be known as "The Jewish People Study" and would have it published that June in the *George Washington University Law Review*. After a lengthy preliminary correspondence between Berger and Assistant Secretary of State Phillips Talbot, a forty-one-page draft of Mallison's article was sent to him on March 14.[66] On April 20, 1964, Talbot formally replied in what Berger would initially interpret as the victory he had been after for the last twenty years but would prove woefully anticlimactic:

> The Department of State recognizes the State of Israel as a sovereign State and citizenship in the State of Israel. It recognizes no other sovereignty or citizenship in connection therewith. It does not recognize a legal-political relationship based upon the religious identification of American citizens. It does not in any way discriminate among American

citizens upon the basis of their religion. Accordingly, it should be clear that the Department of State does not regard the "Jewish people" concept as a concept of international law.[67]

In a memo to the Council membership, Berger exclaimed: "It is, in the first place, an unequivocal declaration of policy that the central legal-political claims of the Zionist-Israeli sovereignty, often embodied in law, are inconsistent with the fundamental, constitutional rights of United States citizens. It is a significant contribution to, and clarification of, international law bearing on the relationship of Jews in countries other than Israel to the Israeli state."[68] Typical of the Zionist response to the letter was the letter of protest to Assistant Secretary Talbot from Philip Bernstein:

> I would point out to you that the Balfour Declaration, the League of Nations Mandate, and resolutions of the U.S. Congress have all referred to the concept of the Jewish people. But it is malicious distortion to suggest, as the American Council for Judaism pretends, that those who hold to the concept of the Jewish people believe there to be legal obligations between that people and the State of Israel. Unfortunately, your letter restated the Council's view, and your failure to dissociate yourself from it is misinterpreted to mean that you accept the Council's strictures.[69]

Talbot himself was likely deeply bemused by the whole affair, emphasizing in his letter to Berger: "I remain doubtful that a formal meeting of the type you describe would lead to useful results."[70] Bernstein, for his part, was disingenuous: in addition to fastidiously citing the dubious precedents set by a defunct empire, an international body that no longer existed, and the non-binding resolutions of a yet-separate national legislature, Bernstein seized on the red herring of "legal" obligations of Jewish peoplehood to obfuscate the political. Indeed, in the lives of American Jews, this was a red herring, and Berger did overemphasize possible legal implications of Zionist ideology rather than the ideology itself. Nevertheless, his collaboration with Mallison had not been merely an exercise in legalistic crankery. Israel had indeed claimed the force of law in the name of the Jewish people in the Eichmann case, and with the Talbot letter the State Department would effectively draw the lines along which the Israel lobby could operate in the years ahead. In so doing, the State Department, however much with a whimper, would formally reject the premise of a legal Jewish "nationhood" underlying both the Balfour Declaration and the 1947 partition.[71]

And yet Berger somehow recognized that this would be his ultimate pyrrhic victory. Immediately after the letter was publicized, Clarence Coleman issued a hostile memorandum to the leadership of the Council, accusing Berger of aggrandizing the significance of the letter to advance his own career at the expense of the Council and dealing with his contacts in Washington as a free agent.[72] There was also growing concern among many in the Council about the increase in Berger's contacts with Arab groups, particularly his regular contributions to the publications of the Organization of Arab Students.[73] Coleman's motivations were complex. On the one hand, the substance of his memo revealed that he was more concerned with egos than with serious policy differences. On the other hand, he was obviously feeling the social pressure for his association with the Council and was thus compelled to moderate its views. As it happened, the very day of receiving Coleman's memorandum, Elmer and Ruth attended a UN reception where they chatted amiably with King Hussein of Jordan, after which Berger nearly had a nervous breakdown in contemplating what was to come.[74]

By the spring of 1965 Berger wrote to Coleman threatening to resign from the Council, charging it with a lack of vision and becoming increasingly disorganized and overly bureaucratized. On top of everything else, Berger was undoubtedly shaken that same season by the death of Abraham Cronbach, the only one of his rabbinic mentors to remain loyal to the end and who embodied the Council's enduring claim to be following in the path of a cause greater than itself. A memorial service was held at the Council's annual conference that year, with Berger giving a eulogy that may well have also been a reflection on himself:

> Despite his long and fruitful years, Abraham Cronbach may have lived before his time. But then, so has almost every man who has lived beyond his death. In all the far corners of the world where there are seekers of truth and fighters for justice, this man of truth and peace has sustained others, and the memory of his life must inevitably inspire them again and again, when they weary to hold in the truth and turn their faces from justice.[75]

Several months later Berger would continue to warn of the Council's apocalypse at an executive committee meeting in which he essentially declared that the battle against the Zionist revolution in American Jewish life had been once and for all lost:

> How does it happen our Community Centers are being directed by Israelis? How does it happen a member of the Council cannot be

elected head of the "non-political" New York Federation of Jewish Philanthropies? How does it happen our religious schools are flooded with Israeli indoctrination texts? How does it happen the mass news media never miss relating Jews to the State of Israel?[76]

Finally, at the end of 1966, Leonard Sussman, who for almost twenty years Berger had considered a sort of protégé, left the Council to begin a brilliant second career with the human rights watchdog Freedom House. The Council threw a lavish farewell gathering, where, with a surely mighty pathos, Berger paid tribute to his friend in terms Sussman felt were more truly Berger's description of himself.[77]

On June 5, 1967, after a long and complex standoff with an aging Colonel Nasser, Israel attacked Egyptian and Syrian positions that had been amassing near its borders. Within six days, Israel was in possession of the entire Palestine Mandate, the Sinai Peninsula, and the Golan Heights, separating Syria from the Sea of Galilee. While for some, long-standing fears of expansionist Zionism were confirmed, the American Jewish community was overcome by a nearly messianic ecstasy that would not leave anyone in its path. Even the Israeli attack on the U.S. naval intelligence ship *Liberty* could scarcely impact the deep identification with Israel in the wider U.S. public. Lyndon Johnson would reportedly use the lives of the sailors killed aboard the *Liberty* as leverage against Reform rabbis he would meet with who would otherwise speak out against his policies in Vietnam. But this was hardly all that militated in favor of widespread support for Israel. In the deeply pro-military South, Christian Zionism, with its "dispensationalist" theology, was on the rise, helping to create overwhelming sympathy for Israel, shocking many ACJ stalwarts in that region, and turning all of their previous assumptions upside down.[78]

Indeed there were those in the ranks of the Council who felt that they should not actively oppose, if not even join, the spirit of jubilation at Israel's conquests. For his part, Berger even believed that the Council was increasingly populated by wealthy Jews who cynically joined in order to avoid the social pressures of giving $50,000 to the UJA, whereas they could get away with giving only $5,000 to the Philanthropic Fund of the Council.[79] Berger would moreover be shocked to hear the following from his friendliest State Department contact, Roger Davies: "The President has General Earle Wheeler, McGeorge Bundy, and Nicholas Katzenbach in the basement of the White House. Whatever is going on is known only to them."[80] As Berger recalled a decade later:

We had not yet been exposed to the chicanery disclosed in the
Pentagon Papers or instructed by Watergate in the technique of cover-
up. So we did not know, or had too little literary talent, to describe
what we could feel with our sixth sense was taking place. Rumor had
it that Arthur Goldberg would meet with Abba Eban and then phone
the U.S. delegation authoritative instructions. Whether true or not,
that was the way the finished product looked.[81]

Desperate for some daylight with which to make sense of the whole situation, Berger reluctantly accepted the invitation of Richard Korn, who was
now rotating the ACJ presidency with Clarence Coleman, to join him for a
game of golf with his friend Arthur Ochs Sulzberger, who had succeeded his
father as publisher of the *New York Times*. Successfully using the occasion to
secure a feature story in the *Times* on the Council's reaction to the recent war,
the story would quote Berger identifying Israel as the aggressor and criticiz-
ing several leaders of major Jewish organizations. Furious, Coleman wrote to
the new executive director of the Council, Norton Mezvinsky, speaking for
the rank-and-file: "I know that our members, by and large, want to be assured that their continued support for the Council does not mean their undying hatred of the State of Israel or, of even greater importance, their
endorsement of the position and tactics of the Arabs. They are Jews, and share
and delight in the accomplishments of their fellow Jews."[82]

As late as the end of 1967, Berger still harbored some hope that the
Council could be saved, but increasingly expressed his eagerness to retire from
active duty. In a long letter to this effect to Morris Lazaron, he even expressed
the fear that Israel was going to become a staging ground for "police actions"
in the Middle East by the U.S. military: "That is the picture as I see it, and all
I can say is no one in Washington is denying it."[83] Throughout the first half
of 1968, the Council managed to soldier on, despite the severity of its problems, publishing a bold pamphlet on "Israel as a factor in Jewish-Gentile relations in America," by a young firebrand named Michael Selzer, and hosting
the first public lecture in America by the chief rabbi of Moscow. A small but
determined group of Berger's supporters in the Council rallied to his defense
when the reckoning came at the executive committee meeting in June. But by
a wide margin, they accepted Berger's resignation from the Council.

Berger no doubt felt relieved more than anything. In a reply to a letter of
support from Lazaron, Berger stated: "I do not believe they have been 25
wasted years. I know the record will stand and, perhaps, help others to find
that justice without which there can be no peace in the Middle East. And I

think I am philosopher enough to understand the superficiality and the hypocrisy which are at the bottom of this." Taking a direct swipe at Coleman, he continued: "After all, the Prophet did not say 'Zion will be redeemed through the schmaltz handed out in the card room of the Lake Shore Country Club.'"[84] Lessing Rosenwald, though generally assenting to the mood of the Council and to Coleman's leadership, was now most of all completely withdrawn as he entered his twilight years. He and Berger would exchange letters reaffirming their high personal regard for one another in the immediate aftermath.[85] At great remove from his stormy career as the noble dissenter in American Jewish life for two generations, Rosenwald died in 1979.

After the resignation of Elmer Berger, who for all practical purposes was eponymous with the organization for twenty-five years, the American Council for Judaism became all but moribund. In a letter affirming the Council's determination to go forward after the resignation, Richard Korn insisted that "our efforts must be centered on the impact of Zionism on the American scene and on the lives and institutions of Americans of the Jewish faith,"[86] which in this context meant simply avoiding any definitive stands on events in the Middle East or even on relevant American foreign policies. By the 1970s the Council no longer had the resources to even put on the show of holding annual conferences. They maintained a national office until 1988, at which time the ACJ would have almost certainly ceased to exist were it not for the determination of Allan Brownfeld, the onetime youth group stalwart who had become an accomplished right-wing pamphleteer, to personally continue the publication of a quarterly newsletter. Even this, however, took place over the apparent objections of Clarence Coleman, who in his last years would repeatedly plead with Brownfeld to disband the Council.[87]

After the death of William Fineshriber in 1968, only Morris Lazaron remained among the core group of rabbis who had founded the ACJ in living to see the long-term aftermath of the 1967 war. Though his sympathies were squarely with Berger in the drama of the Council's implosion, at the same time he felt compelled in the weeks after the war to formally resign from American Friends of the Middle East, now a pathetic shadow of its former self, after what he felt to be their extreme apologetics for the Arab states.[88] In 1973 Lazaron would write a brief memoir for *Conservative Judaism*, the eponymous magazine of the movement, in which he declared that "Israel has proved by its indomitable courage and the sacrifices of its citizens its right to exist in peace," but also warning, "Extreme nationalism in the Diaspora will inevitably result in isolating Jews from their fellow citizens."[89]

In addition to endorsing the slowly emerging calls for a two-state solution in a letter to the *New York Times* in 1976, Lazaron also anticipated the future of progressive Judaism he would not live to see, saying of the young generation: "We must try to recapture their idealism, show them that mysticism is just as important in Judaism as in the religions of the East, and that social justice is just as important a goal in Judaism as it is in socialism or communism."[90] While a number of voices in the Jewish press took the opportunity to crow that the most stubborn and notorious of the old anti-Zionists, apart from Berger himself, was now making an apparent deathbed penance,[91] this was very far from being the case; Lazaron had been binationalist as a Brandeis Zionist in the 1920s, a loyal friend and supporter of Judah Magnes and his successors during his most active years with the ACJ, and in the aftermath of the 1967 war took what was yet the radical position in supporting a two-state solution. Devoting his last years to his passion for painting, Lazaron died while giving a show in London in 1979.

In the years leading up to 1967, Berger and the ACJ enjoyed a remarkable pyrrhic victory over their adversaries by forcing out into the open the nature of post-statehood organized Zionism and moving the American government to formally clarify its view of this foreign nationalism in its politics. American Zionism would have remained a force to be reckoned with in any event coming out of its trial by fire in the early to mid-1960s, but under ideal circumstances it would have presented American Jews with a clearly drawn choice. The consequence of 1967 would be that the choice would be made amid a pro-Zionist euphoria like nothing that could have been anticipated even in the headiest days of the 1940s. The ACJ could do quite well for itself as long as its raison d'être was the likes of the Zionist Organization of America, a group that became less and less relevant as time passed it by, but it could never have been a match for the political powerhouse that the Israel lobby was becoming.

This euphoria would also give the Israel lobby the cover it needed to transform itself into just another ethnic lobby of Cold War Washington, thereby allowing it to discard its most ostentatious trappings, such as the sale of Israel bonds at High Holiday services. Indeed, the great galvanizing force of the UJA itself largely fell by the wayside, as the financial power of AIPAC could now rest easily on a lean cadre of wealthy committed donors. The more the grassroots were kept at the periphery and were merely "pro-Israel," the less it looked like a true mass movement of American Jews, all the better for the new Israel lobby. The party organizations that had rallied the grassroots to the American Zionist Council were now forced into the larger Conference of Presidents, whose bureaucracy reduced them to shadows of their former selves. In short, because the constraints laid down on American Zionism led directly to the emergence of AIPAC as we have known it for the last generation, they represented for Berger the ultimate pyrrhic victory.

But the 1967 war would end up proving to be the ultimate pyrrhic victory for Zionism, because the price of that victory was the loss of whatever chance Israel ever had to be what Zionist ideology professed it to have always desired to be: a normal country. In effect, by conquering the whole of the Mandate, Israel was reassuming a governing responsibility for the bulk of the refugees it had displaced in the aftermath of the UN partition. While they at the same time governed them and remained steadfast to the ideology of Zionism, Israel would have, to one degree or another, a serious problem of legitimacy. And as this reality would persist, for all the success in the generation to come of reconciling Zionist prerogatives with the mundane reality of American Jewish existence, the Zionist apparatus would not for a moment renounce the doctrines by which it still claimed to govern the American Jewish community, and the institutions of that community remained as devoted to and indoctrinated by Zionism as ever before. Now more than ever the execution of Isaiah's job had fallen squarely to Elmer Berger.

7

ONE VOICE AGAINST MANY

A few weeks before his formal resignation from the ACJ, Elmer Berger traveled to Beirut to be the keynote banquet speaker at a conference hosted at the American University of Beirut. On that trip, an incident would occur while Berger spoke to a group of students at the university that would set the tone for his work for the balance of his life. After giving what had become standard remarks in an informal bull session with the students, one of them arose to earnestly inform him:

> Dr. Berger, all of us know you well. What you have tried do for the cause of justice in this part of the world is something that many of my generation will not forget. But with regret we believe that in terms of practical results you have failed, and now we ask that you understand if we feel we can no longer follow your suggestions for our actions even though we believe we are operating to put into effect the best of your thinking developed over the years.[1]

Indeed, Elmer Berger was now alone among that band of rabbis whom, even in the most optimistic part of the 1940s, he had described as "the last of the Mohicans" in having the opportunity to reflect on that failure and to make some attempt to put that reflection to good use for the sake of future generations. Only with considerable reluctance, however, would Berger even do this. In 1970 he and Ruth bought a house with an eye toward retirement in the seaside community of Long Boat Key in Sarasota, Florida. Were it solely up to him, Berger may well have lived out his days as a virtual recluse in Long Boat Key, giving most of his energy to golf. He wrote to his friend and sympathizer Don Peretz that "permanent escape to the crackers is very appealing. If I am going to be 'alienated' it might as well be where the temperature is warm, the fishing is easy and the golf always available."[2]

But as he wrote those words, Berger had already established an outfit to continue his activities as a free agent. Those who had rallied to defend Berger's honor before the ACJ formally accepted his resignation, led by an energetic Moshe Menuhin, urged him to lead them in a new organization. After accepting Berger's one condition, that he not be paid a dime for his efforts by the group, in February 1969 the group Jewish Alternatives to Zionism was formally incorporated as a non-profit in the District of Columbia:

> Dedicated to conduct an educational program applying Judaism's values of justice to knowledge of the Arab-Israel-Zionist conflict, and attempting to help advance the cause of peace in the Middle East through rejection of Zionist/Israel's "Jewish people" group nationality claims automatically relating Jews to the State of Israel; because these claims are inconsistent with American constitutional guarantees of individual citizenship rights and responsibilities for Jews as for all other Americans. This program, separating church and state, will, we hope, help to preserve and advance the integrity of Judaism's religious values.[3]

Within a couple of years, the group was permanently renamed American Jewish Alternatives to Zionism (AJAZ) in a nostalgic nod to the "Americanism" of the group's older Council supporters, with Berger assenting with the feeling that "a rose is a rose is a rose."[4] Indeed, though AJAZ was formally incorporated with a roster of supporters for tax-deduction purposes, Berger never sought for it to be a membership organization along the lines of the ACJ but rather only an outlet for his own continuing activism.[5] Along with Moshe Menuhin, these early supporters of AJAZ included such longtime ACJ stalwarts as Isaac Witkin, David Berkinghoff, and Minette Kuhn of New York; Leonard Greif, Arthur Gutman, and Edwin Rauh of Baltimore; Lewis Affelder of Cleveland; Theodore Dennery of New Orleans; Bernard Gradwohl of Lincoln, Nebraska; Jack Heiman of St. Paul, Minnesota; and Simon Rositzky of St. Joseph, Missouri.

Rounding out the list were Noel Buckner, son of Berger's most loyal of friends from his Michigan days, and Larry Margolis, a onetime member of the

ACJ staff who went on to a distinguished career in the employ of the National Conference of State Legislatures. A New Yorker named Harry Lesser served as treasurer, eventually succeeded by Berger's nephew Sanford Mendelsohn, son of his sister Adelaide. Before the end of 1969, Norton Mezvinsky was on board with AJAZ after resigning as executive director of the ACJ to pursue an academic career, quickly landing a tenure-track position at Central Connecticut State University. Mezvinsky would serve Berger not only as a loyal friend and supporter but also as an indispensable link to the slowly emerging milieu of anti-Zionist voices in the academic world, including but not limited to the field of Middle East studies.

By this time also Berger had for all practical purposes left the rabbinate. When he was still with the ACJ, he had ceased to pay dues to the Central Conference of American Rabbis and was stunned when, in spite of all the abuse he received in the public statements of that body, he was still personally solicited to continue to pay dues. At the same time, at least one major leader of the CCAR was pushing for formal expulsion proceedings against Berger, but his colleagues resisted this, undoubtedly wary of opening such a potential Pandora's box with a move sparingly reserved for those guilty of crimes or serious ethical violations, and even then in degrees.[6] In any event, Berger was able to leave the CCAR effectively by mutual agreement. In a letter to his old friend and Hebrew Union College classmate Allan Tarshish, who was now ministering to a zealously Classical Reform congregation in Winnetka, Illinois, Berger declared his determination to get on with his life "without the deadening sense of the hypocrisy and the erosion of virtually everything which ever interested me in the rabbinate."[7] However, Berger would for many years lead a seder for his old friends in New York each spring, and as late as the late 1980s, he would often officiate at intermarriages, traveling across Florida from Sarasota.[8]

Perhaps significantly, this juncture neatly coincided with the rapid increase of Berger's involvement with Arab advocates and organizations after he left the ACJ. His earliest Arab contacts in the 1950s had been mostly through Fayez Sayegh, an unofficial Palestinian representative at the United Nations who worked closely with American Friends of the Middle East. By the 1960s he was also frequently consulting with George Tomeh, the longtime Syrian ambassador to the United Nations. Berger's most lasting Arab contacts came through the Organization of Arab Students, which had been established in the late 1950s with the generous assistance of American Friends of the Middle East. Berger continued to collaborate closely with the group as it broadened its mandate by the 1970s after renaming itself the Association of Arab-American University Graduates. Among the leaders of the organization around this time was Edward Said, who would go on to a long career as a pioneering, if controversial, scholar of the Middle East and a leader of Arab American opinion.

By 1971 Berger was also closely collaborating with the new Institute for Palestine Studies in Beirut. Dedicated to relatively dispassionate scholarship, Berger was glad to have a kindred spirit in the institute's founder, Walid Khalidi, whom he felt was a refreshing voice of moderation against the increasingly militant and pro-Soviet orientation of the emerging Palestinian vanguard.[9] Early on, Berger donated all of his yearbooks and other records of the CCAR to the institute, for which they were particularly grateful, determined to help foster an understanding of Jews and Judaism in the Arab world not only by maintaining a large Jewish collection but also by providing courses in modern Hebrew.[10] Berger also furnished the institute with the working papers and other records that had been a result of his collaboration of the past several years with Tom Mallison.[11]

Not surprisingly, all this led to the eager courtship of Berger by Arab governments, to whom he had been grateful but from which he had kept a polite distance in his years with the ACJ. In the summer of 1971 Berger traveled to several Middle Eastern cities along with his new erstwhile disciple Norton Mezvinsky under the aegis of the Arab League, also addressing their international conference.[12] This led many of Berger's detractors to suspect that he was now being supported by Arab money, if they had not already suspected the ACJ of having been as well. As early as the 1950s, to be sure, Berger had been lavished with praise and offers of support from the Arabs, but most of the time he would keep a cool distance. In particular, Berger was consistently irritated by Arab propaganda literature that would mindlessly quote him as a token Jew in support of their views.[13] Nevertheless, he was lavishly treated by his Arab hosts, particularly on this 1971 sojourn. In later years, many visitors to Berger's home might have come away with the impression that the gifts on display from these trips were signs of his dependence on Arab largesse, but they merely reflected the extraordinarily high regard in which the Arabs held him, giving him the sort of gifts normally reserved for heads of state.[14]

More than anything, however, Berger was increasingly radicalized by all he had been exposed to in the wake of the 1967 war. Generally speaking, this radicalization was of a piece with the larger radicalization that had taken place in U.S. society in the late 1960s and into the 1970s. So it was with a considerably more open mind than would have been likely a decade earlier that Berger responded to the rise of the Palestinian Liberation Organization (PLO) as the decade began. In January 1970 the PLO issued a statement from its historic Algiers Conference, which set the strident and ideological tone of Palestinian activism in the years to come: "Zionism is a racist, capitalist, expansionist and colonialist system which constitutes an integral part and a spearhead of world imperialism headed by the United States. It is directed not only against the Palestinian people but against all the Arab peoples and all the other national liberation movements as well."[15] Berger began corresponding with the PLO representative in New York, Sadat Hassan, and that April even shared a stage with the new left radical Stokely Carmichael at "Palestine Week" at George Washington University.[16]

But if Berger was making some startling new radical friends, he was at the same time sure to keep the old. His ties to friendly Protestant clergy remained as strong as ever, serving on the board of the Holy Land Center in New York, led by Norman Vincent Peale, the famed pastor of the Marble Collegiate Church in Manhattan. A loyal friend going back to the days of the Committee for Peace and Justice in the Holy Land was L. Humphrey Walz, who now led the Presbyterian Synod of the Northeast. Probably the most notable of Berger's gentile friends in this era was Christopher Mayhew, the Labour Member of Parliament who was seized by the issue of justice for the Palestinians to honor the legacy of his beloved mentor, Ernest Bevin. After jointly facing off with I. L. Kenen in a debate on the Middle East at the American Enterprise Institute, Mayhew optimistically wrote to Berger that "within our lifetime we shall see the Jewish people recognize in you someone who stood between them and disaster."[17] Defecting from Labour several years later to the fossilized Liberal Party, Mayhew was arguably the father of the modern Liberal Democratic Party, thus leaving a shining legacy in the party of opposition to the New Labour warmonger Tony Blair.

Berger also grew increasingly close in friendship as well as collaboration at this time with Tom Mallison, who had been so moved by his initial contacts with Berger to pursue his calling as an advocate for the Palestinians, frequently as an attorney in international legal forums. Mallison also increasingly served as Berger's eyes and ears in Washington, which was auspicious as military aid to Israel came increasingly within the sights of senators who had achieved prominence as outspoken opponents of the Vietnam War, most notably Mark Hatfield of Oregon.[18] For his part, Berger had also cultivated the support of

Allard Lowenstein, the mastermind of the antiwar presidential campaign of Eugene McCarthy in 1968 who was now serving a single term in Congress from Long Island.[19] Indeed, even if the rise of the new left was leading to the increasing association of the Palestinian cause with revolutionary Marxism, for the time being, the more respectable voices of discontent were discovering the issue in equal numbers. Along with Senator Hatfield, Berger's old friend from earlier battles William Fulbright was now also an increasingly respected and radicalized voice in the wake of Vietnam.

There was no question of the stakes to Berger and his associates, who shrewdly recognized that this was a critical moment in determining the future of American foreign policy. As early as 1969, when the secretary of state in the new Nixon administration, William Rogers, began to articulate a vision for resolving the Middle East conflict generally along the lines that had been promoted by Eisenhower and Kennedy, Berger wrote a letter of support to Rogers but with a candid warning: "The most certain and democratic defense against special interest Zionist pressures is full and ventilating challenge. If in-depth explanations of American policy conclusions are not forthcoming, Mr. Eban will become again Assistant Secretary of State for the Near East."[20] Rogers, however, would prove to be among the most ineffectual secretaries of state in history, with Richard Nixon's foreign policy almost totally dictated by Henry Kissinger. Berger would have extreme contempt for both men and was especially graphic toward Nixon in his personal letters.

It was perhaps fitting then that Berger would make his most memorable, and indeed only, appearance in the U.S. political circus when Nixon ran for reelection in 1972. Nixon's Democratic opponent that year, George McGovern, had been a latecomer to the Senate backlash against the Vietnam War, but by the time he became the Democratic presidential nominee, he was advocating for America to "come home," as few had done since before the Second World War. McGovern did hedge his bets when it came to Israel, calling for aggressive U.S. action to prevent Soviet military penetration of the Arab states. Even this, however, was not enough to prevent his legion of detractors from questioning McGovern's commitment to Israel, with his opponents for the Democratic nomination such as Hubert Humphrey challenging his votes against military aid to Israel, as well as the overall implications for the slowly emerging "special relationship" of McGovern's larger commitment to drastically scale back America's military commitments.

On July 6, 1972, John Roche, one of many Humphrey loyalists who would help build the neoconservative movement over the course of the 1970s, devoted his syndicated column to the subject of McGovern and Israel. After summarizing the broad skepticism of McGovern's pro-Israel noises on the campaign trail by remarking that "in a real crisis, McGovern would send a battalion of the Peace Corps and go to the UN wearing a yarmulke," Roche focused his crosshairs on Rick Stearns, a close campaign adviser whose youth symbolized McGovern's association, for good and ill, with campus radicalism.

In 1965 Stearns, then a Harvard University senior, had helped arrange for Berger to address an Arab student conference, writing in a letter of thanks, "Your speech made the largest single impact of any we heard. Agreement with your position on Palestine, I think, is 100 percent."[21] Roche added, after quoting the letter, "Berger has not merely repudiated the Zionist position, he has, as the use of the code word 'Palestine' in the above letter indicates, denied the very legitimacy of the State of Israel and adopted what is, in essence, a pro-Arab position."[22] Berger first wrote a letter of reassurance to Stearns, confiding: "I hope if the Senator wins the nomination he might really give the most serious consideration to clarifying his position on the Middle East. A really fresh start could be a genuine contribution to 'the new politics.'"[23]

Berger then proceeded to write a letter to the editor in response to the Roche column, stating: "I cannot, of course, speak for Mr. Stearns, much less for Senator McGovern. But it is more important for the American people to understand the complex Arab/Israel/Zionist problem as accurately as possible than to know the opinions of Mr. Stearns, or me, or for that matter, even of Mr. Roche."[24] What this episode illustrated was the centrality of Israel in the disaffection from McGovern of those Cold War liberals who would become the neoconservatives, that is, their fear for the survival of Zionism and Israel if America should once again be a republic, not an empire. As Norman Podhoretz would put it in the definitive statement of his neocon faith:

> There was, to be sure, one thing that even the most passionately committed American Zionists were reluctant to do, and that was to face up to the fact that continued American support for Israel depended upon continued American involvement in international affairs—from which it followed that an American withdrawal into the kind of isolationist mood that had prevailed most recently between the two world wars, and that now looked as though it might soon prevail again, represented a direct threat to the security of Israel.[25]

But even at this early stage, progressive Jewish voices emerged who were determined to resist the rise of neoconservatism. One of the earliest, who even reached out to Berger, was Everett Gendler, an ordained Conservative rabbi who began the *havurah* movement of young Jews inspired by the counterculture to create space for progressive Jewish religion outside the authority of the Conference of Presidents. In 1970 Gendler joined the rising star of the American left, Noam Chomsky, in circulating an open letter to protest the growing repression of dissent in Israel, which Berger gladly accepted the invitation to sign.[26] The following year, the signers of the letter formed an organization, the Committee on New Alternatives in the Middle East (CONAME), whose supporters included Benjamin Spock, Sidney Lens, Todd Gitlin, Michael Lerner, and Abbie Hoffman. Gendler was also joined by his cofounder of the *havurah* movement, Arthur Waskow, who, after an early disillusionment with politics, was one of the first to be ordained by the Reconstructionist Rabbinical College, founded in 1968 by an aging and increasingly disaffected Mordecai Kaplan. Both Gendler and Waskow were old friends of Norton Mezvinsky—Gendler, a family friend from his Iowa youth, and Waskow from the University of Wisconsin.

The executive director of CONAME, Allan Solomonow, would be on friendly terms with Berger and even seek him out for advice, which of course he was happy to give.[27] But Berger was also wary of his new friends on the left and of their commitment, confiding to Mezvinsky:

> What is so distressing is that these people, just seeing the first light of dawn, have largely ignored what you and I and a few others have known and put on the record long ago. I find either a certain pretentiousness about this, or careless study. Or, perhaps, fear to identify with any of us because we have been targeted. Well, if they think they will be any more loved for their late discoveries then they are still too naïve to be in the big leagues.[28]

Still, the Jews of the new left had Berger's unfailing sympathy. As he assured his young conservative admirer Allan Brownfeld: "While, as you know, I am anything but a radical leftist, I think the coordinated attacks of organized Jewish groups on the youth of the left is deplorable. It is motivated, quite openly, by political considerations for Israel and is certain to alienate even more young Jews."[29]

However, at the same time, much of Berger's concern about the commitment of this generation to thoroughgoing anti-Zionism would prove well founded. A number of the more vocal "liberals" of the Reform rabbinate had joined CONAME and would soon form a parallel rabbinical organization,

Breira, which would call for Israel to engage in direct negotiations with the PLO and even look toward the long-term goal of a two-state solution. The key leader of this group was Arnold Jacob Wolf, who sought to coopt the *havurah* movement for Reform and ultimately evolved to the point that he no longer regarded himself to be a Reform Jew. Also notable was Balfour Brickner, whose father had been Louis Wolsey's militant Zionist successor in Cleveland. Always idiosyncratic, a decade earlier he had hosted Palestinian representatives (as well as ACJ friend Norman Thomas) at his Washington, D.C., congregation and now was declaring, "I've never adopted 'My country right or wrong' for America and I'll be damned if I adopt it for Israel."[30]

When Uri Avnery, then a member of the Knesset, came to America in the early 1970s to promote a two-state solution, he was originally scheduled to speak on thirty campuses through Hillel. But by the time he arrived, Brickner was the only one of the thirty rabbis who had not canceled, and he even proceeded to show Avnery the secret memo of the Anti-Defamation League that had led to the cancellations.[31] But Wolf and Brickner remained steadfastly committed to Zionist ideology and quickly grew hostile to the radicalism of Gendler and Waskow. Attempting to hold the middle ground in Breira was Joseph Asher, the German-born rabbi of Temple Emanu-El in San Francisco, but the tortured history of Zionist controversy in that community put him in an extremely delicate spot. Indeed, the Zionist Organization of America had been quick to publish a pamphlet comparing Breira to the American Council for Judaism.[32] All this conspired toward the disappearance of Breira by the late 1970s and the adoption of a new platform by the Reform movement in 1976 that did away with the last remaining traces of ambiguity about Zionism. Brickner was undoubtedly especially haunted by the controversy, given his personal connection to Berger and the battles of his father's generation, and when asked about it years later would descend into an angry obscenity-laden rant.[33]

But Berger had plenty of headaches as well on his left flank, as it were. Around the same time as the founding of AJAZ, Alfred Lilienthal had begun publishing a newsletter, *Middle East Perspective*, which he hoped might fill the void that had been left by William Zukerman and the *Jewish Newsletter*. Lilienthal had grown close to Moshe Menuhin as he grew apart from the ACJ in the 1960s, and it was Menuhin who intervened to get the newsletter off the ground much as he did to rally Berger's loyalists in the ACJ, ultimately leading to the establishment of AJAZ. As early as 1969, Berger was urging his supporters to subscribe to the newsletter and even contributed material to it, but as before remained wary enough of Lilienthal to insist that his name never appear on the newsletter.[34] But Berger's feelings toward Lilienthal were more of pity than of contempt, and they would remain in touch at least through the 1970s. As he stated to an old Council stalwart who raised concerns about Lilienthal's reemergence: "He is a bright boy and, in a way, he is performing a service. My quarrels with Al have all had to do with his paranoia and his total inability to remain on any reasonable working basis with anyone."[35]

As media savvy as he had been in his younger years, in the years that he published *Middle East Perspective* Lilienthal was a genuine rival to Berger as the public face of Jewish anti-Zionism in America, appearing more than once as a guest on William F. Buckley's *Firing Line*. Indeed, this was partly because of Lilienthal's extremism—as early as the 1950s, Lilienthal had been an avowed Arab partisan to a degree never countenanced by Berger. Many of Berger's friends were also alienated by the fact that Lilienthal was increasingly aligning himself with the Neturei Karta, the notorious anti-Zionist Orthodox sect that was rapidly becoming the more favored Jewish voice in Arab propaganda.[36] He ceased the publication of *Middle East Perspective* in 1984 after a failed attempt to hand it over to Allan Brownfeld, who grew distrustful of Lilienthal after being exposed to his paranoid tendencies.[37] Alfred Lilienthal would, however, have the distinction of being the only major actor from the battle against Jewish statehood to live to see the Second Intifada and its aftermath, and would be honored at its peak with a tribute gala by the Jewish peace activists Jeff Halper and Josh Reubner before finally passing away in 2008.

If Berger ultimately had patience for Lilienthal in these late and more radical years, he would, however, eventually have a bitter break with Moshe Menuhin. After Menuhin had been forced to self-publish his definitive tome *The Decadence of Judaism in Our Time* in 1965, a second edition had been published in 1969 by the Institute for Palestine Studies, complete with an updated section on the 1967 war and its aftermath, that included a lengthy discussion of the implosion of the ACJ. By 1972 Menuhin hoped to publish yet another new edition, which was picked up by the Arab League Information Center in New York. Berger, however, was deeply disturbed that this new edition of the book included an extended attack on the younger generation of Jews disillusioned with Zionism, and when Berger informed Menuhin of his concerns, he then proceeded to attack Berger for going wobbly. By the time the new book was published, which Berger regarded as nothing more than an extended diatribe against allegedly faint-of-heart anti-Zionists, Menuhin formally resigned from AJAZ, but not before sending angry letters to the group's other supporters leading to several more resignations.[38]

But a younger and more vibrant generation of "Canaanites" was emerging as Moshe Menuhin tragically alienated every friend he ever had by the end of his long life. With Uri Avnery increasingly becoming the elder statesman of the movement, the new rising star was Israel Shahak, a Holocaust survivor and chemistry professor at the Hebrew University of Jerusalem. Shahak had long regarded Berger as a formative influence, and he became fast friends with Norton Mezvinsky when he entered academia. With the disappearance of Ihud by the time of the 1967 war, Shahak would found a new group, the Israeli League for Human and Civil Rights. After warning in a speech in America that "either Israel will accept the basic values of the western world and become a just society, or it will become an openly fascist state," Shahak became involved in a long war of words with none other than Morton Applebaum, the rabbi who had succeeded Berger in his pulpit in Flint.[39] In 1994 Shahak would begin publishing a series of probative works with *Jewish History, Jewish Religion*, which sought to build on the narrative established by Berger in *A Partisan History of Judaism*.

As Berger got to know the rising stars of the new generation and with their incredible appetite for public controversy inundating him, he had at least one old friend from that generation who essentially remained a kindred spirit. Ned Hanauer, the former stalwart of the ACJ youth group who had Council loyalists on both sides of his family, had been offered the job of executive director of the Council after the departure of Leonard Sussman just before the 1967 war but declined in anticipation of the Council's imminent implosion.[40] By the late 1960s, however, the independently wealthy Hanauer had formed his own advocacy group with the assistance of the Jewish Peace Fellowship, Search for Peace in the Middle East, largely supported by Christian clergy from the antiwar movement and focused almost exclusively on media relations.

Berger was actively consulting Hanauer in his new undertaking, putting him in touch with Tom Mallison and other advocates in Washington for the Palestinian refugees. But Berger was not forthcoming with Hanauer's desire for the financial support that could have created a membership organization to fill the void left by the ACJ and potentially included the new left community, particularly that to which Hanauer was himself close in Cambridge.[41] Never tiring, Hanauer died very suddenly and tragically of pancreatic cancer in August 2006, just weeks after the Israeli war in Lebanon that finally marked the turning point in favor of his life's work.

The year 1973 would begin for Berger with the acquaintance of the young man who would be his most loyal friend in Florida. That January, Justus Doenecke, a young professor at the New College of Florida in Sarasota, wrote to Berger, informing Berger that he was on the mailing list of AJAZ and was eager to meet him, having just learned that Berger had taken up residence in Sarasota.[42] Berger wrote back with equal anticipation, having not yet gotten around to visiting New College and making contacts there.[43] Already a leading scholar of the movement against American intervention in the Second World War as he first entered academia, Doenecke was part of a small vanguard in the scholarly community trying to reassert the tradition of noninterventionism in the wake of the Vietnam War and had thus become greatly interested in the Middle East after 1967. Doenecke thus immediately put Berger in touch with his historian comrades, Leonard Liggio and James J. Martin, along with former ACJ member Murray Rothbard. Berger would write warmly to Rothbard after being reacquainted that "lively conversation is one of the few real pleasures left in this increasingly dismal world," and Rothbard would compliment him in kind, writing that "there is no one I'd rather have praise anything I've written on the Middle East than yourself."[44]

In October of that year, Egypt and Syria once again went to war against Israel in an attempt to avenge their defeat in 1967. In a letter to Ned Hanauer, Berger expressed his exasperation with all the actors:

> In my opinion our great President is up to his usual practices, trifling with the welfare of the country and perhaps the peace of the world, claiming "new initiatives" while doing little more than re-shuffling the old clichés and demonstrated failures. On the Arab side I am deeply disappointed at the evidence which suggests that they have learned nothing about public relations, at least in the United States, since 1967.[45]

Indeed, Berger was deeply alarmed that the United States was finding itself embroiled in the conflict as never before, joining his friend Norman Dacey who issued a press release on behalf of his American Palestine Committee, warning, "For the President to send troops to Palestine without Congressional mandate would go beyond existing precedents."[46] There was undoubtedly cause for alarm when it came to the president, who secretly invaded Cambodia while the Watergate proceedings were in full swing. Richard Nixon ultimately sent an airlift of arms to Israel but went no further.

But the October war would be a watershed for Israel as it began to come back to reality after the euphoria of 1967 and to contemplate the possibility that not all of its problems could be solved militarily. This was helped along in 1974 when the Arab League formally declared the PLO to be the sole legitimate representative of the Palestinian Arabs. With this came formal admission of the PLO to the UN General Assembly and a momentous address that year to that body by the chairman of the PLO, Yasser Arafat. Berger issued a formal statement of welcome to the PLO on behalf of AJAZ, stating that "this is only the latest episode in an unfolding—and still unfinished—process of fulfilling historic justice."[47] The day after Arafat addressed the General Assembly, Berger had his one and only meeting with him in Arafat's hotel suite, in which he generally complimented the speech and gave what he described as his standard public relations advice to the Arabs.[48]

By this time, however, Berger was beginning to back away from many of his more radical flourishes that marked the early and most active years of AJAZ. In responding to a letter from Justus Doenecke expressing serious concerns about Arafat, Berger assured him: "I too criticize both my leftist Israeli friends and those of a similar stripe from among the Arabs for losing the impact of what they say in the clichés of Marxism. In fact I made this very criticism of Arafat's speech to the General Assembly."[49] Berger clarified his views further in a letter to Leonard Sussman, who remained a close friend and whose employers at Freedom House were none too pleased with the turn in the international arena of which the rise of the PLO was ineluctably a part: "I won't comment on all the judgments about the UN bias. To a large extent they are true. But I am disgusted with the simplistic commentary offered about it by most of the wiseacres."[50] Thus, while the following year Berger spoke of "the recent, fairly frenetic effort of the U.S. at the UN to oppose the accurate labeling of Zionism as 'racist'," he had good cause to also be skeptical of how political such a move was.[51] In the same letter, he also presciently declared that "the Kissinger pledge to Israel to oppose, almost automatically, any political moves against Israel in the UN is downright silly."[52]

As Berger began to back away from his more radical associations of the past several years, the shape of the long-term aftermath of the 1967 war was finally beginning to reveal itself. In 1977 Menachem Begin, the onetime leader of the *Irgun* who had been spurned for decades by the liberal base of American Zionism, was elected prime minister at the head of his new Likud Party. This could have been the moment for a real breakthrough by the groups that had emerged in the past decade such as CONAME or even Breira, but a substantive change in the relationship of American Jews to Israel did not materialize. In fact, if anything, what it led to was the ability of these liberals to position themselves as "progressive Zionists," that is, while typically scathing in their criticism of the Israeli right, not only affirming their loyalty to Zionist ideology but also affirming the legitimacy and authority of the "official" Jewish community, represented by the Conference of Presidents and increasingly by AIPAC itself.[53]

Nonetheless, there also emerged a ray of hope in the presidency of Jimmy Carter. In 1978 Berger published his *Memoirs of an Anti-Zionist Jew* with the Institute for Palestine Studies, which was really just the expansion of his synonymous 1975 article in the *Journal of Palestine Studies* into a monograph. Somewhat hopeful at the early stages of the process that led to Israel's peace treaty with Egypt and withdrawal from the Sinai, Berger wrote:

> Mr. Carter continues to give off emanations suggesting he fully understands the portentous dimensions of his choice. He has just said failure to reach a settlement could be a disaster for the whole world. With broad brush but in the clearest language any President of the United States has yet used, he has painted in what is expected of Israel by way of the concessions almost everyone agrees are needed to achieve a just peace.[54]

But Berger also went on to anticipate the problems raised by Carter's diplomacy—the explosion of the U.S. subsidy to Israel and now also to Egypt and how this would mire America in the region's problems as never before. Berger was also no doubt disturbed by what it implied was necessary for an ubermilitant such as Begin to concede just the most utterly impractical of Israel's conquests, the Sinai. All this, of course, was testimony to the rising power of the new Israel lobby.

In 1979 two other events would unmistakably burst the hopeful spirit that had defined so much of Berger's activities in the decade since he left the ACJ. The first was the Iranian Revolution, which overthrew the U.S. client regime installed a generation before by Berger's onetime golfing partner, Kermit Roosevelt.[55] This rude reminder of all he had come to find so woefully misguided on the part of the Council was compounded by the fact that it marked the arrival of Islamic religious enthusiasms into "the problem," as Berger had come to call it in shorthand, an undoubtedly troubling development for a committed anticlericalist who came of age at the Hebrew Union College of the 1920s. But the other event would be more personal and devastating. Ruth, Elmer's devoted wife of thirty-three years and at no time more so than in the past decade as his sometimes personal secretary—and, like

her husband, a heavy smoker—died that summer of lung cancer. For virtually his whole career, and especially during the previous ten years, Elmer
Berger had been one voice against many, but as he entered his twilight years,
he increasingly found himself truly alone.

8

BEFORE THE STORM

Whatever hope had existed for a new beginning for America's place in the world after Vietnam, which had infused such hope into AJAZ in the 1970s, was dashed by the election of Ronald Reagan in 1980. Running with a message that implied the restoration of "national greatness," Reagan saw not only the ascendant neoconservatives flock to him but also a significant portion of the Israel lobby, which resented Jimmy Carter's humbling of Menachem Begin, despite it having likely been the greatest gift a U.S. president ever gave to the long-term security of the State of Israel. In this new order of things, Zionism would now be inextricably linked to the military and propaganda might of the American colossus, and the party of that colossus first began to take recognizable form in the Republican Party of Ronald Reagan. It was, to be sure, a far cry from the Republican Party that had commanded the loyalty of Elmer Berger's pacifist mentor, Louis Wolsey, in the era when successive Republican administrations championed the Kellogg-Briand Pact to outlaw war.

As Berger faced this strange new world without the rock he once had in his wife, Ruth, he would rush into a new relationship. Roselle Tekiner, an Irish Catholic by birth, had been married to a wealthy Turkish importer in New York and was now a professor of Middle East studies at the New College of Florida. Introduced by a couple with whom Berger had helped sponsor a community theater in nearby Siesta Key, and being both of a generation where such marriages of convenience were common, if not customary, Elmer and Roselle were married in 1980. The marriage would be brief, however, and ended in annulment. Berger remained an unbowed chain-smoker even after the death of Ruth, and this was ultimately irreconcilable with Roselle, who suffered from asthma.[1]

The two nevertheless remained close companions for the remainder of Berger's life, and Roselle would become an important new lifeline for Berger to what was happening in the field of Middle East scholarship. Among the new developments on this front was the launch, in response to the growing specter of the Israel lobby after the election of Reagan, of a new magazine, *Washington Report for Middle East Affairs*, in 1982. Its founder and editor was Andrew Kilgore, a veteran of the Foreign Service who had been a protégé of Loy Henderson. Kilgore had been the consul general in Arab Jerusalem during Berger's 1955 visit, when the two men began a long friendship. Other friends of Berger who would be involved with the magazine included Tom Mallison and L. Humphrey Walz.

Much of the balance of Berger's life would curiously, considering his typical modesty, be defined by looking ahead to his legacy. This began in earnest at the beginning of the decade with a PhD student writing his dissertation on the history of the American Council for Judaism. Thomas Kolsky, born in Poland at the height of the Second World War and arriving in Israel with his family in the autumn of 1948, was a passionate student of Zionism when he returned as a postgraduate to study in Israel after his family had immigrated to the United States. His advisers were none other than the leading court historians of Zionism, Howard Sachar and Melvin Urofsky. After Kolsky was initially interested in studying the first Jewish immigrants' encounters with the Palestinian Arabs before Herzl, Sachar and Urofsky convinced him instead to study the ACJ, seeking a psychoanalytic study of the Council that would definitively demonstrate the maladjustment of the "self-hating Jews" who dared to oppose the founding of a Jewish state. But Berger quickly found in Kolsky a serious and independent-minded student, writing to Leonard Sussman: "I am rather involved with a graduate student who is doing a doctoral dissertation on the Council. Off and on I have spent a good deal of time answering very good questions he has put to me."[2]

In fact, Sachar, who was now Kolsky's formal adviser at George Washington University, was so appalled that Kolsky would not write an ideological treatise that he eventually cut him off, at which point a friend of Kolsky on the faculty—Leo Ribuffo, a noted scholar of American Protestantism—had to see him through. One other notable ally Kolsky had in his research was Jacob

Marcus, who personally underwrote his research at the Archives of Hebrew Union College. All this still did not ultimately spare Kolsky the withering abuse of both Sachar and Urofsky when they were impaneled at his thesis defense.[3] The incredible uproar over Kolsky's essentially even-handed dissertation provides an indispensable window into the fanaticism that, well over a generation later, Berger and the ACJ still inspired in the Zionist imagination. Even as the twentieth century was nearing its end, the totalitarian impulse of Zionist ideology to brand any opposition as illegitimate and intolerable was alive and well.

Any remaining doubt that Zionist unity was beginning to crack by this time—the shortcomings of the new left challenge notwithstanding—was put in hand by the Israeli invasion of Lebanon in 1982. For the first time, unfailingly Zionist American liberals were beginning to seriously question Israeli policies and objectives. The Reform rabbis who had earlier belonged to Breira were condemning the war from their pulpits, if also lashing out at more radical Jewish critics. Shortly after the war in Lebanon began, Berger headlined an antiwar rally in Florida with former Senator James Abourezk of South Dakota, an Arab American who had been an ally since the 1970s.[4] Having no doubt that the war in Lebanon marked a turning point, Berger wrote to Leonard Sussman: "But now, the sneaky cultivation of the 'anti-Semitic' smear strengthens my opinion that the quintessential Zionist, and even some theoreticians of the Labor Alignment, are afraid the recent adventures may lead to a serious investigation of the ideological basis of the state and one of the major considerations of its foreign policy."[5]

In May 1983, as the war dragged on, Berger helped organize a large conference in Washington on the fallout of the war whose speakers included such friends as Tom Mallison, Norton Mezvinsky, Don Peretz, Walid Khalidi, and Allan Solomonow, along with such other Washington friends as Congressman Pete McCloskey of California, journalist Georgie Anne Geyer, and a member of the Neturei Karta.[6] But Berger also had a very practical concern arising out of the Lebanon war. Years earlier, against the advice of both Norton Mezvinsky and Justus Doenecke, Berger had decided to give the papers of AJAZ to the Institute for Palestine Studies in Beirut. The institute had been a victim of Israel's bombing campaign, but it took a long time before both the literal and figurative rubble could be cleared to assess the scope of damage to its archives. But the historical record of AJAZ would be saved, thanks to the intervention of Jacob Marcus, who was then entering his nineties but was active as ever with the American Jewish Archives.

Berger had a considerable exchange with his old professor while he attempted to secure a microfilm of the AJAZ papers for his archives, as it also coincided with an invitation Berger received to a banquet honoring Marcus. Berger took the opportunity to assure his dear friend and teacher: "I am what I am mostly because of my years at the College, when its mission was clear and its character displayed integrity. Your instruction was a large part of what for me were character-forming days and I rejoice in the inheritance."[7] Taking the opportunity for reflection in acknowledging a letter from Marcus informing him that the archives had received the AJAZ microfilm, Berger confided: "My biggest regret is that I have never had the time to try to write a real critique of Zionism, both as an ideology and a political/national movement, and now as a state. Most of what we have on the subject is rather simplistic history. But I have never found the time to do a systematic and really coherent, complete analysis."[8]

As he began to enter a truer state of retirement, Berger found himself increasingly aloof from the passing scene. Whereas some might have given points to Ronald Reagan for his ultimate withdrawal from Lebanon and general coolness to Israel throughout his administration, Berger retained enough of the radicalizing effect of the 1970s to resist this: "The less said about his so called Middle East policy, the better. How anyone with an ounce of sense could have either encouraged or condoned an Israeli solution for Lebanon is an answer for only cabalists to unearth."[9] Berger was even sympathetic to the presidential campaigns of Jesse Jackson in the 1980s, but not enough to act on it in any way.[10] Indeed, much of his activism, such as it was, in these twilight years was of a nature typical to men of his age. In one particularly colorful example, Berger wrote a long letter, along with his regular $100 contribution, to his local PBS affiliate complaining about the "Civilization and the Jews" series narrated by Abba Eban and received a favorable response from the head of the affiliate.[11]

In 1985 Berger keynoted a conference of the Arab-American Anti-Discrimination Committee, which had just been founded by James Abourezk. He used this occasion to focus on the rising phenomenon of Christian Zionism in America, particularly as championed by Jerry Falwell. After sardonically commenting that "if the Moral Majority has its way, and rebuilds the old sacrificial Temple, in all likelihood the moneychangers driven out by Jesus will be welcomed to help pay off the mortgage, probably held by the Histadrut," Berger warned of the danger posed by this rising power in U.S. politics:

We who believe in the separation of church and state, who consider free and responsible public debate of issues in the public domain the lifeblood of democracy cannot accept the attempt of a Falwell to inhibit this right with such totalitarian cant as the following, quoted from his "Old Time Gospel Hour" on January 30, 1980—"We are so pro-Zionist, pro-Jewish, we are the only thing, the only one driving force in America that will not allow Washington to lift her hand of support from Israel."[12]

Remarkably, Berger even ended this speech on an optimistic note at this late and weary stage of his life and witness: "I sense something of a soaring human spirit which will not be denied, of the resurrection of the Old Testament Prophets and their Judaism and the Christianity of Jesus and the universalism of Islam."[13]

The following year, Berger also addressed a gathering of the African National Congress, at the height of the struggle against apartheid. Berger remained at least peripherally engaged with the larger scene of pro-Palestinian activism in this era. He was the keynote speaker in 1986 at a dinner honoring Paul Findley, the onetime ranking Republican on the House Foreign Relations Committee who had been victim of one of the most notable AIPAC "scalpings," with the publication of his book attacking the Israel lobby, *They Dare to Speak Out*. Proving himself as perceptive about AIPAC as he had been about the more ostentatious forms of the Zionist apparatus in his day, Berger emphasized in this speech:

> There is very little real secrecy about these activities and, in a strict sense, certainly no deep, dark conspiracies. In fact, the AIPAC managers boast of their achievements, no doubt believing that nothing succeeds like success and to underline, perhaps even to exaggerate the public perception of their power increases the efficacy of their intimidation potential.[14]

Berger's entire speech was even praised and entered into the record in a special order speech on the House floor by John Conyers of Michigan.

Berger was also honored that year with a banquet put on by Samir Rabbo, a wealthy Arab American in Brattleboro, Vermont, who ran a small vanity press, Amana Books. The event was held August 23, 1986, at the Unitarian Church of Peterborough, New Hampshire, and the papers presented were eventually published in a *festschrift* titled *Anti-Zionism: Analytical Reflections*.

The book would not be published until 1989, however, after Berger came to suspect that Rabbo had constructed the whole project as an elaborate embezzlement scheme and filed a lawsuit before settling out of court.[15] Despite this obstacle, the book still served as an effective fulfillment of Berger's wish to have written a comprehensive critique of Zionist ideology. With several carefully and specifically focused pieces by other authors, the book began with a reproduced comprehensive pamphlet Berger had written for AJAZ in 1981.

In this essay, he emphasized that Zionist ideology has never been addressed in the international, particularly American, efforts to resolve the Israeli-Arab conflict:

> Recognition of this "Jewish people" nationality concept is the first priority of Zionism's diplomacy. It is the cornerstone of the Zionist state's system of nationality rights and obligations. Appreciation of the centrality of this factor is indispensable to any assessment of Israel's long-range adaptability to the Middle East. It is therefore indispensable to any evaluation of any formula touted to solve the Palestine problem with the desired "just and enduring peace."[16]

Edited by the two individuals who had effectively become Berger's family, Norton Mezvinsky and Roselle Tekiner, the other contributions to the volume included Tom Mallison on Zionism and international law, Israel Shahak with an early exposition of his groundbreaking work on the late-medieval/early-modern period of Jewish history and its significance for Zionism, and Mezvinsky's thoroughly researched requiem for Reform anti-Zionism.

On the heels of this book, Berger would receive what must have been a truly unexpected surprise with respect to the interest in his legacy. In 1989 he would be contacted by a rabbinical student at Hebrew Union College who was interested in writing his dissertation on him. Mark Glickman, who had grown up in the onetime ACJ stronghold of the Chicago North Shore, was inspired to enter the rabbinate by his uncle Robert Marx, who had been a protégé in Chicago of Arnold Jacob Wolf before forming his own congregation of a more Classical Reform orientation. A militant voice in protesting Chicago's racial inequalities, Rabbi Marx had become notorious around this time for remaining a loyal friend to Jesse Jackson after he had fallen out of favor with much of the Jewish community and had even been a friendly acquaintance of Clarence Coleman. Glickman had first become interested in studying Berger after he had learned about the ACJ in an undergraduate course on Zionism and the Middle East and made them the subject of his term paper for the course.[17]

As Glickman shrewdly prefaced his dissertation:

I have always been fascinated by heretics. Interestingly, heretics rarely define themselves as such—rarely does a person adopt a stance which he or she feels at the outset runs contrary to the fundamental precepts of a given community. Instead, they usually feel that their views are logical extensions of those very same principles upon which their community is founded. Heretics are therefore usually deemed such by others, and thus the study of them reveals a negative image of the community from which he or she dissents. In other words, a study of a heretic from our own community is a study of what we are not, and by learning what we are not, we also learn a great deal about what we are.[18]

Whereas Thomas Kolsky focused his dissertation on the ACJ in its battle against Jewish statehood, Glickman focused on Berger's thought or "ideology" and secondarily on his biography, along with a considerable discussion of Berger in the Zionist imagination.

Glickman began predisposed to a negative view of Berger but nonetheless accepted his invitation to spend a weekend with him in Florida and interview him for would become an indispensable oral history. Berger opened up to this young student for the rabbinate with a warm regard for his memories of Hebrew Union College, as he had expressed a few years earlier in writing to Jacob Marcus. It was, perhaps, for this reason that Berger was extremely private about this dissertation and did not even discuss it with many of his closest friends.[19] Berger also revealed in his interviews with Glickman a remarkable moderation in where his views on the Middle East had evolved—he now favored a two-state solution but along lines of mutual cooperation envisioned by the original UN partition, and he spoke for his highly Westernized Arab friends such as Edward Said and Walid Khalidi in expressing their benighted view of Yasser Arafat, that he was unsavory but "did what had to be done."[20] All this prompted Glickman to remark with shock in the middle of the interviews to Berger that "you are not an extremist,"[21] and he ultimately concluded his dissertation by declaring that, after much soul searching, he was now in favor of an eventually "de-Zionized" Israel.[22]

This dissertation was being written at the height of the First Intifada, which began in 1987, and the prospect for a two-state solution emerged following the speech by Arafat to the United Nations in 1988, which opened the door to that possibility. This also coincided with the initial exposure of the depths to which the Israel lobby, particularly through its indispensable neoconservative allies, was plumbing Washington in foreign policy intrigue. This occurred with the conviction not only of Jonathan Pollard for Israeli espionage but of such operatives as Elliott Abrams in the Iran-Contra scandal. The growing menace of neoconservatism and its implications for the future of Zionist calumny seem to have been totally lost on Berger, who simply attributed Iran-Contra to the same old Washington power games: "In Washington, there is no end of sanctimony and pontificating to the Iran-Contra engineers. Oh, for the good old days of simple skullduggery like Teapot Dome and such lovable philanderers as Warren Harding!"[23]

This pattern held in Berger's response to the Gulf War in 1991, completely ignoring the growing number of voices such as Gore Vidal and Pat Buchanan who indicted the Israel lobby for precipitating this war to inaugurate a "new world order," if he was even aware of them at all:

> I found the whole thing disgusting. The sanctions would have worked and we could have avoided the cost which I have seen run up to $1.6 billion a day. But it seems clear to me Bush wanted the war. Its organization became for him a tour de force and erasing, for the moment, his image as a wimp. It will now be easier to win support for the defense industries to sustaining economic "prosperity" in the face of a recession—and to hell with long term effects of inflation and the neglect of peacetime consumer production.[24]

Still, the vast consequences of the war for "the problem" were hardly lost on him: "Bush has brushed off suggestions that it will be necessary to address Israel's aggressions and violations of international law in order to cut Saddam down to size, but long term I believe the Iraqi's bullying may force some things that the U.S./Israeli combine has successfully evaded in previous 'diplomacies.'"[25] Berger may well have been chastened by his radical experiences of the 1970s against joining the brutal polemical warfare of others. In any event he surely felt he was getting too old for it.

He therefore decided to devote his remaining years to dispassionate scholarship. In the late 1980s, Anis Kassem, a Palestinian graduate student of Tom Mallison at George Washington University, approached Berger about writing a journal article interpreting the newly declassified U.S. documents on the armistice negotiations of 1948–49. Before long the project had exploded into a full-fledged book. Indeed, Berger's public appearances in these last active years were increasingly focused on the dry facts of this diplomatic history going all the way back to the Zionist memorandum presented at Versailles in 1919. The final product was *Peace for Palestine: First Lost Opportunity*, published by the University of Florida Press in 1993. Berger declared in this last and most impressive of his books: "This detailed analysis of the 1948–49 armistice talks does not presume to be a panacea. But insofar as it highlights the causes for the failure of those talks—in fact, insofar as it discloses that glossing over the basic issues assured a continuation of war—it may identify those basic issues."[26] Don Peretz, Berger's old friend and now an elder scholar of this field, wrote a foreword to the book with the confident assurance: "There are many who will refute this book without a glance at the first page because it was written by Elmer Berger. The loss is theirs."[27]

The timing of the book's publication was extremely fortuitous. Just weeks after its release, on September 13, 1993, Yasser Arafat and Yitzhak Rabin, the prime minister of Israel, signed an agreement on the White House lawn affirming their mutual commitment to negotiate a two-state solution to the Israeli-Palestinian conflict. This likely came as somewhat of a surprise to Berger, who quite erroneously predicted in his interviews with Mark Glickman that the sliver of hope for such a pass rested not with Rabin but with his more hawkish rival in the Labor Party, Shimon Peres.[28] Berger likely held this view because of his memories of Rabin as an aggressive Israeli ambassador to the United States a generation earlier. Yet, while Rabin famously said of his negotiations with the Palestinian Liberation Organization that "this is a divorce, not a marriage," he and Arafat were remarkably similar men. They both were hardened militants who each recognized, for reasons of their own, that with the end of the Cold War they had to get the best deal they could while it was on the table. Both men were also the only ones who had even a prayer of being able to sell such a deal to their respective peoples. But even that, of course, was extinguished with the assassination of Rabin by an Israeli hardliner in 1995.

Many of Berger's friends were severely critical of this new peace process. Edward Said went so far as to compare it to the humiliation of Germany at Versailles. In his book *Jewish History, Jewish Religion*, published shortly after the agreement, Israel Shahak had a particularly devastating critique. A serious critic of Marxism and of its adoption by the leadership of the PLO, Shahak observed that it was precisely because of this Marxist outlook that the PLO embraced the Israeli "peace camp" of a similar bent, and that this arrangement by its very nature led the PLO to become Israel's enforcer in the Palestinian territories.[29] Berger undoubtedly had some sympathy for this view, but he would be generally hopeful, though wary, about the peace process. He certainly could not go along with Shahak's attempt to revive the more extreme antireligious views of the *haskalah*, for Elmer Berger was, indeed, the last of the last in remaining true to the faith of Isaac Mayer Wise and the Pittsburgh Platform. He also remained an admirer of his old radical friend Arthur Waskow, whose followers were now beginning to organize themselves in the movement known as Jewish Renewal.[30]

Most of all, though, Berger was confident as the end approached that the days were numbered for his greatest adversary, the "official" American Jewish community organized in the Conference of Presidents. In a letter acknowledging his eighty-sixth birthday, Berger declared confidently that "although events in the Middle East are as messy as ever, Zionism operates as only a diminishing vestigial force in the U.S. among culturally lagging politicians, and some unknown number of fat cat Jewish bureaucrats running a tangle of Zionist-controlled bureaucracies with diminishing sex appeal."[31] Most presciently, Berger also observed, "Israel's value as a 'strategic asset' of the U.S. is on a decline. Rabin knows this, even if an abundance of American Jews do not."[32] But if Berger felt confident that his enemies in the American Jewish community were doomed, he was not optimistic, to say the least, about any future for his old faith. He drearily assumed that younger generations of American Jews would simply leave Judaism altogether rather than seek out a progressive alternative.[33]

In the late winter of 1995 Berger's health began to sharply decline. What must have amounted to over seventy years of chain-smoking was finally catching up to him. He had severe coughing spells since the 1980s and had been in and out of the hospital for five years before being diagnosed with lung cancer. In a memorandum he prepared for obituary editors, Leonard Sussman quoted a sort of final testament that Berger had recently confided to him:

> I never veered from my enthusiasm for the transcendent and univer-
> sal principles of the Judaism of the great literary Prophets of the Old
> Testament. Yet the widespread public debate over the political destiny
> of Palestine, the unwarranted and basically fallacious Zionist claim to
> represent something called "the Jewish people," the deliberate omis-
> sion of any political justice for the indigenous Arab inhabitants of
> Palestine—all led me to intensify my study and understanding of the

conflict in Palestine at a time when increasing numbers throughout the western world were becoming concerned with postwar plans for peace.[34]

Elmer Berger died the evening of October 5, 1996, at his home in Long Boat Key. Norton Mezvinsky, his most devoted of friends, was at his side. The *New York Times* ran a short, terse, but respectful obituary, mostly quoting the *Times* review of Thomas Kolsky's published dissertation and identifying Berger as merely "a foe of Zionism as well as Israel."[35] A more hostile obituary was issued by the Associated Press (AP), which claimed that Berger was about to write an introduction to a book by the reputed French Holocaust denier Roger Garaudy. Roselle Tekiner wrote a letter to the editor refuting this, which led the AP to discover that it had no source, and resulted in a correction.[36] Apparently, even in death Berger could inspire hysterical hearsay from his enemies.

Mezvinsky wrote a moving obituary for *Washington Report for Middle East Affairs*, declaring his epitaph: "He beseeched the State of Israel to develop as a truly democratic state, to be just and merciful to all people, and thus to walk humbly with God."[37] A yet lengthier tribute would come in the following issue from Naseer Aruri, who proclaimed Berger the heir to Isaac Mayer Wise and Judah Magnes. In part, Aruri recalled:

> Not only did Dr. Berger speak with a voice of conviction and authority on the issue of Zionism and its implications for both Jews and Arabs, but he also exhibited a profound knowledge of the scriptures. In his numerous speeches and debates, he often quoted from the scriptures with tremendous ease and confidence, often making his opponents uncomfortable and bewildered.[38]

But the most poignant epitaph to Elmer Berger would come from Mark Glickman, in the concluding words of his rabbinical dissertation on the man:

> But as a Jew I feel impelled to dream, to dream with the perhaps naïve hope that someday things will be better, that some day we will be able to look each other in the eye, Jew to Jew, Jew to Arab, and that together we will be able to sit under our vine and fig tree, and be afraid no more.[39]

EPILOGUE

In his last years, Elmer Berger would lament that had the American Council for Judaism been able to hold together after the 1967 war, it could have been a serious voice in debating the future of American Judaism as it began to confront the consequences of the peace process. Even if this were true to a point, there is virtually no evidence to suggest that the American Jewish community was ready for that debate in the 1990s. If anything, the peace process was only interpreted as a license for American Judaism to become more closely and intensely identified with Zionism than ever before. Multiple factors contributed to this reality. One was the increasing prevalence of the Holocaust in defining American Jewish identity, peaking right around the time of the 1993 accord with the film *Schindler's List* and the opening of the Holocaust Museum in Washington, D.C. Another was the dramatic increase of Israeli influences on the religious practices of American Jews, whether directly from Israelis themselves or through the intensely Zionist-oriented Jewish summer camps, which defined the exposure of whole generations to Judaism.

By the 1990s, both the Reform and Conservative movements officially observed the three holidays that established a sacred narrative of Jewish history in the twentieth century, which had become equal to if not greater than any biblical narrative: Yom HaShoah, to commemorate the Holocaust; Yom HaAtzmaut, to commemorate the founding of the State of Israel; and Yom

Yerushalayim, to commemorate the 1967 war.[1] In 1999 the Reform movement was compelled to adopt a new platform that was widely seen as a direct repudiation of the Pittsburgh Platform in practically all of its particulars. This included, even now, the issue of Zionism and "Jewish peoplehood" when Reform anti-Zionism was all but completely forgotten. Arnold Jacob Wolf went so far as to declare that the Pittsburgh Platform had been "the original sin" of Reform.[2] That this blast came from one of the movement's most reputed "progressives" is revealing. It demonstrates that what in its day was the "far-left" ideology of Breira was now the dominant perspective of Reform, which led to an embrace of the worship of "peoplehood" as never before.

It may be that this was not altogether new—just a more contemporary, and perhaps more orthodox version of the doctrines of Mordecai Kaplan and Stephen Wise, but this is beside the point. Significantly, this platform was adopted just as Reform was once again overtaking the Conservatives as the largest denomination of American Jews. At the very moment that liberal Judaism was once again surpassing the traditional in commanding the allegiance of American Jews, the Reform movement responded by doubling down on its commitment, in its own words, "that both Israeli and Diaspora Jewry should remain vibrant and interdependent communities."[3] The leadership of the Reform movement thus pledged its devotion to a faith owing more to Moses Hess and Wilhelm Friedrich Hegel than any authentically Judaic source, essentially reducible to the proposition that God so loved the Jews that He sent unto them His only begotten nation-state so that "the Jewish people" would not perish but have everlasting life.

But by the very nature of liberal religious bureaucracy, only a tiny fraction of the roughly one million self-identified Reform Jews in the United States would even be aware of the movement's official platform, let alone of its implications for their Jewish identity. And this would be the reality of American Jewish life that set the stage for the storm of the first decade of the twenty-first century, the disaffection of the Jewish masses, of which Berger had warned at the end of his life. The bulk of American Jewry was now a core component of the liberal upper class, which would soon be subjected to scorn by the Republican Party of George W. Bush. The children and grandchildren of the Jewish masses who flocked to Abba Hillel Silver were now more affluent and assimilated than that era's hate objects of "our crowd" had ever been. Alarm about the dramatic rise of both the rate and acceptance of intermarriage would overwhelm "official" Jewish quarters. As early as 1998, the Labor Zionist ideologue Leonard Fein would lament: "The change is potentially profound, for it involves our transformation from a peoplehood into a faith community. After all these years, it seems to be the American Council for Judaism that has won the ideological argument that we are 'members of the Mosaic persuasion.'"[4]

This natural sociological change in American Jewry would not by itself lead to a serious reconsideration of American Jewry's devotion to Zionism, but the combined impact of events over the next decade would. In 2000 Israel offered a Palestinian state that may have been barely contiguous but in any event would have effectively remained under Israeli military control. When Yasser Arafat was unable to accept this offer, the Palestinian people erupted in a spontaneous uprising as much against Arafat for his failure as against Israel. Thus began the Second Intifada. The following year, on September 11, 2001, George W. Bush responded to spectacular terrorist attacks on American soil by proclaiming that the United States was "at war" in the most possibly abstract terms. This, in turn, allowed the self-appointed leaders of the American Jewish community to boldly proclaim that "we are all Israelis now," a cry that took on ominous implications as the Second Intifada entered an especially bloody period in the spring of 2002. The antiwar movement Bush had inspired was now totally galvanized by the plight of the Palestinians. But the rich tradition of liberal Jewish anti-Zionism embodied by Elmer Berger appeared to be all but extinct. To a young Jew coming of age at this perilous moment, it seemed that in order to be a Jewish anti-Zionist, one either had to join the Neturei Karta or the International Socialist Organization.

But the consequences of the September 11 attacks proved dynamic enough that this would not remain the case for long. Whereas in the first year following the attacks Bush was true to the proposition that the world should be united in its response and eschewed any suggestion of a clash of civilizations, this was to the great chagrin of Israel and its U.S. enablers, with Israeli prime minister Ariel Sharon openly expressing the fear that Israel would be sacrificed to appease the Muslim world, as it was held that Czechoslovakia had been to appease Hitler.[5] But when it became clear after a year had passed that Bush was fanatically determined for reasons of his own to go to war in Iraq, the Israelis recognized and seized their chance. Suddenly, Bush was forced to speak of waging war to bring democracy to the Arab and Muslim world, at the very least implying a clash of civilizations. This may very well have even been what brought the Israel lobby on board in its crucial role in precipitating the

Iraq War—the understanding that for its support, Bush would have to embrace Israel's desire for a clash of civilizations to the point of even invoking such nonsensical phrases as "Islamofascism."

The Iraq War, of course, served to galvanize the American liberal left into fierce opposition to the neoconservative agenda behind it, and while at first the most reliably Zionist of liberal Democrats somehow managed to be vehemently opposed to the Iraq War, the reemergence of liberal anti-Zionism was only a matter of time. The first breakthrough came in October 2003 with the publication of an essay in the *New York Review of Books* by Tony Judt, a historian of the most impeccable liberal and social democratic credentials, prophetically warning of the death of the two-state solution and calling for a binational state:

> The problem with Israel, in short, is not, as it is sometimes suggested, that it is a European enclave in the Arab world, but rather that it arrived too late. It has imported a characteristically late-nineteenth-century separatist project into a world that has moved on, a world of individual rights, open frontiers, and international law. The very idea that a "Jewish state," a state in which Jews and the Jewish religion have exclusive privileges from which non-Jews are forever excluded, is rooted in another time and place. Israel, in short, is an anachronism.[6]

Overnight, the social democratic anti-Zionism of the *Jewish Newsletter* was resurrected from the dead. In response to the predictable barrage of smears and attacks, Judt rejoined the accusation that he was demanding a standard of liberal democracy that was even a stretch for the Western world by emphasizing a point at the very core of Berger's critique of Zionism: the idea that even if it were granted that the Jews were a "nation," Israel should be vested with the sovereignty not only of its own citizens, however exclusively defined, but also of the transnational entity of "the Jewish people of the world," which was completely novel and pernicious. In the wake of the Judt essay, the leadership of Jewish anti-Zionism dramatically shifted from the radical left and increasingly toward the mainstream of American liberalism. A new vanguard of Internet journalists such as Philip Weiss, Richard Silverstein, Tony Karon, and M. J. Rosenberg, to name but a few, was suddenly giving new life to liberal Jewish anti-Zionism. Before long this perspective even dominated such leading print organs of left-liberal opinion as the *American Prospect*.

Not to be discounted in facilitating this breakthrough was the overreaching of the Israel lobby itself. Since the lobby's trial by fire in the 1960s and the emergence of AIPAC as just another Cold War lobby, it could have the run of Washington as long as all it wanted were massive amounts of military aid, the suppression of unfavorable UN resolutions, and the ability to get three-quarters of the House and Senate to sign a napkin, as one AIPAC operative famously put it. Once it could be implicated in the genesis of the Iraq War, AIPAC again crossed the line back into the territory of unadulterated foreign agency. Once it became clear the objective Israel had thus achieved—to place America effectively at war with the entire Muslim world, and thus make Israel's enemies America's enemies—the Israel lobby would only respond by doubling down in beginning to push for war against Iran. By this time, no rational explanation was available for Israel's desire to confront Iran, which increasingly became for Israel a scapegoat for its internal and demographic crisis. But in the wake of the disaster of Iraq, for America to then go to war in Iran would have been utterly catastrophic.

It was largely in response to this most ominous possibility that the major breakthrough came that would begin, slowly but surely, to break the incredible taboo that had emerged over so many years around discussion of the Israel lobby. In March 2006 the *London Review of Books* carried a long article simply titled "The Israel Lobby" by John Mearsheimer and Stephen Walt, two heretofore generally apolitical and widely respected scholars of international relations at the University of Chicago and Harvard University, respectively. After unequivocally stating that "Israel is a liability in the war on terror and the broader effort to deal with rogue states," the article went on to comprehensively cover the incredible extent of the Israel lobby's influence, examine the unusually generous and privileged nature of U.S. military aid to Israel, and thoroughly debunk any case for this support on moral grounds.[7] In the autumn of 2007, the book-length "The Israel Lobby and U.S. Foreign Policy" was a bestseller. Zionists and anti-Zionists alike were totally galvanized by it and its success. While detractors frequently compared the book to the *Protocols of the Elders of Zion*, the elder sage of the Israeli peace movement, Uri Avnery, compared it to *Uncle Tom's Cabin* in its potential to change the course of history.[8]

With the gravity of the charges leveled by the critics of Walt and Mearsheimer, it is imperative to emphasize that the "special relationship" has not been a nefarious conspiracy upon the United States committed by the State of Israel and its U.S. agents. As a younger international relations scholar, Anatol Lieven, has argued, it was not the first time a great power found itself so totally and ruthlessly manipulated by a small client state. The precedent cited by Lieven was the relationship of Russia and Serbia at the dawn of the twentieth century, a relationship that was essentially the trip-wire for the outbreak of the First World War with Russia's commitment to defend Serbia against Austria-Hungary.[9] Whereas Russia and Serbia had been bound together by pan-Slavic nationalism, a more subtle sacred story would bind the United States to Israel. For the United States, Israel has been the ultimate symbol of itself as a force for good in the world, representing the salvation of the Jews as the heroic outcome of the Second World War, the mythic "good war." In other words, what has bound America and Israel together is their shared constant need for another Hitler to destroy.

This incredible outcome could never have been anticipated by the founders of the American Council for Judaism, whose Judaism was inseparable from their love of a very different America. But it was with this reality in mind that Avraham Burg, a onetime speaker of the Knesset who had grown increasingly disillusioned in the wake of Israel's ominous direction since the beginning of the Second Intifada, titled the book in which he most decisively affirmed his "post-Zionist" faith *The Holocaust Is Over; We Must Rise from Its Ashes*. By the time this book would be published in English in 2008, two unimaginably brutal Israeli wars, first in Lebanon in 2006 and then incredibly against the Palestinians of Gaza it was subjecting to a starvation blockade at the end of 2008, would bring the remarkable rise of anti-Zionism of the past decade to an incredible crescendo. This was, again, prompted in no small measure by the increasingly erratic demands being made of the "special relationship." In the presidential election of 2008, the Republican candidate John McCain came the closest of any U.S. leader to directly violating the doctrine of the 1964 Talbot Letter in his insistence that America was duty-bound to prevent another Holocaust—that is, "crimes against the Jewish people"—with respect to waging war against Iran.

Significantly, and perhaps ironically, Avraham Burg would have the closest relationship to American Jewish religious life of any Israeli leader in living memory, if not ever. This would be in his self-identified "spiritual home" during frequent extended stays in New York, Congregation B'nai Jeshurun in Manhattan. Originally a Conservative congregation and even led for many years by the longtime Zionist Organization of America president Israel Goldstein,[10] it would become unaffiliated as it entered the orbit of the nascent Renewal movement, the lodestar of progressive Jewish religion in America at the dawn of the twenty-first century. They have been joined by much of the Reconstructionist movement, which today is as divorced from the doctrine of Mordecai Kaplan as is Reform from the doctrine of Isaac Mayer Wise. In its aesthetic, this milieu could hardly be more different from that of Classical Reform, but in its substance it has proved to be profoundly akin. This has included the general identification of the movement with organizations such as Rabbis for Human Rights and B'Tselem, which have borne witness in the past decade that there yet remain leaders and teachers of Judaism appalled by Israeli militarism and its dispossession of Palestine.

There has also been the unique example of Michael Lerner, a onetime new left radical who would find a higher calling as a Renewal rabbi and become the movement's best-known spokesman through his magazine *Tikkun*. After the disheartening experience of being ostracized by the revolutionary socialist leaders of the antiwar movement at the peak of the Second Intifada, as the tide turned in the years ahead, he would take his stand by, among other things, courageously embracing Walt and Mearsheimer. An indispensable voice for the vitality of progressive Jewish religion, whereas some might argue that the observance of Passover is the ultimate affirmation of "Jewish peoplehood" as a sort of national liberation story, Elmer Berger would have no doubt been delighted by the interpretation offered by Rabbi Lerner:

> We are descended from slaves who staged the first successful slave rebellion in recorded history. The Jewish people began as a multicultural mélange of people attracted to a vision of social transformation. What makes us Jews is not some biological fact, but our willingness to proclaim the message of those ancient slaves—the world can be changed, we can be healed.[11]

From this connection has come what is perhaps the climax of the extraordinary series of events that has seemed to vindicate Berger's life work, a definitive and learned polemic concerning his foremost grievance. *The Invention of the Jewish People*, written by the Israeli intellectual historian Shlomo Sand, spent nineteen weeks as a bestseller in Israel in 2008 before finally being released in an English translation the following year.[12] In many respects bringing the liberal Jewish critique of Zionism to an Israeli audience for the first time, the book employs contemporary theories of nationalism by applying them to the intellectual pedigree of Zionism, relying heavily on the works of ACJ friend Hans Kohn. Sand also roots much of his critique in the perspective toward biblical history by Berger in *A Partisan History of Judaism*, as well as the narrative of the proselyte roots of world Jewry, probably given its most straightforward expression in Alfred Lilienthal's *What Price Israel?*

These narratives were approaching scholarly consensus in the first half of the twentieth century before being obstructed by Zionist historiography in its drive to exalt "the Jewish people" as the eternal seed of Abraham, as carefully detailed by Sand. In short, *The Invention of the Jewish People* may be nothing less than the thorough and definitive critique of Zionism as an ideology that Berger late in life expressed his regret of never having been able to write.

Here, then, we can begin to assess the legacy of Elmer Berger and of Reform anti-Zionism in light of the extraordinary events of the past decade. With respect to their warnings about the consequences of founding a Zionist state in Palestine, one can do no better than to quote the concluding words of Thomas Kolsky's study, words that are if anything more apt today than when they were written over twenty years ago:

> As the ACJ had foreseen, the birth of the state created numerous problems—problems the Zionists had minimized. For example, Israel became highly, if not unusually, dependent on support from American Jews. Moreover, the formation of the state directly contributed to undermining Jewish communities in Arab countries and to precipitating a protracted conflict between Israel and the Arabs. Indeed, as the Council had often warned and contrary to Zionist expectations, Israel did not become a truly normal state. Nor did it become a light to the nations. Ironically, created presumably to free Jews from anti-Semitism and ghetto-like existence as well as to provide them with abiding peace, Israel became, in effect, a garrison state, a nation resembling a large territorial ghetto besieged by hostile neighbors. Ultimately, the Zionists won and their opponents lost. However, the ominous predictions of the American Council for Judaism are still haunting the Zionist venture.[13]

But perhaps more important, the predictions of the Council, and of Berger in particular, about the Zionist takeover of essentially all American Jewish organizational life proved to have an absolutely deadly accuracy. Although it is true that organized activist Zionism declined sharply after statehood and all but disappeared by the 1970s, with astonishingly little resistance, Israeli patriotism, if not hardcore doctrinaire Zionism, became the religion of American Jewry. An ecumenical bureaucracy, set up at Israeli and Zionist instigation and having remarkably little other purpose than to advocate on behalf of the State of Israel and to enforce loyalty to it among its constituents, was freely vested with this authority by all three major branches of American Judaism and all civic organizations of any note in American Jewish life. This, which became the Conference of Presidents of Major Jewish Organizations, would indoctrinate to its constituents, if not also to the public at large, first principles of nationalism and collectivism that in virtually any other context would be rightly met with abhorrence by the American people. Most ominously of all, AIPAC has been the direct servant of this conference and has thereby, at least in theory, broadly implicated the entire American Jewish community in its activities.

A critical fact about Elmer Berger should be noted: at least by the standards of the years following the Second Intifada, his preferred policy prescriptions for resolving the Israeli-Palestinian conflict were remarkably moderate. His true heresy was his denial of Zionism's politicized construction of the Jewish people, if not of Jewish peoplehood altogether. Exactly how anomalous in history the view has been that Judaism is solely a matter of confession is beside the point—what matters is what this meant in practice. The heresy, in other words, was to reject the very legitimacy and authority of a politically organized Jewish community. As has been noted, this rejection had deep roots in the original rebellion of the founders of Reform Judaism against the civil authority of rabbis over their respective communities, which in many cases was backed by the authorities of the old order. The fundamental heresy of Classical Reform—first against Orthodoxy and then against Zionism—was the proposition that it was possible, and perhaps even essential, for a Jew to be an individualist.

We can therefore begin to understand why Elmer Berger and his colleagues became the objects of such vicious hysteria in the Zionist imagination. The ACJ, and eventually Berger alone, was a constant haunting reminder that the individualist heresy had not been eradicated forever, for the Zionists were intolerant of opposition not merely because it was political opposition, but because its very existence was a direct challenge to their collectivist ideal. Indeed, the inflation of the threat posed by Berger and the ACJ in the Zionist imagination can even be attributed to the simple need of any fanatical grouping to have an external enemy to motivate them, perhaps not unlike a similar need of the State of Israel itself.[14] The soaring heights reached by this hysteria were amply demonstrated by Philip Roth in *The Plot Against America* to those very few who were even aware what his subplot about "Jewish collaborators" was supposedly based on. Bill Kauffman memorably stated in his scathing review of the novel that "the scene in which Rabbi Bengelsdorf vivisects FDR's Scottie Fala must have been excised by a wise editor."[15]

Part of the reason this has been so obfuscated over the years has been the association of the historic leadership of American Zionism with American liberalism. The shockingly illiberal language of the Zionists therefore has to be understood in the context of what was fundamentally illiberal about that era of American liberalism. The palpable bloodthirstiness of the celebrated "liberal" Stephen Wise toward "Cardinal Wolsey and his Bishops" is only to be expected when considered beside the zealous witch-hunting of such fellow New Dealers as Max Lerner, Harold Ickes, Walter Winchell, and Archibald MacLeish. Even on into the Cold War years, the outrageously pseudoscientific effort to create the "self hating Jew" as a category of mental illness, though recalling the Soviet use of psychiatry, was but a logical extension of the efforts of such authors as Theodor Adorno and Daniel Bell to reduce all dissent from Cold War liberalism to a mental defect called "status resentment."[16] It is small wonder, then, that the new left, which held out the hope of reviving a more genuine liberalism, especially among Jewish youth, sent so many of these partisans into the panic that became known as neoconservatism.

This, indeed, is one of the most extraordinary aspects of the legacy of the American Council for Judaism—how much its history teaches us about the peculiar demonology of the neoconservatives. As Jacob Heilbrunn argued in his landmark history of neoconservatism:

The best way to understand the phenomenon may be to focus on neoconservatism as an uneasy, controversial, and tempestuous drama of Jewish immigrant assimilation—a very American story. At bottom, it is about an unresolved civil war between a belligerent, upstart ethnic group and a staid, cautious American foreign policy establishment that lost its way after the Vietnam War.[17]

This very specific devil of the old foreign policy establishment can of course be traced back to the State Department, which was best of friends with the ACJ in the 1940s and 1950s. The neocons may have indeed recognized early on that, contrary to the propaganda line being fed to the liberal-voting Jewish masses, Loy Henderson and Henry Byroade were among the most revered architects of Cold War liberal foreign policy. That they were therefore targeted by Joe McCarthy is also significant. This may well have set off the first stirring of the counterintuitive neocon romance with right-wing populist rabble-rousing, most incredibly in more recent years with their alliance to Christian fundamentalism.

More to the point, then, may be this knack of the neocons for such counterintuitive demographic alliances in U.S. politics. The neocons seized on
the coalition of the backlash against the liberal establishment because that
establishment was its enemy, beginning perhaps for the parochial reason of
their Zionist partisanship but by the 1970s for what they regarded as the betrayal of Cold War liberalism on a broader level. Thus, there exists no greater
devil in the neocon imagination than the American Jew who ineluctably casts
his lot with that liberal establishment and puts his loyalties thereto before
any loyalty to "the Jewish people." In our own time, of course, these are the
affluent liberal Jews who are the indispensible denizens of what David
Brooks called "bourgeois bohemia," more commonly referred to as "blue-
state America." But over sixty years ago, they were Lessing Rosenwald, Arthur
Sulzberger, Joseph Proskauer, the San Francisco aristocracy, and the rabbis
who ministered to them as Americans of the Jewish faith. Indeed, like the
original Zionists before them, the neocons seem driven by the psychic need
to prove themselves to be other than their easily stereotyped brethren—the
need, frankly, to counter the negative image of classical anti-Semitism to
themselves.

Without question then, what moves the neocons, particularly in the
forum of *Commentary* magazine, to their rage against the liberal Jewish
masses is their disaffection from the "collective" of "Jewish peoplehood" and
apparent desire, therefore, toward assimilation, or at the very least, as Elmer
Berger preferred to call it, integration. This is not, however, a simple conservative yearning to preserve that which a distinctive culture in a pluralistic society is always under any circumstances at risk of losing, but rather a unique
and utterly foul brew of racialism and narcissism. Through the "worship of
peoplehood," as Berger prophetically called it to Milton Himmelfarb, combined with the almost obsessive self-segregating tendencies in "organized"
Jewish life, the neocons and their allies in the self-appointed American
Jewish leadership have concocted and spread a religion that is nothing less
than racism as a substitute for Judaism. It is indeed difficult to imagine what
could be more at odds with the spirit and temper of American society today.

No discussion of this question would be complete without examining its
intersection with the legacy of Jewish socialism. Since the 1960s, this legacy
has been almost totally defined by those who have claimed it in the neoconservative movement or else at its fringes—beginning with the oddball
faction of neocons who self-identified as social democrats, and then with
the emergence of the English edition of *The Forward* in the 1990s, whose

editors then went on to found the uber-neocon and ultra-Zionist *New York Sun*, continuing to claim that legacy even in those pages. It is true that *The Forward* championed Zionism even before the Second World War. But the fact that this world produced, in the *Jewish Newsletter* and its supporters, the only surviving pocket of Jewish anti-Zionism that could even compare to the American Council for Judaism, including the leader of the Jewish Labor Committee himself, speaks volumes about the treachery by which the name of Jewish socialism, however faint, has been marshaled in the defense of Zionism in the past decade. Yet this merely reflects a deeper divide going all the way back to the movement's heyday, between those who took seriously the liberal ends of Jewish socialism, namely assimilation or integration by other means, and those for whom it essentially became Zionism by other means.

The common thread, therefore, in all of this is the great chronic problem of American Jewish life, which, more than anything, was the root cause of Zionism's success to begin with—assimilation anxiety. At the dawn of the twenty-first century, this anxiety has returned dramatically at a time when the allure of Zionism is, at the very least, seriously tarnished, and the Orthodox option has proven attractive to many but has clearly discernible limits. Leaving the great majority leaning toward some possible version of liberal Judaism, one is compelled to reconsider in this context Elmer Berger's philosophy of emancipation and integration. There can be little argument that this philosophy was seriously flawed, in short because it took for granted the centrality of mainline Protestant worship to American life in the 1950s, and that it would remain compelling for a majority of Americans. This was, of course, merely an indication of the fealty of the Council to an America that by then was either dead or dying.

Berger did try his hand at ritual innovation when his status as the guru of the ACJ was at its zenith, but his failure to deliver would only serve to reinforce the prevailing image of his broader philosophy, that it merely amounted to complete assimilation. The great disadvantage at which Berger was placed in this was that his desire, in his own words, to "harmonize with American life"[18] came at one of the most infamously conformist moments in American history, and therefore any effort to draw from a larger reservoir of American culture would produce utterly dismal results. By the time the *havurah* movement came along and began its more successful innovations, despite the fact that many of its leaders were friends and allies of Berger, he was far beyond caring about such matters. Still, it is important to note in this context that Berger was not at all as zealously committed to the high church aesthetic of Classical Reform as many of his colleagues in the ACJ were, especially when we consider that the relative continuing vibrancy of liberal Judaism as opposed to mainline Protestantism is no doubt in part because it has the rich reservoir of Jewish tradition to draw on for drama and mystery.

On the other hand, the majority of American Jews today would be completely baffled by the suggestion that they were anything but completely emancipated and integrated Americans whose Judaism is primarily, if not solely, a matter of confession. While this could not be said during the majority of Elmer Berger's lifetime, Berger must nevertheless be given credit for recognizing the underlying essential sociological truth of American Jewish life—that regardless of the theological and even sociological merits of the question of Jewish peoplehood, the concept ultimately could not withstand the reality of U.S. society. Various means would be employed to square this circle, such as the identification of the Jews as "ethnic Americans" alongside the Irish and Italians. This was plausible enough, at least until the State of Israel, in which the overwhelming majority of them had never even thought to set foot in 1948, somehow became their "homeland," with Hebrew, rather than Yiddish, somehow becoming their mother tongue.

But in any event, this answer would only be salient for a couple of generations at most, as the other immigrant groups of the Ellis Island generation would be more or less assimilated by the end of the twentieth century. Because, even at that time, of the implications of Zionism, which went quite above and beyond any simple "hyphenated" American identity, the Zionist propaganda surrounding this reality would have significant and far-reaching consequences in U.S. history and society. It appears to be that in the Zionist propaganda of this era, and even specifically that which was used to counter the arguments of the ACJ, was found the earliest articulation of the idea that America is not a "melting pot" but a "salad bowl," that is, that America should not be a culturally assimilated society.[19] This antiassimilationist argument of American Zionism has become especially powerful in our own time as it has been employed in the contemporary debate over immigration to the United States, making it especially difficult to picture a culturally and socially integrated American future.

Yet it spite of this, the first decade of the twenty-first century will have closed with probably the greatest imaginable reproach to the spirit of anti-assimilationism—the election of Barack Obama. Consider, first, what it represents on behalf of African Americans. The rise of the black power movement, broadly defined, in the wake of the civil rights movement had far-reaching consequences in shaping American Jewish identity, as both an example and a negative motivator fortifying for one more generation, on top of the consolidation of the power of the Israel lobby, a cultural reality that militated against any identity as simple Americans of Jewish faith. But beginning in the 1990s, black nationalism became increasingly buried in the past and at the same time began the extraordinary rise and triumph of the black bourgeoisie, dramatically climaxing with the election of Obama.

That the option of emancipation and integration has been so totally and successfully embraced by a people who barely a century and a half ago were human chattel is beyond any conceivable reproach to the bitter Jewish parochialism underlying both Zionism and neoconservatism. It is not surprising, then, that there is a powerful undercurrent of antiblack racism behind the deep Israeli hostility to Obama. Nor is it surprising that he has brought neocon hysteria to a fever pitch, and probably on no matter more so than regarding their fellow Jews, with Norman Podhoretz's exacerbated tome *Why Are Jews Liberals?* being only its most bitter expression. Perhaps most astonishingly, several favorable reviewers of the book in a *Commentary* symposium have expressed themselves most eager of all to cast aside the enduring bonds of Jewish peoplehood in favor of preserving their militant remnant, not unlike, it would seem, the Zealots of the Roman era.[20]

Indeed, we may yet be seeing the repeal of the twentieth century—the century of horror, the century of collectivism, the century of mass destruction and genocide, in short, the century that made Zionism possible. However they go forward, the Jewish people will have to come to terms with the fact that they were totally swept up in a revolutionary movement, and that this has only ended with the same pile of corpses as all revolutionary movements that came before it. As Martin Luther King Jr. said in another context, in this generation we will have to repent not only for the wickedness of the bad but also for the appalling silence of the good. Nevertheless, it would be a mistake to simply reduce Zionism to a malevolent spell that befell a brief century of the Jewish millennia. It was, rather, the ultimate resolution of a long crisis of finding a place in the modern world, the larger story of which has been so woefully neglected.

Still, when we consider the fallen nature of mankind, the record of the Jews remains by far among the better in existence for persistently serving as an example of justice and righteousness. Under the same appalling circumstances of the twentieth century, it is indeed difficult to imagine any other group producing such extraordinary men of conscience as Elmer Berger, Lessing Rosenwald, Judah Magnes, Uri Avnery, and Michael Lerner, to name but a few. Like that of the Prophets of old, their example remains for the time when the world finally begins its retreat from barbarism and looks to those who warned against the madness in seeking how it might but do justly, love mercy, and walk humbly with God. So at this late hour, let it at the very least be said that the words of Isaiah were finally heeded: "Now go, inscribe it in a book, that it may be a testimony for the time to come."[21]

ACKNOWLEDGMENTS

I would be remiss indeed if I did not begin by acknowledging the most unlikely source from whom I first heard of Elmer Berger, the neoconservative propagandist Joshua Muravchik, in a passing mention in the June 2007 issue of *Commentary*. Acknowledgment is also due to his interlocutor in the relevant anecdote, His Royal Highness Prince Turki al-Faisal.

Four individuals stand out for their exceptional contribution to the writing of this book. Leonard Sussman, first and perhaps foremost of these, could not have been more helpful with his sharing of anecdotes buried several decades in his memory and was extremely generous in furnishing me with both primary and secondary sources in his possession. It would be difficult to do justice to the totality of his contribution to this book, and to his emotional investment in my completion of it, so suffice it to say that I have been humbled by his confidence.

Allan Brownfeld deserves the principal credit for setting me on the path of writing this book, through his encouragement when I presented the idea as a protean and long-range notion in my first meeting with him in the spring of 2008. His support throughout the process has been deeply valued.

Norton Mezvinsky, of whom it is no exaggeration to call the closest thing Elmer Berger ever had to a son, I was unfortunately not able to consult to the degree I would have liked. Nevertheless what few conversations we were able to have proved invaluable. I can only hope to have done a reasonable degree of justice to the man he rightly held in such extraordinarily high regard.

Finally, Justus Doenecke, a historian I greatly admired before getting to know him though the writing of this book. It was a privilege to be able to consult so extensively, and his generosity and enthusiasm toward my work was matched in kind. I was extremely fortunate to have in him both the perspective of a casual if close friend of Berger and the inquisitive mind of the historian, having thus obtained from him several of the answers to questions that would be sought out by the future historian.

This book principally relies on primary research, and thus I owe an incredible debt to the two scholars whose writings on this subject provided me with an indispensible foundation—Thomas Kolsky of Lansdale, Pennsylvania, and Rabbi Mark Glickman of Woodinville, Washington. It is no exaggeration to say that without their respective dissertations, the writing of this book would have been impossible.

Thomas Kolsky, who confided to me his own interest a decade ago in writing a full-length biography of Elmer Berger, was unfailingly gracious and helpful, having himself been through the rigors of tackling, being overwhelmed by, and finally recovering from the study of Reform Jewish anti-Zionism. In particular I am extremely grateful to Dr. Kolsky for receiving me in Pennsylvania in order to review the primary documents that remain in his stead, as well as for general interviewing purposes.

Mark Glickman served as nothing less than my rabbi for the purposes of writing this book, and his generosity and encouragement went simply above and beyond. Though I feel that most of my countless queries to him were often of the most tangential nature to my project, he ably received them all without fail, and his perspective as a contemporary Reform rabbi with an exceptionally well-informed grasp of the history of his denomination was truly invaluable. Special acknowledgment is also due to Rabbi Glickman for producing his indispensible oral history interview of Elmer Berger, without which, among other things, it would have been next to impossible to have a satisfactory account of his early years.

I have been in awe of the archival profession ever since my undergraduate days, and nowhere is its tremendous value more deeply felt than in the research of such subjects as that of this book, which have been shoved far down Orwell's memory hole. I therefore have only the most profound gratitude to all the noble members of that profession who assisted in the research of this book: Harry Miller, Richard Pifer, and Marissa Dobrick at the Wisconsin Historical Society; Kevin Proffitt, Vicki Lipski, and Jennifer Cole at the American Jewish Archives of Hebrew Union College; Lara Michels at the Judah Magnes Museum; John Haynes at the Library of Congress; Thomas Lannon at the New York Public Library; Marvin Rusinek at the American Jewish Historical Society; Carol Leadenham at the Hoover Institution; and Mary Huth at the University of Rochester.

Special thanks are also due to the library staff of Hebrew Union College in Cincinnati for sending two original dissertations from before World War II for me to review at their New York campus, as well as to the staff of the microfilm room of the New York Public Library for patiently arranging an interlibrary loan of a microfilm from the American Jewish Archives. I am extremely grateful to several photo archivists for their utmost due diligence, notably Nathan Tallman at the American Jewish Archives and Lisa Marine at the Wisconsin Historical Society. Many thanks to my dear friends Richard Winger and Jerry Kunz for hosting me on my research trip to San Francisco, and Dawa Choedon and Tsering Dorjee on my research trip to Washington, D.C.

Numerous individuals responded to a wide variety of queries in the course of my research, and most responded with the utmost earnestness and generosity, and I thank them all: Uri Avnery, Eugene Bird, Lenni Brenner, Donna Curtiss, Michael Davis, Brian Doherty, Seymour Fromer, Nathan Glazer, Peter Hanauer, Renate Hanauer, Andrew Kilgore, Rashid Khalidi, William T. Mallison III, Gail Malmgreen, Robert Marx, Steve Naman, Daniel Opler, Robert Parmet, Don Peretz, Murray Polner, Darcy Richardson, Sheldon Richman, Moses Rischin, Fred Rosenbaum, Grant Smith, Scott Stanley, Charles Tannenbaum, Max Tonkon, Arthur Waskow, Morris Weisz, Jerome Winegarden Jr., and Karen Wolsey.

My utmost gratitude to Potomac Books, with whom it is an honor to be published, and with particular thanks due of course to my able editor, Elizabeth Demers, for believing in and championing this project through to publication. Very special thanks are also due to Jon Basil Utley for his most generous research grant through the Freda Utley Foundation. His devoted patronage of the cause of peace will be long remembered.

The two unsung heroes of this book are Philip Weiss and Joseph Stromberg. Phil, for giving me the forum through his blog to engage with the questions about the Middle East and American Jewish identity, which are at the heart of this book, and for serving as a resilient example in confronting those issues head on at this critical moment in history. And Joe, for serving as an example of what is possible as an independent historian and for his tremendous encouragement and enthusiasm for my pursuits, particularly his encouragement of my interest in this subject. Special thanks also to Joe's wife, Mary, for providing her services as a professional genealogist in my research. I would still be remiss, though, without mentioning in this context my dear friend and mentor of many years, Ernest Evans.

Finally, I must thank my parents for each in their own way giving me the support, material and otherwise, to pursue the research and writing of this book, as well as believing in my ability to pursue my dream to write history. It is my sincere hope to prove myself worthy of that dream with this offering.

NOTES

For abbreviations used in the notes please see the Bibliography for this book.

Prologue

1. Prime Minister's Speech at the Herzliya Conference.

2. Kolsky, *Jews Against Zionism*, p. 192.

3. Ibid., p. 200.

4. Ibid., pp. 62–65.

5. Ibid., p. 62.

6. Ibid., pp. 124–25.

7. Roth, *The Plot Against America*.

8. For a thorough review and debunking of Roth see Kauffman "Heil to the Chief." As examples of the historical ignorance of other reviewers of Roth, one ill-informed liberal reviewer believed Bengelsdorf to be a metaphor for neoconservatism, while a critical conservative reviewer believed him to be based on Richard Nixon's adviser on Jewish issues, the Orthodox rabbi Baruch Korff.

9. For the definitive history of this episode see Scholem, *Sabbatai Zevi*.

10. On this phenomenon see Matt Goldish, *The Sabbatean Prophets*. Cambridge, Mass.: Harvard University Press, 2004.

11. For a detailed account of the movement's founding period in Germany, with its ties to Freemasonry highlighted, see Graetz, *History of The Jews*, Vol. 5, pp. 559–88.

12. Murray Rothbard, *An Austrian Perspective on the History of Economic Thought*. Cheltenham: Edward Elgar Publishing, 1995.

13. Quoted from Avineri, *The Making of Modern Zionism*, pp. 42–45.

14. This case is made to favorable effect by the neoconservative propagandist Joshua Muravchik in *Heaven on Earth: The Rise and Fall of Socialism* San Francisco: Basic Books, 2002.

15. Ibid.

16. Ibid.

17. Kolsky, *Jews Against Zionism*, pp. 29–30.

18. "The Pittsburgh Platform."

19. Ibid.

20. Karp, *Haven and Home*, pp. 95–102.

21. Ibid., pp. 102–10.

22. Quoted from Kolsky, *Jews Against Zionism*, p. 1.

23. Elon, *The Pity of It All*, p. 288.

24. Heller, *Isaac Mayer Wise*, p. 604.

25. Kolsky, *Jews Against Zionism*, pp. 30–31.

26. Ibid., pp. 29–33.

1. An Earnest Disciple

1. Shuffield, "The Loewenstein Family of Milam County, Texas."

2. Their father, Nathan Lowenstein, was an innkeeper in Philadelphia who had come from Hanover; the different spellings are likely a result of their different and respective immigrations.

3. The practice of a widowed spouse marrying a sibling of the deceased, though common to several tribal societies, has special significance in Orthodox Judaism as it is prescribed in Deuteronomy 25 and also contains an exit clause known as *halizah*.

4. EBOH.

5. Ibid. Though Berger himself would typically describe his father as having had a white-collar job with the railroad, he is listed as an engineer in all other sources, including the U.S. Census.

6. Ibid.

7. Ibid.

8. Ibid.

9. Retrieved at http://www.clevelandjewishhistory.net/silver/temple.html.

10. Edward Calisch to Louis Wolsey, November 15 and December 12, 1922, LW.

11. EBOH.

12. Ibid. Berger recalled learning secondhand that Wolsey, whom he regarded in later years as impetuous, was chronically resentful of never attaining the most elite pulpit either in Cleveland or later in Philadelphia.

13. Significantly, the only other Reform rabbi to publicly protest American entry into the First World War was the ardent binationalist Zionist Judah Magnes.

14. Handwritten note on a copy of the Pledge for Jewish Pacifists, initialed by Cronbach, AC.

15. "Pacifist Is Brave Too, Rabbi Says" *Cleveland Plain Dealer*, January 19, 1924. News clipping, AC.

16. Retrieved at http://www.fairmounttemple.org/history.htm.

17. On this history see Graetz, *History of the Jews*, Vol. 1, pp. 471–503.

18. The word *Hasidim* is itself the Hebrew translation of the Greek *Essenes*. As late as 1870, Graetz still spoke of the "neo-Hasidim."

19. EBOH.

20. Ibid.

21. Glickman, "One Voice," pp. 13–15.

22. EBOH.

23. Brown and Kutler, *Nelson Glueck*, pp. 58–61.

24. EBOH.

25. Berger, "An Examination." On Glueck, see Brown and Kutler, *Nelson Glueck*, pp. 43–45.

26. EBOH.

2. The Lines Are Drawn

1. EBOH.

2. Lapides, "History of the Jewish Community," p. 7.

3. Ibid., p. 8.

4. EBOH.

5. Kolsky, *Jews Against Zionism*, p. 34.

6. "The Columbus Platform"

7. "Stephen Wise Sends an Open Letter to Mahatma Gandhi," *The Jewish Exponent*, May 3, 1935. LW.

8. "Rabbi Wolsey Scores Dr. Wise on the Gandhi Correspondence," *The Jewish Exponent*, June 21, 1935. LW.

9. "Can we achieve Jewish Unity by a referendum? A sermon by Rev. Dr. Samuel H. Goldenson." SG-N.

10. Ibid.

11. Ibid.

12. Stephen S. Wise, "Dr. Goldenson Confuses an Issue," *The Congress Bulletin*, June 3, 1938. SG-N.

13. Lipsky, Louis "Temple Emanuel Voices An Obsolete Complaint." *The Congress Bulletin*, June 3, 1938. SG-N.

14. Rosenbaum, *Visions*, pp. 186–87.

15. Irving Reichert to Lincoln Steffens, February 7, 1934. IFR.

16. Rosenbaum, *Visions*, p. 186.

17. Ibid., p. 184.

18. "One Reform Rabbi Replies to Ludwig Lewisohn," in *Judaism and the American Jew*, p. 131.

19. Ibid., p. 132.

20. Louis Wolsey to Irving Reichert, March 17 and March 30, 1936, IFR.

21. "Temple Beth El History"

22. Interview with Justus Doenecke, April 6, 2009.

23. Berger, *Memoirs*, p. 32.

24. EBOH.

25. Berger, *Memoirs*, p. 4.

26. EBOH. It should be noted how quickly the party line changed from this to the raising of an exclusively Jewish army, the very issue that prompted the founding of the American Council for Judaism.

27. Ibid.

28. Ibid.

29. Kolsky, *Jews Against Zionism*, p. 27.

30. H. L. Mencken to Morris Lazaron, February 26, 1937, MSL.

31. Mencken to Lazaron, December 10 and 17, 1937; Lazaron to Mencken, December 15, 1937, MSL.

32. Mencken to Lazaron, June 2, 1938, MSL.

33. Joseph Proskauer to Felix Warburg and Morris Lazaron, September 29, 1937; Lazaron to Proskauer, October 7, 1937, MSL.

34. "Homeland or State: The Real Issue," MSL-N.

35. Ibid.

36. Mencken to Lazaron, March 9, 1940, MSL.

37. Kolsky, *Jews Against Zionism*, pp. 37–39.

38. Edith Rosenwald, "The Council's Ten Years as I Remember Them," *Council News*, March 1953.

39. The very fact that Julius Rosenwald chose to name his first son after the German Enlightenment philosopher is itself a powerful testimony to his Classical Reform convictions.

40. Owen Rall to Lessing Rosenwald, October 11, 1940; Rosenwald to Rall, October 17, 1940, LJR.

41. Sidney Sternbach to Lessing Rosenwald, October 19, 1940; Rosenwald to Sternbach, October 30, 1940, LJR.

42. Though there is no record of either Hertzberg or Lipsig becoming directly involved in the American Council for Judaism, both were members of the Union for Democratic Socialism led by Norman Thomas at the height of his friendship with the ACJ in the mid-1950s.

43. Ira Hirschmann to Lessing Rosenwald, November 1, 1940, LJR.

44. Lessing Rosenwald to Robert Wood, December 3, 1940, LJR.

45. Lessing Rosenwald to Alfred Knopf, June 27, 1941, LJR.

46. Interview with Justus Doenecke, March 7, 2009.

47. "Rosh Hashanah Sermon, September 21, 1941," IFR.

3. Staking Everything

1. Kolsky, *Jews Against Zionism*, p. 42.

2. Berger, *Memoirs*, p. 5.

3. "Why I Am a Non-Zionist," EB-N.

4. Ibid.

5. Julian Morgenstern to Elmer Berger, May 21, 1942, ACJ-W.

6. Kolsky, *Jews Against Zionism*, p. 58.

7. Interview with Jerome Winegarden Jr., March 23, 2009.

8. Frank Sundheim, "The Beginnings and Early History of the American Council for Judaism," term paper for Dr. Jacob R. Marcus, History 5, Hebrew Union College, November 1957, American Jewish Archives, Hebrew Union College, Cincinnati, Ohio, p. 9.

9. Ibid., p. 11.

10. Kolsky, *Jews Against Zionism*, p. 42.

11. Ibid., p. 43.

12. Morris Lazaron to Nelson Glueck, March 18, 1942; Glueck to Lazaron, March 22, 1942, MSL.

13. Kolsky, *Jews Against Zionism*, p. 44.

14. Ibid.

15. Ibid., p. 46.

16. David Philipson to Louis Wolsey, April 13, 1942, LW.

17. Wolsey to Philipson, April 16, 1942, LW.

18. Irving Reichert to Louis Wolsey, April 23, 1942, LW.

19. Elmer Berger to Louis Wolsey, April 27, 1942, LW.

20. Berger to Wolsey, May 7, 1942, LW.

21. Norman Buckner to Elmer Berger, May 1, 1942, LW.

22. Kolsky, *Jews Against Zionism*, p. 47.

23. Ibid., p. 40

24. Ibid., pp. 40–41.

25. Ibid., p. 48.

26. Samuel Goldenson and Louis Wolsey to their colleagues, May 12, 1942, LW.

27. Goldenson and Wolsey to colleagues, May 15, 1942, LW.

28. Norman Gerstenfeld to Louis Wolsey, May 19, 1942, LW.

29. "Program of Atlantic City Meeting of non-Zionist Reform Rabbis," LW.

30. "Jewish Postwar Problems," MSL.

31. "The Flint Plan: A Program of Action for American Jews," EB-N.

32. Ibid.

33. "Statement of Principles by Non-Zionist Rabbis," LW.

34. Kolsky, *Jews Against Zionism*, pp. 54–55.

35. Elmer Berger to Louis Wolsey, November 25, 1942, LW.

36. Bernstein was a national officer of the Keep America Out of War Committee as late as early 1941, following many years of activism in the shadow of his mentor, Stephen Wise. Years later, Bernstein would not allow his pacifist past to prevent him from using his version of events to attempt to smear Berger as a deserter.

37. Kolsky, *Jews Against Zionism*, p. 55.

38. Ibid., p. 66.

39. Berger, *Memoirs*, pp. 10–11.

40. Morris Lazaron to his colleagues, November 19, 1942, MSL.

41. Kolsky, *Jews Against Zionism*, pp. 203–5.

42. The best-known incident, suggesting a widespread practice, concerned ACJ member Lloyd Dinkelspiel of San Francisco, who discovered to his outrage that a proxy vote had been cast in his name at the Conference. Rosenbaum, *Visions*, p. 197.

43. Kolsky, *Jews Against Zionism*, p. 76.

44. Ibid.

45. Lessing Rosenwald to his colleagues, October 15, 1943, ACJ-H.

46. Kolsky, *Jews Against Zionism*, p. 77.

47. Nelson Glueck to Arthur Sulzberger, September 7, 1943, MSL.

48. "Mrs. M. P. Epstein Named Hadassah Head," *New York Times*, October 28, 1943. Press clipping, MSL.

49. Arthur Sulzberger to Abba Hillel Silver, November 2, 1943, MSL.

50. For a detailed account of the "Sulzberger myth" and its promoters see Blank, "The *New York Times'* Strange Attack."

51. "Where Do You Stand?," in *Judaism and the American Jew*, p. 135.

52. Ibid., p. 143.

53. Rosenbaum, *Visions*, pp. 197–98.

54. Kolsky, *Jews Against Zionism*, p. 62.

55. Ibid., p. 80.

56. "Why I Oppose Zionism by Rabbi Elmer Berger," American Council for Judaism pamphlet, IFR.

57. Elmer Berger to Hyman J. Schachtel, November 26, 1943, ACJ-W.

58. Elmer Berger to Harry Wise Sr., July 6, 1944, ACJ-W.

59. Kolsky, *Jews Against Zionism*, p. 81.

60. Abraham Cronbach to Bernard Gradwohl, October 4, 1944, AC.

61. Julian Morgenstern to Louis Wolsey, June 9, 1944, ACJ-W.

62. Berger to Wolsey, January 6, 1945, LW.

63. Reichert to Wolsey, January 11, 1945, LW.

64. Isaac Bernheim to Leopold L. Meyer, January 25, 1944, AC.

65. EBOH.

66. Interview with Thomas Kolsky, February 28, 2009.

67. Kolsky, *Jews Against Zionism*, pp. 92–95.

68. "The Jewish Times, February 25, 1944—Immaterial and Irrelevant!," Transcription, ACJ-W.

69. Kolsky, *Jews Against Zionism*, p. 93; Curley to Berger, April 18, 1944; Lemke to Berger, June 30, 1944; Wadsworth to Berger, July 31, 1944; Voorhis to Berger, December 4, 1944, ACJ-W.

70. Wolsey to Berger, June 30, 1944, LW.

71. Norman Thomas to Elmer Berger, February 4, 1944, NMT.

72. Berger, *Memoirs*, p. 32.

73. Jack Altman to Elmer Berger, April 11, 1945, ACJ-W.

74. "Address by Lessing J. Rosenwald, January 14, 1945," ACJ-H.

75. Quoted from Kolsky, *Jews Against Zionism*, p. 111.

76. Berger, *The Jewish Dilemma*, p. 10.

77. Ibid., p. 90.

78. Ibid., p. 35.

79. "Some Advance Comment on *The Jewish Dilemma*," ACJ-H.

80. Melvin Berger to Elmer Berger, November 19, 1945, ACJ-W.

4. The Righteous Stand

1. Kolsky, *Jews Against Zionism*, p. 116.

2. Ibid., p. 123.

3. Ibid., p. 124.

4. Ibid., p. 132.

5. Ibid., p. 133.

6. "For Release On or After Monday, June 3rd," ACJ-W.

7. Among the exceptions were Senator Burton Wheeler, Democrat of Montana and as close as any U.S. Senator to a Norman Thomas socialist, and Congressman Howard Buffet, Republican of Nebraska, always a radical among the isolationists and father of the billionaire Warren Buffet.

8. Lilienthal, *What Price Israel*, p. 112.

9. For this analysis, the author is indebted to Justus Doenecke, a leading scholar of isolationism who was also a friend of Elmer Berger.

10. Kolsky, *Jews Against Zionism*, pp. 144–46, 153.

11. Ibid., p. 146.

12. Ibid., p. 149.

13. Ibid., p. 152.

14. Quoted in Smith, *America's Defense Line*, p. 35.

15. "The Policy and Program of Reform Judaism," in *Judaism and the American Jew*, p. 36.

16. Brown and Kutler, *Nelson Glueck*, p. 110.

17. Ibid., p. 112.

18. Ibid., pp. 102–4.

19. Kolsky, *Jews Against Zionism*, p. 159.

20. George Levison to Lessing Rosenwald, February 24, 1947, GLL.

21. Rosenwald to Levison, March 1, 1947, GLL.

22. Kolsky, *Jews Against Zionism*, p. 160.

23. Ibid., p. 163.

24. Judah Magnes to Joseph Proskauer, September 19, 1946, GLL.

25. "Statement of the American Jewish Committee submitted to the United Nations Committee of Inquiry into Palestine," GLL.

26. Kolsky, *Jews Against Zionism*, p. 164.

27. Alfred Lilienthal to Elmer Berger, July 30 and August 19, 1947, GLL.

28. Kolsky, *Jews Against Zionism*, pp. 166–67.

29. Ibid., pp. 168–69.

30. Elmer Berger to George Levison, September 11, 1947, GLL.

31. Kolsky, *Jews Against Zionism*, p. 170.

32. Ibid., pp. 171–72.

33. Ibid., p. 173.

34. Ibid., p. 175.

35. Ibid.

36. "Address opening the academic year 1947–48, by J. L. Magnes, President of the Hebrew University," ACJ-W.

37. Lessing Rosenwald to Judah Magnes, November 11, 1947, ACJ-W.

38. Kolsky, *Jews Against Zionism*, p. 176.

39. Ibid., pp. 177–78.

40. Rosenbaum, *Visions of Reform*, pp. 203–6.

41. Kolsky, *Jews Against Zionism*, pp. 178–79.

42. Ibid., pp. 180–81.

43. Morris Lazaron to Kermit Roosevelt, February 25, 1948, MSL.

44. Kolsky, *Jews Against Zionism*, p. 181.

45. Judah Magnes to Virginia Gildersleeve, March 8, 1948, ACJ-W.

46. Leon Simon to Judah Magnes, March 7, 1948, ACJ-W.

47. Magnes to Simon, March 16, 1948, ACJ-W.

48. Kolsky, *Jews Against Zionism*, pp. 183–84.

49. Smith, *America's Defense Line*, p. 35.

50. Saposs, *Communism in American Politics*, pp. 81–83.

51. "For Justice and Peace in Palestine," MSL.

52. Kolsky, *Jews Against Zionism*, p. 185.

53. Kermit Roosevelt to Lessing Rosenwald, April 15, 1948, LJR.

54. Kolsky, *Jews Against Zionism*, p. 186.

55. Though the Council deliberately sought to avoid any appearance of an international Jewish anti-Zionist movement, in addition to the Fellowship in Britain and the Ihud, the ACJ would also over the years have contacts among like-minded Jews in Australia, South Africa, and the Netherlands.

56. Ibid., p. 187.

57. "Why I Withdrew from the American Council for Judaism," ACJ-W.

58. Wolsey to Rosenwald, June 1, 1948, LW.

59. Untitled Press Release, ACJ-W.

60. "Rabbi Berger Answers Rabbi Louis Wolsey," *Jewish Exponent*, June 4, 1948. Press clipping, EB-N.

61. Untitled Statement, MSL.

62. Ibid.

63. Elmer Berger to Abraham Cronbach, June 3, 1948, ACJ-W.

64. Elmer Berger to I. Edward Tonkon, June 16, 1948, ACJ-W.

65. "Not So Fast Dr. Silver!," ACJ-W.

66. "Draft of Proposed Letter to *New York Times*," ACJ-W.

67. Kermit Roosevelt to Elmer Berger, June 2, 1948, LJR.

68. "Integrated Americans of Jewish Faith or A Permanent National Minority of Jews," *The Council News*, August 1948, IFR.

69. "Western Union—Mrs. Judah L. Magnes, Mayflower Hotel, New York City," ACJ-W.

70. EBOH.

5. A Council for Judaism?

1. Glickman, "One Voice," pp. 90–91.

2. "Zionists Reveal Plan to Control U.S. Jewry," *The Council News*, December 1949, PSB.

3. Ibid.

4. "Statement of the Synagogue Council of America to the American Council for Judaism," ACJ-W.

5. Irving Kane to Lessing Rosenwald, June 30, 1950, ACJ-W.

6. Ibid.

7. "On the NCRAC Statement," ACJ-W.

8. Zukerman was cited in this connection not only by Berger in *The Jewish Dilemma* but also by Irving Reichert in his famous Kol Nidre sermon of 1943.

9. "Excerpt from Jewish Newsletter, April 21, 1949," ACJ-W.

10. "The Party of Opposition in American Jewry," ACJ-W.

11. William Zukerman to Lessing Rosenwald, February 2, 1950, LJR.

12. "Facts and Comments—An Opportunity Missed," ACJ-W.

13. William Zukerman to Elmer Berger, June 23, 1950, ACJ-W.

14. Lilienthal, "Israel's Flag Is Not Mine." Retrieved from http://pulsemedia.org/2009/03/29/israels-flag-is-not-mine/, accessed January 3, 2011.

15. Ibid.

16. Joseph Kaufman to Elmer Berger, June 7, 1949, ACJ-W.

17. Leonard Sussman to Alfred Lilienthal, February 20, 1950, AML. For Lilienthal's own account of the event in question, see Lilienthal, *What Price Israel?*, pp. 141–42.

18. "Jewish Youth in the Balance—Reprinted from *The Council News*." Pamphlet, ACJ-W.

19. Ibid.

20. "Council News Article about NFTY Institute," ACJ-W.

21. "Israeli Premier's First Official Declaration Clarifying Relationships Between Israel and Jews in the United States and other Free Democracies Hailed by Blaustein as 'Document of Historic Significance.'" Press release, American Jewish Committee Archives. Retrieved from http://www.ajcarchives.org/AJC_DATA/Files/508.PDF, accessed January 3, 2011.

22. "Elmer Berger Raps Blaustein, Zionists, UJA, Defense Agencies, Ben Gurion," *Intermountain Jewish News*, November 23, 1950. Press clipping, ACJ-W.

23. Lessing Rosenwald to Jacob Blaustein, September 5, 1951, ACJ-W.

24. "Summary of Minutes of National Executive Committee Meeting, January 22, 1952," GLL.

25. "Memorandum—July 15, 1952," ACJ-W.

26. Lessing Rosenwald to Jacob Marcus, June 15, 1950; Marcus to Rosenwald, June 22, 1950, ACJ-W.

27. Glueck to Rosenwald, July 31, 1950; Glueck to Berger, August 1, 1950, ACJ-W.

28. Balint, *Running Commentary*, p. 17.

29. Lewis Strauss to Arthur Sulzberger, January 28, 1947, LLS.

30. Berger, *A Partisan History of Judaism*, pp. 100–102.

31. Ibid., pp. 114–15.

32. Himmelfarb, "A Partisan History of Judaism by Elmer Berger."

33. "Judaism and the Jewish People," *Commentary*, April 1952.

34. Ibid.

35. On this history see Miller, *Karaite Separatism*.

36. Interview with Leonard Sussman, September 27, 2008.

37. Sussman, *A Passion for Freedom*, p. 60.

38. "Memo to the Executive Staff—June 12, 1950," ACJ-W.

39. Barbara Levine to Elmer Berger, May 15, 1952, ACJ-W.

40. Interview with Leonard Sussman, September 27, 2008.

41. Interview with Justus Doenecke, September 5, 2008.

42. "Getting Back to Fundamentals," in *Judaism and the American Jew*, p. 9.

43. Ibid., p. 14.

44. Roland Gittelsohn to Irving Reichert, April 22, 1952; Reichert to Gittelsohn, May 2, 1952, IFR.

45. Victor Reichert to Lessing Rosenwald, August 13, 1952, ACJ-W. Capitalization in original.

46. "The Impact of Jewish Nationalism on Judaism and Jews by Dr. Morris S. Lazaron," ACJ-W.

47. Sheean was the principal basis for the composite character "Vincent Walker" played by Martin Sheen in the 1982 film *Gandhi*.

48. "Denver Post—For Release Sunday, March 20," ACJ-W.

49. Elmer Berger to Norman Thomas, April 7, 1949, ACJ-W.

50. Berger, *Memoirs*, p. 35.

51. On this history of Presbyterianism, see Malcolm Magee, *What the World Should Be: Woodrow Wilson and the Crafting of a Faith-Based Foreign Policy.* Waco, TX: Baylor University Press, 2008.

52. Norman Thomas, "A Menace to Fraterntiy," *Council News*, September 1952.

53. Samuel Friedman to Norman Thomas, September 12, 1955, NMT.

54. Interview with Don Peretz, February 19, 2009.

55. Krome, "A Rabbi and the Rosenbergs."

56. Berger, *Memoirs*, p. 40.

57. Levison to Rosenwald, January 3, 1953, GLL.

58. Kolsky, *Jews Against Zionism*, p. 191.

59. Kolsky, *Jews Against Zionism*, p. 192; Berger, *Memoirs*, p. 41.

60. "Dulles Recommendations on Middle East Hailed by American Council for Judaism," ACJ-W.

61. "Press Release from American Zionist Council," ACJ-W.

62. Henry Moyer to *Time* magazine, May 22, 1953; Dulles to Moyer, June 18, 1953; Moyer to Dulles, June 23, 1953, ACJ-W.

63. It is worth noting, at the same time, that these figures were generally aligned with George Kennan, who as the author of "containment" would be highly critical of its ostensible implementation by Truman.

64. On this history, see Cole, *Engaging the Muslim World*, pp. 87–90.

65. Berger, *Memoirs*, p. 42.

66. Ibid.

67. Ibid., pp. 42–43.

68. "Council Challenges Sharett's right to speak for Jews outside of Israeli State," EB-N.

69. Louis Lipsky to John Foster Dulles, July 15, 1954, PSB.

70. Oral history interview with Henry Byroade by Niel M. Johnson, Harry S. Truman Library, September 19–21, 1988. Retrieved from http://www.trumanlibrary.org/oralhist/byroade.htm, accessed January 3, 2011.

71. Berger, *Memoirs*, pp. 63–65.

72. Ibid., p. 67.

73. Ibid., pp. 68–70.

74. Berger to Lazaron, March 11, 1952, ACJ-W.

75. Lazaron, *Olive Trees in Storm*, pp. 73–76.

76. Ibid., p. 92.

77. Lilienthal, *What Price Israel?*

78. See, for example, Charles Shulman, "Portrait of a Judaist Rabbi," *Congress Weekly*, June 15, 1953. Press clipping, EB-N.

79. Regnery, *Memoirs*, p. 120.

80. Ibid., p. 121. It is worth noting the extreme contrast between Regnery the man and his namesake today. The Regnery Company, now a middle to lowbrow trade publisher of the "conservative movement," has reverted not only to its founder's polar opposite views on the Middle East, with its subsidiary Pajamas Media running the columns of such virulent Zionists as Michael Ledeen and Ronald Radosh, but has also, in shocking contrast to the legacy of Henry Regnery, published a book defending Japanese internment.

81. Kolsky, *Jews Against Zionism*, p. 193.

82. "Anti-Zionist Judaism"

83. Leonard Sussman, "What Do Council Schools Teach?," *Council News*, March 1953.

84. Ibid.

85. Harold Green to Leonard Sussman, May 26, 1953; Sussman to Green, May 29, 1953, ACJ-W.

86. Kolsky, *Jews Against Zionism*, p. 193.

87. "Complete excerpt of that portion of the Address by Rabbi Fink dealing with the Schools for Judaism," ACJ-W.

88. Ernest Lee to Joseph Fink, undated, ACJ-W.

89. "Central Conference of American Rabbis Report of Special Committee on American Council for Judaism Schools," ACJ-W.

90. Samuel Baron to Roland Gittelsohn, June 10, 1955, ACJ-H.

91. A native of Algeria who spent most of his adult life as a rabbi in London and Amsterdam, Sasportas was a confidant in London of Menasseh ben Israel, the Jewish intriguer who convinced Cromwell to emancipate the Jews. The sometimes-violent opposition of Sasportas to the following of Shabtai Tzvi was no doubt partly inspired by the belief of Menasseh ben Israel that the dispersion of the Jews all throughout the world was a necessary precondition for the messiah, in contrast to the proto-Zionism of Shabtai Tzvi. "The same basic qualities of harshness, irascibility, arrogance, and fanaticism are much in evidence in his letters on the Sabbatian movement." Scholem, *Sabbatai Zevi*, p. 567.

92. Glickman, "One Voice," p. 78.

93. "Statement of Principles—Lakeside Congregation for Reform Judaism," ACJ-H.

94. Berger's friend Justus Doenecke, for one, suspects that he never believed in a personal God.

95. Glickman, "One Voice," p. 76.

96. Interview with Justus Doenecke, October 20, 2008.

97. "On Religious and Synagogal Programs—March 11, 1951," ACJ-W.

98. Glickman, "One Voice," p. 42.

99. Elmer Berger, "This is Fohrenwald," *Council News*, January 1953.

100. "Statement by Lessing J. Rosenwald, March 2, 1953," ACJ-W.

101. Retrieved from http://www.philipweiss.org/mondoweiss/2008/06/cfr-heavy-walter-russell-mead-says-americans-love-israel-like-cherry-pie.html.

102. Form letter by Harry Snellenburg, December 1, 1956, ACJ-H.

103. Glickman, "One Voice," p. 112.

104. Berger, *Who Knows Better Must Say So*, pp. 8–9.

105. Ibid., p. 10.

106. Ibid., pp. 32–33.

107. Ibid., p. 36.

108. Ibid., p. 52.

109. Ibid., pp. 52–53.

110. Ibid., p. 70.

111. Ibid., p. 85.

112. Israeli Labor Federation.

113. Ben-Gurion's Ruling Party, which would eventually evolve into the Labor Party.

114. Ibid., p. 86.

115. Ibid., p. 105.

116. Ibid., p. 111.

117. Glickman, "One Voice," p. 115.

118. "Facts—February 1956," LLS.

119. Glickman, "One Voice," p. 117.

120. "Resolution Adopted by the National Community Relations Advisory Council," ACJ-H.

121. "Resolution Adopted by the Central Conference of American Rabbis," ACJ-H.

122. Irving Reichert to Clarence Coleman, July 19, 1956, IFR.

123. Sidney Wallach to Irving Reichert, July 26, 1956, IFR.

124. Interview with Leonard Sussman, September 27, 2008.

125. Interview with Fred Rosenbaum, March 18, 2009.

126. Morris Lazaron, "In the Shadow of Catastrophe," *Council News* December 1956.

127. Berger, *Memoirs*, p. 76.

6. Pyrrhic Victories

1. Norman Thomas to Morris Polin, January 30, 1957, NMT.

2. Harry Rogoff to Norman Thomas, February 7, 1957, NMT.

3. Polin to Thomas, February 13, 1957, NMT.

4. William Zukerman to Norman Thomas, February 17, 1957, NMT.

5. Ibid.

6. James Wechsler to Norman Thomas, February 20, 1957, NMT.

7. Swanberg, *Norman Thomas*, p. 402.

8. Ibid., p. 403.

9. Interview with Don Peretz, February 19, 2009.

10. Stove, "The Man Who Knew Too Much."

11. Parmet, *The Master of Seventh Avenue*, p. 97.

12. Herrick, *Jumping the Line*, p. 243.

13. "The Hebrew Manifesto—Principles of Semitic Action," ACJ-H.

14. Menuhin, *The Decadence of Judaism in Our Time*, p. 62.

15. Ibid., p. 61.

16. Interview with Uri Avnery, December 25, 2008.

17. Morris Lazaron, "Why Do They Hate My Father?,'" *Issues*, Summer 1965. MSL-N.

18. "Judaism Today and Tomorrow: A Nuclear-Age View," ACJ-H.

19. "What Is a Jew?," *Time*, May 19, 1961. Herberg is today remembered for his walk-on role in the epoch of the "conservative movement" as the onetime religion editor of *National Review*, even though he remained, among other things, an advocate of trade unionism. In his true calling, as a philosopher of Judaism, he remains tragically obscure.

20. Nash, "Forgotten Godfathers." Three of the five remaining subjects—Frank Meyer, Willi Schlamm, and Marvin Liebman—would convert to Catholicism, leaving Eugene Lyons, a lifelong atheist, and Ralph de Toledano, an ethical culture devotee turned self-described "Catholic fellow traveler" the only one of the seven to ever become notably pro-Zionist. It is also worth noting that Chodorov and Ryskind were the only two to come unambiguously out of the anti-Stalinist left.

21. Chodorov, "How a Jew Came to God."

22. Nash, "Forgotten Godfathers."

23. Chodorov, "Some Blunt Truths About Israel."

24. Rothbard is so listed on a roster of all ACJ members in the Greater New York area available in ACJ-H.

25. Interview with Leonard Sussman, January 2, 2009.

26. An early student of Stephen Wise at the Jewish Institute of Religion, Schultz was a rising star in both the Reform movement and the Zionist Organization of America before becoming ostracized for his collaboration with McCarthy, and he later became an activist with the White Citizens Council from a pulpit in Clarksdale, Mississippi. Though some might see in Schultz an interesting parallel to Berger as pariah, as an acolyte of Stephen Wise who turned sharply to the right, Schultz more convincingly appears as a premature neoconservative.

27. Nash, "Forgotten Godfathers."

28. Ibid.

29. Utley, *Will the Middle East Go West?*, p. 1.

30. Ibid., p. 136.

31. Berger's parents spent their last years in Dayton, Ohio. His mother died in 1958, his father in 1962.

32. Berger, *Judaism or Jewish Nationalism?*, p. 100.

33. Ibid., p. 101.

34. Norton Mezvinsky to Elmer Berger, November 15, 1959; Elmer Berger to Clarence Coleman, November 23, 1959, ACJ-H.

35. Berger to Coleman, May 6, 1959, ACJ-H.

36. "The UJA Funds 'Reorganization,'" by Lessing J. Rosenwald. Pamphlet, ACJ-W.

37. Ibid.

38. "Jewish Newsletter, May 2, 1960," EB-N.

39. Parker T. Hart to Clarence Coleman, undated (though acknowledging letters of June 17 and 29, 1960), ACJ-H.

40. "Special Issue—Israel's Eichmann Exploitation," ACJ-W.

41. "Moral and Ethical Problems Arising in the Eichmann Trial," ACJ-W.

42. Berger, *Memoirs*, p. 135.

43. Ibid., p. 46.

44. "In Memoriam: William Zukerman," AC.

45. Brown and Kutler, *Nelson Glueck*, p. 167.

46. Clarence Coleman to Maurice Eisendrath, July 23, 1963, ACJ-H.

47. J. William Fulbright to Elmer Berger, February 5, 1959; Bill Gottlieb to *New York Post* City Editor, December 14, 1960, ACJ-H.

48. Berger, *Memoirs*, p. 92.

49. Smith, *America's Defense Line*, pp. 120–34.

50. Ibid., p. 133.

51. "National Policy and Public Opinion—By Senator J. William Fulbright," ACJ-H.

52. Smith, *America's Defense Line*, pp. 138–39; Scott McConnell, "Obama's Israel Test," *American Conservative*, March 10, 2008.

53. On this history see Hersh, *The Samson Option*.

54. "Rabbi Philip S. Bernstein, Sunday, May 5, 1963," PSB.

55. "Zionist 'Agents' in the United States—By Elmer Berger," ACJ-H.

56. Ibid.

57. Smith, *America's Defense Line*, pp. 142–43.

58. Ibid., pp. 146–48.

59. Ibid., pp. 152–43.

60. Ibid., p. 153.

61. Quoted in Shahak, *Jewish History, Jewish Religion*, pp. 71–72.

62. These yearbooks with Berger's difficult-to-read handwritten notes are available in ACJ-W.

63. For a thorough discussion of these parallels see Cronon, *Black Moses*, pp. 199–200.

64. It is worth noting that a key early civil judgment against Garvey in 1923 was handed down by future ACJ supporter Jacob Panken, who did not hesitate to vigorously condemn Garvey and his movement from the bench, no doubt inspired by his anti-Zionism.

65. Avineri, *The Making of Modern Zionism*, pp. 76–77.

66. Glickman, "One Voice," pp. 127–29.

67. Phillips Talbot to Elmer Berger, April 20, 1964, ACJ-H.

68. Glickman, "One Voice," p. 130.

69. Philip Bernstein to Phillips Talbot, May 13, 1964, PSB.

70. Talbot to Berger, April 20, 1964, ACJ-H.

71. Mallison would later claim through his own sources that the Israeli government would for years pressure the State Department to retract the letter, to no avail. "In Memoriam: William Thomas Mallison Jr. (1917–1997)," *Washington Report for Middle East Affairs*, January–February 1998.

72. Glickman, "One Voice," p. 131.

73. See, for example, "New Insights into the Zionist-Israel-Palestine Problem," *Arab-Ute Reporter*, May 15, 1964. Excerpted, PSB.

74. Glickman, "One Voice," pp. 132–33.

75. "In Memory of Dr. Abraham Cronbach," ACJ-H.

76. "Statement by Elmer Berger—January 28, 1966," ACJ-H.

77. Interview with Leonard Sussman, January 2, 2009.

78. On this history, see Evans, *The Provincials*, pp. 105–8.

79. Interview with Norton Mezvinsky, January 10, 2009. It should still be noted, however, that even this is a shocking indication of the fanatical religious devotion enforced in this era to the United Jewish Appeal.

80. Berger, *Memoirs*, p. 111.

81. Ibid., p. 112.

82. Glickman, "One Voice," pp. 137–38.

83. Elmer Berger to Morris Lazaron, October 31, 1967, MSL.

84. Berger to Lazaron, July 3, 1968, MSL.

85. Elmer Berger to Lessing Rosenwald, July 5, 1968, LJR.

86. Richard Korn to Council Membership, October 1, 1968, ACJ-W.

87. Interview with Allan Brownfeld, August 22, 2008.

88. Morris Lazaron to Alford Carleton, June 27, 1967, MSL.

89. Morris Lazaron, "Looking Back," *Conservative Judaism*, Winter 1973. Press clipping, MSL-N.

90. Ibid.

91. See, for example, Philip Smilovitz, "Purely Commentary: The Lazaron Role and the Story of an Antagonist's Repenting," *Detroit Jewish News*, October 7, 1977. Press clipping, MSL-N.

7. One Voice Against Many

1. Berger, *Memoirs*, p. 142.

2. Elmer Berger to Don Peretz, December 28, 1970, AJAZ.

3. Jewish Alternatives to Zionism letterhead, ACJ-W.

4. EBOH.

5. Interview with Leonard Sussman, May 17, 2008.

6. Interview with Mark Glickman, May 27, 2009.

7. Elmer Berger to Allan Tarshish, March 14, 1972, AJAZ.

8. EBOH.

9. Elmer Berger to Walid Khalidi, March 29, 1971, AJAZ.

10. C. K. Zurayk to Elmer Berger, April 15, 1971, AJAZ.

11. Elmer Berger to Walid Khadduri, July 16, 1971, AJAZ.

12. Elmer Berger to Ahmed Anis, June 7, 1971, AJAZ.

13. Interview with Leonard Sussman, March 22, 2009.

14. Interview with Justus Doenecke, November 15, 2008.

15. "Part of Political Statement from Algiers Conference," AJAZ.

16. Hugh Jencks to D. M. Duff, April 10, 1970, AJAZ.

17. Christopher Mayhew to Elmer Berger, November 17, 1972, AJAZ.

18. W. T. Mallison Jr. to Elmer Berger, June 29, 1970, AJAZ.

19. Berger to Mallison, January 14, 1970, AJAZ.

20. Elmer Berger to William Rogers, December 17, 1969, AJAZ.

21. John P. Roche, "George McGovern and Israel," syndicated column. Press clipping, AJAZ.

22. Ibid.

23. Elmer Berger to Richard Stearns, July 6, 1972, AJAZ.

24. Elmer Berger to Thomas Teepen, July 19, 1972, AJAZ.

25. Podhoretz, *Breaking Ranks*, p. 336.

26. Everett Gendler to Elmer Berger, September 9, 1970; Berger to Gendler, September 10, 1970, AJAZ.

27. Allan Solomonow to Elmer Berger, April 14, 1971; Berger to Solomonow, August 2, 1971, AJAZ.

28. Elmer Berger to Norton Mezvinsky, July 26, 1972, AJAZ.

29. Elmer Berger to Allan Brownfeld, April 6, 1971, AJAZ.

30. Holley, "Rabbi Balfour Brickner."

31. Avnery, "Two Knights and a Dragon."

32. Rosenbaum, *Visions of Reform*, pp. 266–68.

33. Interview with Mark Glickman, November 12, 2008.

34. Elmer Berger to Alfred Lilienthal, December 2, 1969, AML.

35. Elmer Berger to Theodore Dennery, July 24, 1970, AJAZ.

36. "Reb Amrom's Last Request," AJAZ.

37. Interview with Allan Brownfeld, May 9, 2008.

38. Berger, *Memoirs*, pp. 135–39.

39. "Israelis Becoming Persecutors," "Israeli Speaker's Views Disputed," AJAZ.

40. Interview with Peter Hanauer, February 7, 2009.

41. Interview with Justus Doenecke, March 7, 2009.

42. Justus Doenecke to Elmer Berger, January 22, 1973, AJAZ.

43. Berger to Doenecke, January 25, 1973, AJAZ.

44. Elmer Berger to Murray Rothbard, July 3, 1974; Rothbard to Berger, July 10, 1974, AJAZ.

45. Elmer Berger to Ned Hanauer, October 4, 1973, AJAZ.

46. "The American Palestine Committee: October 6, 1973," AJAZ.

47. "Statement of Welcome to the Palestinians," AJAZ.

48. EBOH.

49. Elmer Berger to Justus Doenecke, November 20, 1974, AJAZ.

50. Elmer Berger to Leonard Sussman, November 25, 1974, LRS.

51. Berger to Sussman, October 22, 1975, LRS.

52. Ibid.

53. An incredible essay outlining how the "Jewish polity" was able to begin to delineate the boundaries of legitimate and illegitimate dissent, entirely on the basis of what was "good for Israel," was published by Jack Wertheimer, professor of American Jewish history at Jewish Theological Seminary and frequent contributor to *Commentary*. See Wertheimer, "Breaking the Taboo."

54. Berger, *Memoirs*, p. 145.

55. Berger even recalled being with Kermit Roosevelt as the 1953 coup was taking place and Roosevelt confiding the developments as he became aware of them. Interview with Justus Doenecke, July 6, 2009.

8. Before the Storm

1. Interview with Justus Doenecke, September 5, 2008.

2. Elmer Berger to Leonard Sussman, July 20, 1982, LRS.

3. Interview with Thomas Kolsky, February 28, 2009.

4. "Elmer Berger Still at It," *Jewish Post and Opinion*, July 30, 1982. Press clipping, EB-N.

5. Elmer Berger to Leonard Sussman, October 3, 1982, LRS.

6. "Tentative Program for Symposium," LRS.

7. Elmer Berger to Jacob Marcus, October 26, 1982, Elmer Berger-Jacob Marcus Correspondence.

8. Berger to Marcus, February 21, 1983, Berger-Marcus Correspondence.

9. Elmer Berger to Leonard Sussman, August 24, 1983, LRS.

10. Interview with Justus Doenecke, July 6, 2009.

11. Elmer Berger to Mark Damen, November 24, 1984; Damen to Berger, December 19, 1984, LRS.

12. "The Promise—September 6, 1985," LRS.

13. Ibid.

14. "Daring to Speak Out: Hon. John Conyers of Michigan—Extension of Remarks," *Congressional Record*, May 22, 1986.

15. Elmer Berger to Leonard Sussman, October 8, 1989, LRS.

16. Berger, *Anti-Zionism*, p. 14.

17. Interview with Mark Glickman, December 3, 2008.

18. Glickman, "One Voice," p. iv.

19. As examples, Leonard Sussman was only made aware of the dissertation shortly before Berger's death, and Justus Doenecke had not ever known about it until told by the author.

20. EBOH.

21. Ibid.

22. Glickman, "One Voice," pp. 169–74.

23. Elmer Berger to Leonard Sussman, January 21, 1988, LRS.

24. Berger to Sussman, March 17, 1991, LRS.

25. Berger to Sussman, August 18, 1990, LRS.

26. Berger, *Peace for Palestine*, p. 241.

27. Ibid., p. xii.

28. EBOH.

29. Shahak, *Jewish History, Jewish Religion*, pp. xi–xii.

30. Interview with Justus Doenecke, July 6, 2009.

31. Elmer Berger to Leonard Sussman, June 23, 1994, LRS.

32. Berger to Sussman, September 20, 1994, LRS.

33. Interview with Leonard Sussman, May 12, 2009.

34. "Background for an obituary; Rabbi Elmer Berger," LRS.

35. Eric Pace, "Elmer Berger, 88, a Foe of Zionism as Well as Israel," *New York Times* October 9, 1996. Press clipping, LRS.

36. "Rabbi Who Opposed Jewish Homeland Dies"; "Remembering Rabbi, Factually" *Sarasota Herald-Tribune*, October 11–15, 1996. Press clipping, LRS.

37. Mezvinsky, "In Memoriam."

38. Naseer Aruri, "A Tribute to Rabbi Elmer Berger," *Washington Report for Middle East Affairs*, January–February 1997.

39. Glickman, "One Voice," pp. 173–74.

Epilogue

1. Significantly, these holidays are not observed by even the most avowedly Zionist of Orthodox Jews, regarding them as violations of the Omer, the sacred seven weeks that simulate the journey out of Egypt at Passover to arriving at Sinai at Shavuot.

2. Kaplan, *Contemporary Debates*, p. 9.

3. "A Statement of Principles for Reform Judaism."

4. Brownfeld, "Jews Are 'Trading in Peoplehood for Faith.'"

5. "Analysis: Sharon's Appeasement Warning."

6. Judt, "Israel: The Alternative."

7. John Mearsheimer and Stephen Walt, "The Israel Lobby," *London Review of Books*, March 23, 2006.

8. Avnery, "Two Knights and a Dragon."

9. Lieven, *America Right or Wrong*, pp. 186–90.

10. It should also be noted, however, that the pulpit of B'nai Jeshurun was briefly held by none other than Judah Magnes in the early 1910s.

11. "A Passover Seder Haggadah Supplement by Rabbi Michael Lerner."

12. Sand, *The Invention of the Jewish People*.

13. Kolsky, *Jews Against Zionism*, p. 201.

14. Glickman, "One Voice," pp. 158–59.

15. Kauffman, "Heil to the Chief."

16. Though the concept of "Stockholm Syndrome" did not yet exist in this era, Zionism essentially believed that this was the condition suffered by anti-Zionist Jews—identification with their "captive" gentile society.

17. Heilbrunn, *They Knew They Were Right*, pp. 14–15.

18. Glickman, "One Voice," p. 76.

19. See, for example, *False Witness: The Record of the American Council for Judaism*. New York: American Zionist Council, 1955. In fact, the very term "cultural pluralism" was coined by the Zionist ideologue Horace Kallen.

20. "Why Are Jews Liberals? A Symposium," *Commentary*, September 2009.

21. Isaiah 30:8. The Holy Scriptures, Jewish Publication Society of America.

BIBLIOGRAPHY

Archival Collections

American Council for Judaism Papers, Wisconsin Historical Society, Madison, WI (ACJ-W).

American Jewish Archives, Hebrew Union College, Cincinnati, OH.

American Council for Judaism Collection (ACJ-H).

Abraham Cronbach Papers (AC).

Morris Lazaron Papers (MSL).

Louis Wolsey Papers (LW).

Elmer Berger Nearprint File (EB-N).

Samuel Goldenson Nearprint File (SG-N).

Morris Lazaron Nearprint File (MSL-N).

Elmer Berger-Jacob Marcus Correspondence, Small Collection.

Lessing Rosenwald Papers, Library of Congress, Washington, DC (LJR).

Irving Reichert Papers, Judah Magnes Museum, Berkeley, CA (IFR).

Norman Thomas Papers, New York Public Library, New York, NY (NMT).

George Levison Papers, in possession of Thomas Kolsky, Blue Bell, PA (GLL).

Alfred Lilienthal Papers, Hoover Institution, Stanford, CA (AML).

Lewis Strauss Papers, American Jewish Historical Society, New York, NY (LLS).

Philip Bernstein Papers, University of Rochester, Rochester, NY (PSB).

Personal Correspondence of Leonard Sussman, courtesy of himself to the author (since deposited with American Jewish Archives, Hebrew Union College, Cincinnati, OH) (LRS).

American Jews for Alternatives to Zionism Papers, Institute for Palestine Studies, Beirut (Microfilm, American Jewish Archives, Hebrew Union College, Cincinnati, OH) (AJAZ).

Articles and Dissertations

Berger, Elmer. "An Examination of the Meanings of selihah, hemlah, rotzon, and hen in the Bible." Rabbinical dissertation, Hebrew Union College, Cincinnati, OH, 1932.

Glickman, Mark. "One Voice Against Many: A Biographical Study of Elmer Berger, 1948–1968." Rabbinical dissertation, Hebrew Union College, Cincinnati, OH, 1990.

Lapides, Abe. "History of the Jewish Community of Pontiac, Michigan." *Michigan Jewish History*. July 1977.

Nash, George. "Forgotten Godfathers: Premature Jewish Conservatives and the Rise of National Review." *American Jewish History*, 1999.

Sundheim, Frank. "The Beginnings and Early History of the American Council for Judaism." Term paper for Dr. Jacob R. Marcus, History 5, Hebrew Union College, November 1957. American Jewish Archives, Hebrew Union College, Cincinnati, OH.

Wertheimer, Jack. "Breaking the Taboo: Critics of Israel and the American Jewish Establishment." In *Envisioning Israel: The Changing Ideals and Images of North American Jews,* edited by Allon Gal, 397–419. Detroit: Wayne State University Press, 1996.

ACJ Publications (bound volumes courtesy of Leonard Sussman)

Council News 1951–1953, 1955–1957.

Issues 1958–1959, 1965–1966. (Since deposited in Swarthmore College Peace Collection, Swarthmore, PA.)

Author Interviews

Leonard Sussman: May 17, September 27 (2008); January 2, March 22, May 12 (2009).

Justus Doenecke: September 5, November 15 (2008); March 7, April 6, July 6 (2009).

Mark Glickman: November 12, December 2 (2008); February 11, May 27 (2009).

Norton Mezvinsky: July 18, 2008; January 10, 2009.

Allan Brownfeld: May 9, August 22 (2008).

Uri Avnery: December 25, 2008.

Seymour Fromer: February 6, 2009.

Nathan Glazer: November 29, 2008.

Peter Hanauer: February 7, 2009.

Thomas Kolsky: February 28, 2009.

Don Peretz: February 19, 2009.

Fred Rosenbaum: March 18, 2009.

Jerome Winegarden Jr.: March 23, 2009.

Oral History

Elmer Berger interview by Mark Glickman, November 29–30, 1989; Oral History Collection of the American Jewish Archives, Hebrew Union College, Cincinnati, OH (EBOH).

Oral History Interview with Henry Byroade by Niel M. Johnson, Harry S. Truman Library, September 19–21, 1988.

Books

Avineri, Shlomo. *The Making of Modern Zionism: The Intellectual Origins of the Jewish State.* New York: Basic Books, 1981.

Balint, Benjamin. *Running Commentary: The Contentious Magazine that transformed the Jewish Left into the Neoconservative Right.* New York: Public Affairs, 2010.

Berger, Elmer. *The Jewish Dilemma.* New York: Devin-Adair Company, 1945.

———. *A Partisan History of Judaism.* New York: Devin-Adair Company, 1951.

———. *Who Knows Better Must Say So.* New York: The Bookmailer, 1955.

———. *Judaism or Jewish Nationalism? The Alternative to Zionism.* New York: Bookman Associates, 1957.

———. *Memoirs of an Anti-Zionist Jew.* Beirut: Institute for Palestine Studies, 1978.

———. *Anti-Zionism: Analytical Reflections.* Brattleboro, VT: Amana Books, 1989.

———. *Peace for Palestine: First Lost Opportunity.* Gainesville, FL: University of Florida Press, 1993.

Brown, Jonathan M., and Lawrence Kutler. *Nelson Glueck: Biblical Archaeologist and President of Hebrew Union College-Jewish Institute of Religion.* Cincinnati: Hebrew Union College Press, 2006.

Cole, Juan. *Engaging the Muslim World.* New York: Palgrave Macmillan, 2009.

Cronon, E. David. *Black Moses: The Story of Marcus Garvey and the Universal Negro Improvement Association.* Madison, WI: University of Wisconsin Press, 1954.

Elon, Amos. *The Pity of It All: A History of Jews in Germany, 1743–1933.* New York: Henry Holt and Company, Metropolitan Books, 2002.

Evans, Eli. *The Provincials: A Personal History of Jews in the South.* Chapel Hill, NC: University of North Carolina Press, 1973.

Graetz, Heinrich. *History of The Jews.* Breslau: 1870, reprinted Brooklyn, New York: DeVinne-Hallenbeck Company, 1927.

Heilbrunn, Jacob. *They Knew They Were Right: The Rise of the Neocons.* New York: Doubleday, 2008.

Heller, James. *Isaac Mayer Wise: His Life, Work, and Thought.* New York: Union of American Hebrew Congregations, 1965.

Herrick, William. *Jumping the Line: The Adventures and Misadventures of an American Radical.* Madison, WI: University of Wisconsin Press, 1998.

Hersh, Seymour. *The Samson Option: Israel's Nuclear Arsenal and American Foreign Policy.* New York: Random House, 1991.

Judaism and the American Jew: Selected Sermons and Addresses of Irving Frederick Reichert. San Francisco: Grabhorn Press, 1953.

Kaplan, Dana Evan. *Contemporary Debates in Reform Judaism.* New York: Routledge, 2001.

Karp, Abraham J. *Haven and Home: A History of the Jews in America.* New York: Schocken Books, 1985.

Kolsky, Thomas A. *Jews Against Zionism: The American Council for Judaism, 1942–1948.* Philadelphia: Temple University Press, 1990.

Lazaron, Morris. *Olive Trees in Storm.* New York: American Friends of the Middle East, 1955.

Lieven, Anatol. *America Right or Wrong: An Anatomy of American Nationalism.* New York: Oxford University Press, 2004.

Lilienthal, Alfred. *What Price Israel?* Chicago: Henry Regnery Company, 1953.

Menuhin, Moshe. *The Decadence of Judaism in Our Time.* Beirut: Institute for Palestine Studies, 1969.

Miller, Philip. *Karaite Separatism in 19th Century Russia.* Cincinnati: Hebrew Union College Press, 1993.

Parmet, Robert. *The Master of Seventh Avenue: David Dubinsky and the American Labor Movement.* New York: New York University Press, 2005.

Podhoretz, Norman. *Breaking Ranks: A Political Memoir.* New York: Harper and Row, 1979.

Regnery, Henry. *Memoirs of a Dissident Publisher.* Chicago: Regnery Books, 1985.

Roth, Philip. *The Plot Against America.* New York: Houghton-Mifflin, 2004.

Rosenbaum, Fred. *Visions of Reform: Congregation Emanu-El and the Jews of San Francisco, 1849–1999.* Berkeley, CA: Judah Magnes Museum, 2000.

Sand, Shlomo. *The Invention of the Jewish People.* London: Verso, 2009.

Saposs, David. *Communism in American Politics.* Washington, DC: Public Affairs Press, 1960.

Scholem, Gershom. *Sabbatai Zevi: The Mystical Messiah.* Princeton, NJ: Princeton University Press, 1973.

Shahak, Israel. *Jewish History, Jewish Religion: The Weight of Three Thousand Years.* London: Pluto Press, 1994.

Smith, Grant. *America's Defense Line: The Justice Department's Battle to Register the Israel Lobby as Agents of a Foreign Government*. Washington, DC: Institute for Research of Middle East Policy, 2008.

Sussman, Leonard. *A Passion for Freedom: My Encounters with Extraordinary People*. Amherst, NY: Prometheus Books, 2004.

Swanberg, W. A. *Norman Thomas: The Last Idealist*. New York: Charles Scribner and Sons, 1976.

Utley, Freda. *Will the Middle East Go West?* Chicago: Henry Regnery Company, 1957.

Periodicals

"Anti-Zionist Judaism." *Time* November 3, 1952.

Aruri, Naseer. "A Tribute to Rabbi Elmer Berger." *Washington Report for Middle East Affairs*, January–February 1997.

Avnery, Uri. "Two Knights and a Dragon" *The American Conservative*, October 22, 2007.

Blank, David Eugene. "The *New York Times*' strange attack on Classical Reform Judaism." *Issues*, Fall 2002.

Brownfeld, Allan. "Jews Are 'Trading in Peoplehood for Faith' Declares Leonard Fein." *Special Interest Report*, March–April 1998.

Chodorov, Frank. "Some Blunt Truths About Israel." *American Mercury*, July 1956.

"Daring to Speak Out: Hon. John Conyers of Michigan—Extension of Remarks." *Congressional Record*, May 22, 1986.

Himmelfarb, Milton. "A Partisan History of Judaism by Elmer Berger." *Commentary*, February 1952.

———. "Judaism and the Jewish People." *Commentary*, April 1952.

Holley, Joe. "Rabbi Balfour Brickner, 78; Founded D.C.'s Temple Sinai." *Washington Post*, September 1, 2005.

"In Memoriam: William Thomas Mallison Jr. (1917–1997)." *Washington Report for Middle East Affairs*, January–February 1998.

Judt, Tony. "Israel: The Alternative." *New York Review of Books*, October 23, 2003.

Kauffman, Bill. "Heil to the Chief." *The American Conservative*, September 27, 2004.

Lilienthal, Alfred. "Israel's Flag Is Not Mine." *Reader's Digest*, September 1949.

McConnell, Scott. "Obama's Israel Test." *The American Conservative*, March 10, 2008.

Mearsheimer, John, and Stephen Walt. "The Israel Lobby." *London Review of Books*, March 23, 2006.

Mezvinsky, Norton. "In Memoriam: Rabbi Elmer Berger (1908–1996)." *Washington Report for Middle East Affairs*, November–December 1996.

Stove, R. J. "The Man Who Knew Too Much." *The American Conservative*, December 15, 2003.

"What Is a Jew?" *Time,* May 19, 1961.

"Why Are Jews Liberals? A Symposium." *Commentary,* September 2009.

Internet

American Jewish Committee Archives. http://www.ajcarchives.org/.

Anshe Chesed Fairmount Temple. "Temple History." http://www.fairmounttemple.org/history.htm.

BBC News. "Analysis: Sharon's Appeasement Warning." http://news.bbc.co.uk/2/hi/middle_east/1581280.stm.

Central Conference of American Rabbis. "A Statement of Principles for Reform Judaism." http://ccarnet.org/Articles/index.cfm?id=44&pge_id=1606.

Chodorov, Frank. The School of Cooperative Individualism. "How a Jew Came to God." *Analysis,* March 1948. http://www.cooperativeindividualism.org/chodorov-frank_autobiographical-story.html.

Jewish Virtual Library. "The Columbus Platform: The Guiding Principles of Reform Judaism." http://www.jewishvirtuallibrary.org/jsource/Judaism/Columbus_platform.html.

Krome, Frederic. Union for Reform Judaism. "A Rabbi and the Rosenbergs." http://tmt.urj.net/archives/2socialaction/032905.htm.

"The Loewenstein Family of Milam County, Texas." http://www.loewensteins.org/Files/LoewensteinFamily2.html.

"The Pittsburgh Platform." http://www.renewreform.org/docs/PittsburghPlatform.pdf.

"Prime Minister's Speech at the Herzliya Conference." January 23, 2008. http://www.pmo.gov.il/PMOEng/Communication/PMSpeaks/speechherzelia230108.htm.

Temple Beth El History. "Remembering Our Past, Celebrating Our Future." www.templebethelflint.org/temple_beth_el_history.htm.

Temple Tifereth Israel. http://www.clevelandjewishhistory.net/silver/temple.html.

Tikkun. "A Passover Seder Haggadah Supplement by Rabbi Michael Lerner." http://www.tikkun.org/article.php/seder_2009.

INDEX

A Partisan History of Judaism (Berger), 28, 99–100, 129, 160, 182

Abourezk, James, 167, 168

Abrams, Elliott, 172

Acheson, Dean, 74, 76, 106

Adorno, Theodor, 185

Affelder, Lewis, 151

African National Congress, 169

Agudath Israel, 12, 94. *See also* Neturei Karta

Albright, William Foxwell, 27

Altman, Jack, 67

America First Committee, 5, 15, 45–46

American Council for Emigres in the Professions, 117

American Council for Judaism (ACJ), 2, 3, 4, 5, 7, 15, 16, 22, 24, 27, 29, 35, 36, 43, 46, 52, 57–58, 61–64, 66, 69, 71–73, 74, 76, 77, 81, 83, 89, 90, 91, 95–98, 101, 111, 112, 118, 119, 124, 125, 126, 127, 128, 129, 131–33, 134, 136–37, 140, 141, 143–45, 148, 150, 151, 152, 153, 158, 159, 160, 161, 163, 166–67, 170, 171,176, 178, 181, 182, 183–85, 187, 188; addressed by Fulbright, 138; after resignation of Berger, 147; call to investigate UJA, 120; conference of 102–4; on Eichmann trial 134–35; founding conference of (Atlantic City), 55–57; founding of philanthropic fund, 11–17;

NCRAC denunciation of, 92–93; 1945 conference of 67–68; 1948 conference of, 81–82; response to establishment of Israel, 86–89; 1952 Eisenhower Administration and, 106–9; release of original platform, 59–60; religious education program of, 112–14; response to 1967 war 145–n46; and UN Palestine debate 77–80

American Enterprise Institute, 154

American Friends of the Middle East (AFME), 109–11, 117, 118, 120, 147, 152

American Friends Service Committee, 88, 117

American Humanist Association, 135

American Israel Public Affairs Committee (AIPAC), 43, 134, 137, 138, 140, 148–49, 163, 169,180, 184. . *See also* American Zionist Council, American Zionist Emergency Council

American Jewish Alternatives to Zionism (AJAZ), 3, 151–52, 158, 160, 162, 165, 167–68, 170

American Jewish Committee (AJC), 41, 42, 43, 51, 54, 57–58, 60, 61, 78, 89, 90, 92, 93, 94, 97–98, 99–100, 105, 111, 124, 125

American Jewish Conference, 59–60, 61, 62, 67, 92, 195n42. *See also* NCRAC, Conference of Presidents of Major Jewish Organizations

223

Breira, 157–58, 162, 167, 177. *See also* CONAME

Brickman, Jay, 115

Brickner, Balfour, 158

Brickner, Barnett, 23, 32, 57

Brooks, David, 186

Brownfeld, Allan, 132, 147, 157, 159

B'Tselem, 182

Buber, Martin, 2, 59, 111, 126, 128

Buchanan, Pat, 172

Buckley, William F., 130, 159

Buckner, Noel, 151

Buckner, Norman, 48, 53, 125

Buffet, Howard, 196n7

Bundy, McGeorge, 145

Burg, Avraham, 181

Burleson, Omar, 132

Bush, George H. W., 172

Bush, George W., 10, 177, 178–79

Buttenweiser, Herman, 27

Buttenweiser, Moses, 27, 28

Byroade, Henry, 2, 106, 107, 108–9, 118, 185

Cahan, Abraham, 105

Calisch, Edward, 52

Carleton, Alford, 125

Carmichael, Stokely, 154

Carter, Jimmy, 75, 163, 165

Cavert, Samuel McCrea, 70

Central Conference of American Rabbis (CCAR), 32, 36, 48, 50–51, 53, 98, 113–14, 120, 141,152, 153

Central Synagogue (New York), 44

Chanin, Nathan, 105, 125

Chavez, Hugo, 126

Chicago Sinai Congregation, 45, 112

Chicago Tribune, 74

Chodorov, Frank, 128–29, 202n20

Christian Century, 82, 83, 99

Chomsky, Noam, 157

Churchill, Winston, 51

Citizens Committee on Displaced Persons, 76, 82

Clifford, Clark, 84

Coffin, Henry Sloane, 83

Cogley, John, 110

Cohen, Eliot, 98

Cohen, Henry, 52

Coleman, Clarence, 112, 115, 120, 121, 133, 134, 144, 146, 147, 170

Columbus Platform, 32

Commentary, 98–99, 100–101, 186, 189, 206n53

Committee for Peace and Justice in the Holy Land, 83–84, 85, 89, 109, 110, 154

Committee for the Return of Confiscated German and Japanese Property, 106

Committee on New Alternatives in the Middle East (CONAME), 157–58, 162. *See also* Breira

Committee on Unity for Palestine, 60, 96

Committee to Aid and Defend the Allies, 46

Commonweal, 110–11

Condell, Charlotte, 101

Conference of Presidents of Major Jewish Organizations, 60, 65, 141, 163, 174, 184. *See also* American Jewish Conference, NCRAC

Conservative Judaism, 147

Conyers, John, 169

"Cos Cob formula", 54, 97

Coughlin, Charles, 38

Cromwell, Oliver, 6, 201n91

Cronbach, Abraham, 4, 5, 23, 28–29, 33, 46, 52, 64, 88, 105–106, 113, 115–116, 124, 125, 136, 144

Curley, James, 66

Cyrus the Great, 99

Dacey, Norman, 161

Davies, Roger, 145

Dennery, Theodore, 151

Der Tag, 94

Deutsch, Gotthard, 28

Deutsch, Monroe, 71

Devin-Adair Company, 69, 99, 111, 131

Dewey, John, 4, 13–14

Dinkelspiel, Lloyd, 195n42

Dodge, Bayard, 83

Doenecke, Justus, 46, 116, 161, 162, 167, 196n8, 201n94, 207n19

Dubinsky, David, 67, 125

Dulles, John Foster, 2, 107, 108, 109, 124

ABOUT THE AUTHOR

Jack Ross is a freelance writer based in Brooklyn, New York. His work has appeared in the *American Conservative, Mondoweiss, History News Network,* and *Washington Report for Middle East Affairs.* He is presently at work on a complete history of the Socialist Party of America.